MASTERY: THE PATH OF INNER ALCHEMY

Also by Zulma Reyo

Morte e Renascimento: A Alquimia Suprema,
Portuguese edition:
Aquariana, 1990
Muerte y Renacimiento: La Suprema Alquímia
Spanish edition:
Kier, 1990

Karma e Sexualidade: A Experiencia Alquimica Humana
Portuguese edition:
Ground, 1992
Karma y Sexualidad: La Experiencia Alquímica Humana
Spanish edition:
Kier, 1992

Mastery:
The Path of Inner Alchemy

Zulma Reyo

JANUS PUBLISHING COMPANY
London, England

First published in Brazil
by Ground Ltda, 1989
First English edition published in Great Britain 1994
by Janus Publishing Company
Duke House, 37 Duke Street
London W1M 5DF

British Library Cataloguing-in-Publication Data
Reyo, Zulma
    Mastery: Path of Inner Alchemy
    I. Title
    131

ISBN 1 85756 084 1

Printed and bound in England by
Antony Rowe Ltd, Chippenham, Wiltshire.

Contents

CONTENTS

Figures

FIGURES

In eternal remembrance
of the one Truth and the Love
of the Godman
for us all and within us all.

To beloved Saint Germain
for his patience with me for so long!
I pay homage in deep humility.

To my mother Rosina,
who led me back into the practices of the Light,
eternal gratitude.

To my son Max,
whose innate wisdom drew me back into the world,
appreciation.

To my students,
who showed me the power of human love,
respect.

In acknowledgement and thankfulness
for all those who believe in the power of Light.

I AM

Foreword

Who are we? What are we? Is there 'life' beyond the physical, three-dimensional world we inhabit? Is there such a thing as God, and what do we mean by it? What is nature in general and what is our relationship to it? In short, what is a human being? – yes, this is what all these questions are aiming at.

In the history of human development, approaches to solutions to this multiple question have ranged from utter superstition to total denial of spiritual or even psychic realities, from unthinking gullibility to unremitting scepticism, from religious acceptance and surrender to unseen or imagined external forces to an arrogant conviction that there is nothing beyond the evidence of the five senses and linear logic.

In modern times in the West empiricism held sway, and still does, over the thinking of science and philosophy. It is a type of reasoning that grounds itself in the apparent veracity of the senses and the security of inductive argument. It asks piecemeal questions and receives piecemeal answers. Sometimes it is a successful approach, but whenever this occurs in a wide area, as in physics for instance, this is invariably achieved by slight of hand. This happens when it introduces surreptitiously concepts and ways of thinking such as: intuition, generalisation, general concepts, universals, which it is not, strictly speaking, allowed to do according to its principles. Such concepts and forms of cognition are illegitimate in strict empiricism, and yet life would be inconceivable without them. They are part of life, they are ingrained in it, they constitute the essential web of human nature.

It is enlightening to observe how empiricism trips over itself as it becomes successful, for inevitably it becomes metaphysical – which is precisely what it sets out to deny or destroy. Modern science which is extremely successful is also extremely metaphysical. But then, speaking scientifically nowadays is hardly different from speaking mystically. The perennial question is: Where do these ideas, concepts, understandings, knowledge come from? How are they formed and in what kind of space do they function? The gnostics would argue that they have always been there – or rather, *here*, in every human being – and that not only concepts but everything that exists is to be found in a human being. In religious terms it makes sense to say that if the whole world is the embodiment of God then a human being is made in his image. The Delphic Oracle propounded the admonition that in order to gain real knowledge of the world you had to 'Know Thyself'. Modern science realises that we are linked with the world around us at a sub-atomic level and that we influence, and are influenced by, it. Psychology has begun to move in that direction too. We are what we think, what we believe, what we intend, because we are literally constantly swimming in the stuff of our beliefs, thoughts, feelings and intentions and we are linked to them at source in a way that is dictated by our nature at the level of these thoughts, emotions, and so on.

To move from the belief that things exist out there independent of us to the understanding that they are out there as well as inside us is an important step, but it is only one part of the story of human evolution, and it is not an entirely new insight either. In the 5th century BC Plato argued that in order to see it is not enough for the image of the object to reach the eye but the eye must also project its own light to the object. Aristotle argued that our understanding always functions in terms of images, implying that we cannot even perceive without imaging. Not long ago, Immanuel Kant reasoned sedulously that human understanding is conditioned by human nature, meaning that whatever we perceive and conceive is conditioned by a kind of grid we wear in our nature which is like unremovable tinted spectacles and that therefore there is no way we could get to know 'things in themselves'.

What is proposed in the present book is that there *are* ways of getting to know 'things in themselves'. The rub, however, lies in the requirement to effect ontological and epistemological changes in ourselves. The central thesis of the book is, in fact, on ontology and epistemology, on what we are and how we get to know what we are. It is a type of anthroposophy. Man is the measure of all things, but not in the original sense of the expression, rather in that man represents everything that exists. In this sense he is made in the image of God, he is God himself. His purpose, the blueprint on which his existence is predicated is to godify himself, to identify himself in all his spiritual glory as God. This is neither wild ambition and phantasy nor unbridled pride. How is he to achieve this?

Zulma Reyo takes us through a series of explanations and exercises both to set the 'theoretical' framework and to assist the serious reader/practitioner to discover the way himself. Indeed, the two, theory and practice, must go together if the explanations are not to sound like phantasies. The 'theory' is what one should eventually come to experience as reality through the practice of exercises and meditations. The explanations and the exercises together constitute what Zulma calls the path of inner alchemy which leads to mastery of one's nature and by extension – as a result of – the rest of the created world. It is the ancient Greek admonition again: Know Thyself. The hub of the whole structure is Love. Man's lower nature may comprise all manner of negative feelings, thoughts and intentions, but in order to identify himself as God he must identify himself as Love; this is the *sine qua non* of godification. It implies going beyond one's ordinary, everyday nature and discovering the real ontology underneath which is akin to that of archangels and planetary rulers.

The epistemology itself, the altered way(s) of knowing, lies in the exercises-meditations which take one beyond the generally accepted world of the five senses and three-dimensional thinking. This is in the Initiatic tradition. Some are old and established exercises, others are new or adapted. Zulma draws from worldwide sources and backgrounds as well as from her own experience. Some of it is magic, some is therapy, pure psychology or prayer. What it is not is phantasy.

We have spent so much time thinking in a piecemeal, polarised, linear manner that we find it extremely difficult to open up to a more global way of thinking and experiencing. And yet it is not so difficult to, at least, begin to have an inkling of what this wider understanding holds for us. Try this: Relax, quieten your thoughts and emotions and concentrate relaxedly on an object; a stone, a plant, a building, a person or whatever. Soon you will surprise yourself with the knowledge that might inundate you concerning the object of your concentration. This is psychism, and it is only scratching the surface, but it is already changing your way of gaining knowledge. Next, study the way you think, feel, act and react with a view to understanding yourself. At some point you will begin to appreciate how other people experience their own lives. Gradually, you will experience the great similarities between you and other people, and then between you and the world at large. It is at this stage that you may begin to become flooded with Love for people and things around you, and it is at this stage that you will begin to experience people and things not as external objects, but as being part of you. You are then clearly on your spiritual path. You may catch yourself praying joyfully, pouring out your Love-filled heart with thanksgiving. You are in contact with yourself, the God within.

But why drag religion into this, you might ask. I posed the same question many years ago to a Great Brother. His answer was that there was no way round it, that everyone on the Path would have to come to that stage sooner or later, that it was a natural progression. I could not accept it. It took me years to come to experience it. The quickest, and safest, way is to fix our gaze on ourself, the God within, and work at it. In effect, we become what we think; today's thought is tomorrow's man. In this manner, by aiming at our higher nature, by identifying with the God within, we become that God. This is not self-hypnosis; it is re-investing energy in what we really are, it is remembering ourselves.

The big, arrogant mistake of strict empiricism, of accepting as true and real only what the five senses and linear logic dictate, is that 'empiricism', which stands for knowledge through experience, ignores multi-dimensional kinds of experience. These are the sort that contain the important epistemological and ontological changes, and to ignore them or deny them is no less than selling ourselves short. Zulma sets great store by them, and rightly so. Such experiences connect us with our inner self through the various conglomerates of energies we might call bodies, which function at numerous levels all the way to the source. Our purpose is to return to the source having acquired full consciousness – it is the path of inner alchemy. To achieve this is to be God, no less.

Andreas Mavromatis PhD
London, February 1994

Preface

It often seems to me as if I am constantly dying and being reborn. Sometimes I cannot relate to the person I was last year ... last month ... and yet something of whom I was then, as it were thirty years ago, filters through to link up all the people I have been. Each one brings a talent, an experience, a depth, an energy or irradiation. You might call these psycho-spiritual personalities, which grouped together present me as a multi-talented, versatile and flexible individual. I have learned to grow with and use to my advantage even the most trying situations to this very day. The lessons never end. School never lets out.

I am the student and I am the teacher, but I am no different from you. I teach what I have lived in the totality of myself, not what I have learned intellectually. In fact I hardly read books anymore. I teach what I have experienced in my life with many people of diverse cultures, religions, countries and backgrounds. I have travelled extensively. I speak Spanish, French and Italian. I have taught people from Europe, Asia, the Middle East and the three Americas, North, South and Central. And they have taught me. I couldn't begin to say who gained the most.

I have lived 'life' on the fringe. It seemed to me that was where the life force was. I grew up in the sixties, a time of alternative life styles. In childhood I had mystical and psychic leanings, as I travelled from country to country without roots. I became a high school language teacher and turned therapist shortly afterwards, after entering primal therapy with Dr Arthur Janov. That process became the scenario for my first formal apprenticeship. I gained tremendous knowledge from the devastating upheavals and reintegration of the physical, emotional and mental aspects of myself. I began learning

15

management and control of the different psychological functions of the psyche, leading me yet further into deeper studies of the self and the occult. Through entering the psychology of the present, I contacted similar psychologies of the past. I moved to England and into the second intensive playground of the self.

In the UK and later in the East I entered the world of esoterica through familiarity with theosophy, anthroposophy, Sufi and Druidic traditions. I became fascinated by religious philosophies and their psychologies; the Eastern contrasted and blended with the Western points of view. Zen . . . Tao . . . Hinduism . . . Tantra . . . The return journey to the West fifteen years later demanded yet another intense reorientation: apprenticeship with the computer generation and familiarisation with the technological mindset.

In conventional terms I'm not sure I could answer who or what I am. And yet I know who and what I am . . . a state of knowing that has spanned my entire lifetime. Very early on I knew that my particular quest was to link who I am with what I am. I have a mind, I have thoughts, I have emotions and feelings . . . Where do they come from? I have a personal history. Why *that* particular history? Since childhood I had strange faculties . . . Why? My quest has been to make some sense out of my life, the energies and materials within it and its moods, which extended way beyond the reaches of psychology. I asked myself: 'Am I weird and different? Or is everyone secretly like me? *How* secretly?'

I have sought to bridge the inner reality and the outer, the rational aspect and the irrational, the mind and the no-mind, the form and the formless, the being-state behind all forms and cultures. I spoke many psychological, cultural and social languages as well, to people in the arts, the sciences, intellectuals, mystics. Each had their own energy, their own style. Within each was the same life. I found myself in each one.

When I first returned to the US after all the years spent in meditative introspection in the East, I had not only to relearn what people were doing and being here in the West but to think of something to call myself. A glance at the profusion of psychotherapists and new age workers in the local alternative directory was overwhelming. Further acquaintance with practitioners in fields related to mine proved even more frustrating. I was immediately pegged, labelled, catalogued, without being heard or seen. I came to see that many people were certainly practising the new age crafts but with little if any depth or breadth. Specialisation had set into the world of the esoteric, the spiritual and the psychological. A kind of new age Renaissance woman, I found that I belonged to all of these and yet to none. In the midst of my frustration, after giving up entirely and working first as a vegetarian cook and later as an executive secretary, I had an insight that changed the course of my life. All the me's aligned. I discovered that I had been on the path of alchemy.

Alchemy is the art-science of transmutation from the lesser to the greater. I saw how I had always sought a universal key that would unlock all manifestation, whether physical or non-physical . . . a key that would unlock form and draw the formless into form. This was alchemy!

Insight followed insight, pictures, feelings and knowing upon knowing. I seemed to remember other lives, other times. I connected directly with a source of knowing that gave access to information that really blew my mind. Alchemy was not only a method, it was a perspective. Alchemy furnished a window into the remote past and the immediate future. Dimensional doorways through time and space opened within me. I knew this was what I had come to teach. I had so embodied the process that I couldn't see it until I had gained some distance from it. And the key to this alchemy and its method was within me, in my consciousness. Alchemy was a state of *being*. Everything fell into place then and in a flash I received the picture of my logo, the symbol which I use for the Centre for Inner Alchemy.

The upright triangle in the symbol is violet, representing the alchemical or transmuting fire, the purification which must happen in order for lead to become gold. This transmuting fire is primary to all creation. The inverted triangle is gold and brings down cosmic light, the energy from the sun or the central sun, the God-Self. The oval sphere around the symbol is the causal body, which I saw in silver. I noticed that the violet flame cut through it as well, indicating dimensions beyond. Man finds himself right in the middle of the symbol. The central sun or source point (symbolic of the Godhead) is located over the chest or heart. Within this central sun, of a luminosity far greater than the physical sun, lay eternity, like a crystal ocean of sacred fire. I called the work Inner

Alchemy to distinguish it from the other, although in truth it was . . . is . . . one.

This book is my gift of love to you, just as its message has been the gift of life to me. May you grow and glow with it until we meet in the crystal temples beyond time.

Zulma Reyo

Preface to English Edition

I am filled with great joy that this, my first book, is able to appear in its original English through a British publisher. As I write these lines six years after the completion of the book, and so many years since its publication in Portuguese and Spanish, I am taken back many more years to London, Kent and Sussex, where the conscious journey towards my Self really began for me.

For the inspiration, revelation and insight which this soil provided for me in those early times of mystical and spiritualistic confusion and for the work which emerged as a consequence I wish to acknowledge a very dear and special friend who is no longer on this Earth but whose memory lives in my heart, Valerie Mackenzie. With her come the eternal bluebells and the English countryside, which nourished my body and soul. I also wish to thank that young mystical man who was Jules Hillyar for standing by me in brotherhood from the inner planes.

Although I came here from the California growth movement, bringing with me the practice of Primal Therapy received with great enthusiasm in those days of squats, communes and alternative lifestyles, it was from here that I parted to the fold of the Great Mother, India.

My journey deepened within the innermost recesses of my soul into darkly fertile and darkening conditions through the Rajneesh teachings and fraternal life for 12 more years. Much of the work sprang from that American, English, Indian amalgam of the 1960s and 1970s. My spirit then led me to embrace the philosophy of Mr and Mrs Guy W. Ballard in North America and the discovery of true Western esotericism through the directed power of Light.

This book was written after the conception of Inner Alchemy and while I had set up a practice in New York City. Inner Alchemy expanded and took root, as the flow of my life's calling took me to South America and the exotic depth and wisdom of that land from where I now work.

How was I to know that in Brazil I would meet two of the most beautiful and humanitarian souls, Elizabeth and Tadeusz de Gromoboy, whose continual joy of life and dedicated helpfulness connected me with the British publisher!

So it is that in the never-ending spiral of my aspirations I find myself here again from where I offer this book to the English-speaking world in gentle, humble gratefulness.

London, April 1993

Introduction

Overview

Heritage

Each one of us has a particular song to sing, a particular dance to dance. Sometimes it is obvious in its simplicity. Sometimes it is complex and confusing, hidden within the recesses of a beingness as yet unknown. All of us have come to do something unique, to express our individuality and its desire for greater life and perfection. When we find what that expression is we find great joy and fulfilment, and our evolution, the rhythm of our lives, seems to accelerate. We are happy, connected to life whether selling real estate or managing finances, being a mother, sweeping the floor, shopping for groceries or choreographing a Broadway play. At these points, all the struggle with disparate or discordant elements makes sense: we come to see it teaches us the art of mastering life – managing the self. An integration has taken place. The break-throughs in the outer world seem to coincide with some kind of completion within, a lesson learned. And even if there is no dramatic outer signpost, living itself becomes exciting. Maybe not more easy but certainly more rewarding, more flowing. Life suddenly has a purpose and you suddenly have a say. At that point you've become an active co-creator with the Godhead. Complete mastery is just a matter of time.

Let's face it. Life is not a bed of roses for anyone. It *is* painful. We've come here to learn . . . something. If we have money, we may not have health, if we have health, we may not have emotional stability. Before life as before death, that greatest of all equalisers, there are no privileged ones. Life provides us with a never-ending curriculum in administration – the management and control of our selves and our world. We learn the laws of life through different languages and symbols, and by trial and error we learn its principles through our own expansions and contractions, through the energy systems governing our bodies, our minds, our emotions, our physical expressions and manifestations ... Man is indeed a microcosm. The ancients knew that 'As above, so below'. They knew that the laws governing life – inner and outer – revolve around principles of vibration, the vibrations which are the mainstream of alchemy.

Traditionally, alchemy refers to that body of gnostic literature and formulas that conjure up images of demons, witches and warlocks, spider-webs and cauldrons. The alchemist is seen as ageless, mysterious and indomitable, at best a Merlin. Behind the melodramatic complexities and intricate symbolisms covering the principles of alchemy lies the overwhelming feeling of enormous force, a power embodied by the alchemist himself in his ability to extract primal energies and substance from his environment and to generate, direct and transmute this energy and substance into other forms. There has been much fear surrounding alchemy, a fear generated by the ignorance and manipulativeness of superstition and of thwarted demi-truths, legacies and bygone times when the inner laws governing alchemy had been misused. Subliminal memories of distortion and fear have filtered through to the modern times.

But alchemy goes further back than the Middle Ages and the mythical Merlin to the beginning of time, when man first came into embodiment. At that time alchemy was a natural knowledge and ability, the *modus operandi*. At that time man was aware of his very special role as intermediary between physical and subtle realities, between the human and the divine. He was aware not only of his dual nature as intelligence in matter, but of his dual energetic systems. He was also aware of his power or ability to create through the manipulation of energy and substance. He knew that the key to this power lay within his own state of consciousness. The key to manifestation, precipitation, dematerialisation, levitation, in fact, all the expression of man's natural powers, lies in the understanding and use of consciousness. It is the state of consciousness itself that determines the use of the laws governing energy and matter. These laws are mysterious only in the same proportion as the states of consciousness are unexplored and incomprehensible to the self.

Nature of Consciousness

Consciousness is a mechanism of perception. This mechanism may express itself in a variety of ways, comprehending various levels of awareness and behaviour. The Buddhists clearly outlined different states in their elaborate depiction of the journey of the soul through the afterlife. These states, or 'bardos', correspond to moods or types of humanity and maximise salient characteristics: anger, envy, apathy, pride and piety. The truth is that consciousness may be sensation-oriented or intellectual, it may be emotionally addicted or psychically cognitive, it may even be spiritually attuned and aligned to cosmic forces. It may be any combination thereof. Each level of activity in our human spectrum corresponds to a state of consciousness, meaning the state from which the activity originates. And each state sets off a vibration, an energy frequency. Man in his faculty of consciousness is a very sensitive and highly complex creator of infinite possibilities of being.

The usual way in which humanity approaches life is haphazard. If we succeed it is often accidentally, through dogged persistence in hit-and-miss methodologies. We have not only lost our abilities to focus, we have lost the full potency of our energy, our power. Rather than a central pooling faculty (a source-power), there exists a state of continuous dispersal (activity and outer focus), which creates a fragmentation of our faculties. And through this we perceive fragmentation. We not only have forgotten that there is a wholeness to life, we have forgotten the capacity and knowledge of our inherent mastery over substance and vibration. Like the proverbial prince-turned-frog we have become locked within one or another system of our own creation. We do not remember that we were and always will be a creator. We have become fascinated and identified with our creations, entrapped within a level of reality we conceive to be the whole.

The normal process of consciousness is to expand and intensify. This happens with or without our cooperation. Without our cooperation, our willingness, to relinquish our identifications and attachments, there is pain and suffering. But pain and suffering is *not* an intrinsic part of life. Over time, with our cooperation, our consciousness comes to flow like a river through different permutations of substance and energy, unhampered and undivided. Life is seen as a flow, a continuous changing play of forces. The focus has been withdrawn from the effects (the distraction and ramifications of our attention) to the cause (the central consciousness). That which perceives change is the supreme intelligence, the highest state of consciousness.

The process of life appears to be a pooling of disparate elements in which our power (our vested interest, our attachments and identifications) is stored and which keeps us divided. In the pooling, the force which was propelling energy outward collects inward now, into a source point, increasing in intensity. That momentum within the collected reservoir is all powerful. Mystics and magicians know this. Occultists know this. Even Hitler knew this! But humanity still doesn't know it, preferring to invest power in external authority, in bearded daddies in the sky, gurus, teachers, authority figures, doctrines, teachings and organisations . . . Within each individual lies the Godhead, a state of consciousness from which just about anything is possible, because consciousness, like energy, is neutral. It is a double-edged sword. In the hands of the light-bearer it becomes god mastery; in the hands of selfish individuals it becomes chaos, disharmony and destruction.

Inner or Divine Alchemy

The original formula of alchemy became veiled in symbolism to protect its practices from misuse by the impure. What has come down to us, although immensely powerful and capable of transmuting matter, is still a lesser alchemy. The alchemy practised by the remote ancients such as the Atlantean and Mayan civilisations is an action of the Godhead, a direct circuit with the supreme source of life and light. To practise this divine alchemy is to tap into the highest vibrational frequencies of which we can conceive and which alter all levels of reality beneath them. Going beyond even the vibration of gold itself is represented by the crystalline substances of the earth: the precious jewels from the crystal to the diamond.

The key to alchemy lies in the understanding of energy and substance. Transformation, and ultimately transmutation, is only possible through understanding. It does not happen accidentally. Matter is energy. Light is energy . . . Everything is energy, in different states of concentration. Life itself, as all alchemists know, is a vibration which quickens substance, and substance is energy. The

24

deepest understanding goes to the very primary vibration: the sacred fire breath of God, or Cosmic Light. There are laws governing all manifestations, even spiritual ones. Bliss . . . grace . . . miracles . . . these happen through the working of immutable laws of Light. God himself, as the ancients conceived Him (particularly the Mayans), is 'the giver of form and measure', 'the giver of life'. Unless we acknowledge the realm of cause, the essence or source – the Godhead – we will forever be shuffling effects and never gain true mastery.

Not only is there a cause to everything under the sun, this cause is intelligent. Everything manifestated is an expression of the energetic life force and is intelligent. Energy responds to man's activity. It responds to thought and direction. It can be manipulated. Man has a unique role in creation. He is the only species that has the power to manipulate life forces, to create, the only species that partakes of the creator and of the created. Physical embodiment is the expression of a commitment to the planet earth: man takes on its very substance, coats himself in it. But the essence of man is not a physical entity. Man is something like a visitor within physicality. He is actually an intelligence, the light of consciousness with its multi-dimensional potentiality, a possibility that goes beyond his emotional and mental self. Man is a presence, a God-presence within matter. Knowing this, accepting this identification, allows him to connect directly with the voltage of the source. The conscious use of this power gained by identifying with God-possibility rather than with material nature, brings about the highest form of manifestation.

Purpose and Mechanics

The purpose of Inner Alchemy is simple. It seeks to raise the vibrational rate of all matter to the level of spirit, or light. It also seeks to create an immortal vehicle through which it may continue to express mastery. Matter has different levels of density and vibration, including etheric and psychic, sound, and ultraviolet gradations of light and colour oscillating into infinite frequencies. Beyond magnetism (which includes physical, mental, emotional and psychic forces) are superior and more intense forces or pulsations which are operated by the God-Self and not by the personality. The material substances, exemplified by gravity and physicality, are positive (solid) energies. The consciousness of the God-Self is the link between the polarities of spirit and matter, negative and positive. Just as every higher force controls the lower, consciousness, expressing itself through higher mind, operates through a force that is vibrationally higher than any speed of physical nature. As such it is capable of controlling all nature and natural processes, including death and old age.

The consciousness of the higher mind is a faculty of the Self with access to a state of knowing that goes beyond intellect and encompasses all knowledge because it is the source of all knowledge. It doesn't concern itself with method or process but with cause, with being. It is God-Self: 'I AM'. A simple way of conceiving of higher mind is to see and feel it as the supreme presence of ourselves: the awareness of the wholeness and intensity of ourselves when we are fully present in the moment, with all our faculties and energies, including physical, focused and accessible.

Training Requirements

The training begins with the self, with the study of behaviour patterns and reactions, with the comprehension of human energy dynamics and the human body, and finally with an understanding of the process of purification and refinement. The alchemy we've known has concentrated on the vegetable and mineral kingdoms and uncovered inner laws of physics and chemistry through objective study. The traditional alchemist possessed a capacity to penetrate substance and modify the frequency of energy. Inner Alchemy on the other hand focuses on the study of the self – physical and non-physical. From the realm of non-physicality the Inner Alchemist attempts to penetrate all manifestation. The end result is the same. A metaphysical leap into what has been termed faith is required. That leap is the alchemical marriage with the Godhead – the very source of all life and all power in the macrocosm as in the microcosm.

Another way of looking at this is to say that medieval alchemy dominated elemental forces, but Inner Alchemy joins the human realm not only with the elemental but also with the angelic principle as well. The elemental kingdom governs all substance; the angelic kingdom governs all principles of light or irradiation. But the angelic kingdom, unlike the elemental, cannot be contaminated and partnership with it brings miracles far more elevated than this recorded history has known, although vestiges of it might be inferred through Druidic examples.

Inner Alchemy also creates a bridge within the individualised self, between its human and divine aspects, between matter and spirit, between mind and higher mind.

Understanding that we are neither body or mind but a presence within life, we can see that the dense material body is the physical expression of the mind (mental set) and vice versa. The study of mental behaviour might entail retracing humanity's steps to early life and other embodiments. In Inner Alchemy it is simultaneously imperative that the physical body be kept balanced and aligned with developing intensities of vibration: these intensities accelerate as blocks and solidified thoughtforms dissolve in the purification process and release extra energy into the energetic system. Coincidental to the dual process of alignment and integration is the restructuring of the mind itself, as it unravels inefficient belief systems and ways of perception. Working in tandem with the purification and unravelling process is the systematic rediscovery and validation of impersonal transcendent data concerning the nature and mechanics of energy and substance.

The practical result of Inner Alchemy is that it teaches the skill of transforming destructive energy into constructive energy. Anger or hate becomes love, sexuality and possessiveness become sensitivity and freedom, fear is transformed into creativity and joy. In this way energy is not only conserved, it is raised to a higher vibratory rate and fused into a system which is gradually being prepared for greater and greater frequencies.

The Three Powers

The purpose of life is not only to grow, expand and return to the source amplified as Light but also to bless, transmit and create; or better still to co-create with God. From the creation of worlds to the manifestation of physical symptoms in the body, all manifestation must follow a formula which requires the use of what we might call the three creative powers. Hermes Trismegistus earlier, and the Count of Saint Germain most recently, have revealed the basic ingredients of all manifestation. In man these powers are thought, feeling and the spoken word. These powers in fact constitute the basic alchemical formula.

The power of thought is easy to understand. We have the capacity to think, to draw a form or a mental blueprint of an idea or concept and are constantly creating all sorts of pictures, consciously or unconsciously.

The power of feeling is more difficult to grasp. We have a capacity of feeling which goes far beyond emotion or sensation. The power from emotional generation and response is immense. In actuality it provides the fuel for all creation. The world is, indeed, created by the vibratory frequency of love. Love is the greatest force in existence. It contains the maximum momentum of energy because it is a concentration of the activity of Light as purity. And what is purity if not a form of essence-activity which not only attracts to itself but irradiates simultaneously? Love is then a force that engenders cohesiveness and perpetuates a self-sustaining activity. Love is such a concentration of the feeling energy that wherever it is directed it triggers manifestation or wish fulfilment. But we don't yet know the power or force of love, mainly because we no longer understand the power of purity.

The power of the spoken word creates the resonant field for manifestation or materialisation. It is hardly regarded as a power and yet the spoken word is responsible for aligning or disturbing our worlds.

The mechanism is this: the thought, or blueprint, like a negative, is propelled by feeling and is set into form by the spoken word. Sound and the spoken word (which is vibration in form) provides the material for creation. Hence we have our 'abracadabras' and 'open sesames', our alchemical fiats and decrees demonstrating the methodology implied in the biblical statement, '. . . and the Word was made flesh'. Decrees and affirmations are depicted visually through symbols and runes. The particular art of employing the right tone and pitch as well as a word into which the sound was sealed, has been lost.

Creation begins as intent and comes into form only through the use of the three powers. From subtle thought to physicality, manifestation of reality is governed by rules or principles. If you know the rules you are able to bring about the manifestation. The mechanics of Inner Alchemy go beyond rules and point to the individual who applies them. Within man himself is the alchemical magic. It is he, through the use of his five senses and the five elements, who raises matter and alters all substance. Man himself in his consciousness is the alchemical stone. Rules were merely guidelines to be applied when there was not sufficient mastery within the self.

Alignment and Discernment

The misuse of alchemy came about through the use of methods devoid of personal integrity. For instance: distanced from the God-head, the traditional alchemist began to believe that the only source for life resided within the ectoplasm of a living organism. The belief and the desire to become a god and create life-forms led to countless murders of living things, from ancient sacrifices and ravages to experiments that run right up to modern times.

It must be understood that life, like power, does not come from the outside. It comes from above; it comes from within. To postulate power in outer sources, including rules or methods, is to relinquish our very godhood. Life is a substance which can be drawn from above, from those finer vibrations which inject and affect matter. It can also be recreated through the process of transmutation. But, seeker-after-power, beware! Only God can do this. The trick is in the alliance with God.

To become a true alchemist, to create harmoniously and effectively, we need to have conquered the characteristics in ourselves that foster misuse and miscreation. We use our powers to create lack, limitation, disease, discord. Instead of love we generate fear, doubt, hatred, uncertainty. Our vocabulary empowers negative words and concepts. We qualify our world, our creations by projecting our own state of unconsciousness onto it. As we are always creating, we may well learn to use the law to create consciously, to create harmony, purity, light, opulence, joy and health in our own worlds.

Outer methods exist for those who can't discern the real from the unreal, the inner from the outer, the good from the evil. The study of Inner Alchemy promotes discernment because it raises consciousness. In the process we learn to gain access to information

29

directly from the source without the need for intermediaries. The time is coming where libraries of all that has been taught in the past will be rendered obsolete. Even now, occult seals have been broken, old occult laws no longer hold true. There is, in reality, no more need for secrecy, individual retribution, the indulgence of self-pity and suffering, hallmarks of the previous age. The trend is towards active responsible participation within life. We are turning our attention now to the god within. The bearers of Light are bridging worlds. We are ready for the next step: god consciousness.

We begin with ourselves and through example can show others what might be done. When we change ourselves we acquire a different frequency of energy. When we transmute the various parts of ourselves, through the use of Inner Alchemy, we perform the highest act possible to man. We become a blessing to life merely by our catalytic presence. Anyone who touches you or your world becomes graced by the harmony and purity of your energy field. Everywhere you go you bring a little more peace, a little more light or clarity.

Aloneness and Wholeness

Truly to experience our aloneness is to discover deeply our wholeness.

In aloneness, we uncover the mechanisms that blindly seek habits. A habit engenders unconsciousness and mechanical behaviour; it takes the energy away from the awareness of the present moment. In consciousness there is constant and total freedom of choice and with that freedom comes a growing responsibility. We are responsible for absorbing and processing energy according to our level of consciousness. At the higher levels we are responsible for affecting others as well as our own worlds.

A person who has experienced the totality of himself will not look outwardly for gratification, for meaning, for direction. Seeking outside oneself for the answers to life is in fact infantile: it is a sucking of energy from the environment. Maturity comes with the courage to be alone, and in that aloneness come the fullness, the power, the overflow, the blessing. Usually we give our power away to parents, boyfriends and girlfriends, husband and wives, bosses ... We empower others who we think possess that ability that we can't find in ourselves. To regain our power and the vision of ourselves as we truly are we need to stand alone and in that aloneness rediscover the all-potentiality that we are.

This rebirth can only be done by the individual. No one else can do it for us without reprogramming us. We seek freedom from *all* programmes. Our life is a series of repetitive acts of behaviour. We keep getting into the same kinds of relationships, the same kind of situations over and over again. Mental activity as the lower mind is, frankly, robotic.

In arming ourselves with the courage to be alone we start to become conscious. As conscious agents we no longer seek contractual agreements of interdependency. We no longer participate in subtle powerplays which keep us divided in our power and from the experience of our godliness. We are no longer prone to confusion or to being misled by people and ideologies. In our own integrity we can easily detect the traps and flaws of anything less than truth and purity and the spirit that yearns for it.

The capacity to discern is of utmost importance in our age, where so many beautiful words are being flaunted about by people who do not live them. Inner Alchemy teaches us how to return to our divinity, to the source within, by pooling our energies and reaching deep within our own individuality and the totality of the self, including physicality. Although it teaches us how to transcend the limitations of physicality and the body consciousness, this cannot be done without being totally in the body, physically, emotionally and mentally. The truth is that we cannot become masters *in absentia*.

Anatomy of Being Human

This book on Inner Alchemy constitutes the contents of a basic course on *Alchemy and the Human Energetic Anatomy*. It outlines the principles of alchemy and points to their application at the different levels of expression available to man through his faculties. We need to understand the anatomy of being human. How do the parts work and how do they fit together? How do we learn to channel and attune ourselves directly to the source from which all knowing originates? This begins with *you now* in the present moment, in alignment with who and what you really are, in this moment and interdimensionally.

We know something about the anatomy of the physical body from Eastern and Western medical practices, which outline the energetic circuits in physical and etheric substance, including the meridians of acupuncture and the lines of force of the martial arts. We think we know about psychology and the working of the mind, which is in fact but a tiny fraction of what Mind really is. We will see that what psychologists define as mind is actually lower mental phenomena. We will discover that there is a higher mind and a higher intelligence only partially glimpsed through some of the Eastern psychologies and philosophies. We will come to know that there is a consciousness beyond the highest intelligence that we are capable of embracing.

We possess an emotional body of energy which is quite distinct from the mental field. What is its anatomy? What is the anatomy of the mental body? Of the physical and etheric energy fields? How do they interrelate? And what about interrelationships between people? What happens to the individual energy fields in relationships? How do we come to lower our power, our insights, our boundaries? We barter, sell, trade our energy, create hybrids and abominations, not knowing how or why we did it.

Inner Alchemy teaches how the parts fit into a central picture. What is the real function of chakras? The seven rays? The seven bodies? How can we actually transform anger and fear permanently at a core level? It is not what we learn about these things that affects our lives, but what we become with that knowledge; most importantly how we integrate this knowledge into our everyday activities. Any technique may be used on the path of Inner Alchemy, but the state of consciousness of the one who uses it must be pure and masterly.

The delphic oracle urged us: *Know thyself!* The study of Inner Alchemy is indeed the study of the Self. We acknowledge the fact that we contain within us the replica of the universe. We are the source of all universes. Through the study of our anatomy, particularly the subtle energetic centres, forces and networks, vibratory fields and the receiving and transmitting apparatus, we again discover the interdimensionality, correspondence and interrelationship of manifestation. There is only one substance, one energy, one source, which we may call God. Attuned to his God-Self, man is linked directly to spirit and matter; the first through higher faculties, the second through physicality.

Balancing the Threefold Nature

Before any alchemical formula can be applied, the need of the age is to balance the emotional nature of individuals: where it is too active it needs to be harmonised, where it is inactive it needs to be awakened. As feeling, emotions are the generating fire which placed within the furnace of the being transforms not only lead into gold and coal into diamond, but ultimately fire itself into Light.

The emotional network is a vibratory field surrounding and inter-penetrating the physical body, extending beyond the ordinary boundaries of the mental frequency as well. Emotions themselves are like whirls or vortices in the aura which act as kinds of disturb-ances, easily agitated and in turn irritating to both body and mind when ungoverned. They interrelate with sensation to cause excitement and passion, and also its opposites, frustration and despair. The aim of ancient religious practices, as well as of modern psychology, is to subdue these whirls through spiritual, mental or psychotherapeutic means. But to subdue or control these whirls permanently, the energy contained within them would need to be channelled into and through the consciousness of the heart.

All of man's energies, in fact, need to be directed into the heart, where they can be requalified by a lucid mentality before being transmuted and returned to the universal in the form of deepened understanding and general goodwill. Alchemical force, faculty and power reside in the chamber of the heart.

The threefold nature of man's physicality (body, mind and feeling) needs development, balance and integration. Without physical life force freely circulating through the body, the mind has no anchor through which to express itself in matter; it therefore remains elusive and fragmentary. On the other hand, physical life force without clear mental direction is open to excesses and con-tamination. Once the threefold nature is harmoniously integrated, alignment with the higher frequencies of the Self is facilitated. This process doesn't happen in a linear progression of development but rather through a circular feeling-process, cyclically intuiting greater and greater portions of the Self and slowly integrating fragments into the threefold physical self or personality.

Law of the One

There is only one power, one intelligence and one substance: God. Beyond behaviour (psychology) lie the higher energy dynamics of matter and spirit; the interaction of the components of personality with psychic environmental forces and spiritual and cosmic factors. In Inner Alchemy, psychology and religion are once again coming together in a unity they outpictured in the ancient times of the Vedas, of Patanjali and most recently of Lord Buddha. Psychology and religion are coming together because matter (physical, emotional and mental or psychic) and spirit (essence, being or cosmic light) are indeed one.

The ultimate purpose of Inner Alchemy is the transmutation of matter into light. This includes cellular matter, transcending illness, death and decay. Historical precedents of this form of alchemical transmution have been provided by records of Lord Buddha, by the legend of Quan Yin in China, by the biblical statements on Jesus of Nazareth and his mother Mary in their 'ascension', and by many others, including the legendary alchemist, the Count of Saint Germain, believed to be working in this physical dimension through his immortal body of light. Masters who have embodied the Law of the One move within humanity today as they did in the beginning of time, when they were called gods. Only the alchemist or student of light has the heart capacity to know and to see.

Alchemy draws from all disciplines, because initially all disciplines derived from alchemy. Although alchemy is a process to be lived, it is also the beginning and the end of all spiritual practice and of all physical manifestation as well. Man is actually a beam of light that has projected itself into matter. Man's essence comes from the realm of light and again returns to it after embodiment. Establishing the circuit between matter and spirit is the first step towards becoming whole again.

Becoming Light: The Ascension

Throughout this text I will suggest that the purpose of life is the expansion or the raising of substance to a higher frequency of vibration, that of light. What this actually means to us individually, is that the human body – the composite of the physical, mental and emotional bodies – is recalibrated, refined. In the process we lose our identification with the heavier forms which represent separation and transcend the laws of matter, including gravity and decay. The vehicle of the personality becomes youthful, healthy and beautiful. Psychologically speaking we experience lightness, joy, freedom from bondage (for it is only matter, including emotional and mental substance, that clings to itself, that gains weight and density). Spiritually speaking this process brings about enlightenment: freedom from karma or the law of cause and effect (which like the former phenomenon also relates to the matter of the emotional and mental bodies that seek adherence and continuity).

The greatest alchemist in our recorded history is Jesus of Nazareth, whose very life was a reaching-out, and whose specific task was to show us *how* to attain to mastery over the lower energies. His teachings have not been fully understood as inner science and the art of transmutation of the physical body into light. There are many unknown masters who have attained within themselves a level of purity and identity with the godhead that has enabled them to gain mastery over the mechanisms of the physical, mental and emotional bodies. Seeming miracles occur in their vicinity, because the rate of vibration of their bodies is so accelerated that it heals, blessing whatever they contact. They are often held in esteem as religious figures or as ordinary remarkable folk, always bringing peace and light.

An ascended being by this definition has mastered the law of physicality and has gained complete control over the vibratory activity of each of the lower bodies. He is able to pool or align his vibrations to those of his light-bound being. Death has been a continuous process of requalification and absorption, of re-creation and integration. He literally creates himself anew in a malleable substance of light. This is why it is said that he knows no death and is immortal. It may be said that at the moment of 'death' he has come to transmute the very substance of his body into an immortal vehicle which can be made to resemble a human form.

The ascension is not myth or poetic fantasy. It completes the cycle of embodiment or physical recycling. The ascension represents the activity of expansion of life, as redeemed substance returns to the source with added lustre or consciousness. The work of illumined physicists, such as Itzhak Bentov, clearly demonstrates this expanding consciousness within matter. The goal of mystical

35

or divine alchemy, or what I am today calling Inner Alchemy, is the redemption of matter and the creation of the immortal body of light for *all* humanity.

Into Space Consciousness

Just as individuals ascend and raise the vibratory rates of all life on the planet by transmuting physical substance, mind consciousness, which is part of matter, is also raised. This process of evolution has now taken a significant leap into another dimension, into what I call Christed or space consciousness, that is a qualitative vibrational leap into a more refined or illuminated structure.

The work of Inner Alchemy is to reactivate the circuits between form and the formless to enable conscious creation to take place. Inner Alchemy is the natural vehicle of the Christ consciousness as it bridges the higher vibratory realms above with matter below by raising the frequency of matter itself. 'As above, so below'.

This next step requires a change in the gestalt from solidity to light, from density to space. Instead of identifying ourselves with our physicality, we identify with the God-Self, with that part of us that is intelligent cosmic light substance. It is this very consciousness that will enable the reawakening of our inherent and long-forgotten powers and our brotherhood, not only with all life in this planet but with all life everywhere in the universe of sentient expanding Light. Inner Alchemy is the religiousness of the future, the methods that lead to the consciousness of space. Inner space . . . outer space. . . . It remains to be seen how the conquest of inner space will open the dimensional doorways into outer space, including the farthest reaches of our physical universe.

Creativity

Creativity is the very flame or essence of Life. Our every act is creative. Mastery is life's supreme expression.

Everyone is capable of transmuting his emotions, elevating his thoughts, manifesting endless creativity and wealth, generating goodness . . . without destroying even a part of himself or of another. We don't take anything away from anyone. Mastery is a skill that once learned allows us to have our cake and eat it too.

We could say that alchemy is a composite of intuitive science and universal religiousness projected through artistic expression. Science and religion meet with art in alchemy as they met in the golden ages of the remote past. Alchemy is the process of creation itself, one abundant endless outflowing from the fount.

Life is the greatest teacher, and the greatest teaching is the observation of the inner life, that ebbing and flowing of forces which create outer manifestation and in turn affect the inner states. The East has known this secret but has forgotten to apply the dynamics to the outer. The West has known how to utilise the data derived from outer expressions, but has forgotten the inner dimensions. Ancient civilisations knew both inner and outer reality. We are again approaching the wholistic vision of life individually.

The alchemical method, like all great truths, is simple. All we need to do is to dare to look and discover who and what we *really* are, to step aside from the little self and the environment and the world of effects, for just a moment. There we can tap into the wealth of is-ness, of being, to discover again and again that we are the microcosm. We are breaking away from the patterns and beliefs of the past and learning to see in a fresh way. Inner alchemy returns us to ourselves, and, as we return to ourselves we rediscover that our nature is alchemical.

The basic perspective of the new roadmap is the view of all life as energy, as fluctuating patterns of different vibrations. As we become empty of the denser ingredients in our being we create a kind of light-vacuum within that attracts the finest frequencies of Light to us. Alchemy is the science or art of vibration symbolised by the alchemical marriage of fire and water: the fire of the spirit, the water of life. We have too long invalidated ourselves through projected power invested in our priests and politicians, our systems and organisations. We can now reach in and tune into God directly. Everyone can feel and know all there is to feel and know.

The Alchemical Practice

How do we practise alchemy consciously? Through ritual. Everyone likes to do something in a specific way, as aesthetically, expressively and spontaneously as possible. How we perform our rituals is a direct reflection of our taste, sensitivity and quality of lovingness. We might, then, begin the alchemical journey by setting the stage: designing a particular place and selecting a definite period of time for its enactment. In other words, we create a holy place where we anticipate communing directly with the Source. Setting the atmosphere externally creates the receptacle which gives expression to the inner longing for completion. Creating a time-frame gives a chance for continuity. Regularity builds up momentum and force that construct and strengthen the very circuitry that we use in alchemy.

The next step is to focus the attention on the project at hand. We make sure that we will have the privacy that we require and that we will not be interrupted. Then we sit, comfortably and silently, and tune into our delicate perceptive mechanisms, in the way that works best for us. This is discovered through our choice of different spiritual and psychological processes that foster discernment and the ability to detect the real from the illusory, as well as build up the staying power through which we learn to sustain the perceptions and the energy acceleration. We know that we have tuned into our core when we reach a deep inner peace, when we feel perfectly relaxed and within ourselves; when no outer disturbance pulls us.

Once we have stilled the outer senses (and some people might require physical activity before they can do this, some way in which they can release as well as generate the physical energy that allows the perception of the feeling networks), we begin the ritual with the *invocation*: the calling to God, or the God-Self. This calling triggers a vibratory reaching into the highest frequencies of our own being, that source-point which projected us into matter in the first place and which continues to feed us life. An invocation is different from prayer in the sense that we are *summoning* in the name and authority of our God-Self. We call in partnership with God. We call for the descent of light, for the law of light to exert its dominion over matter. It is best if this is done verbally, although in certain instances where this may not be possible, the intent alone can serve to evoke the elicited energy. Understand that it is the impulse of love which provides the reaching power that allows us to connect with that frequency which in a linear map is located 'up there'. Note too that as we call 'up' to God, it answers. It *has* to: it IS the Self!

Acknowledging this allows us to earth the God power through our body. It makes us the conduit for cosmic forces.

The invocation is completed when we sense a flow pouring through and into our bodies. This is experienced by some as grace, bliss, ecstasy . . . Alchemy then draws that energy into expression. We have created the alchemical circuit, the electronic current that enables both the descent of light and the ascent of matter. In alchemical terms these are the currents for the magnetisation and etherealisation processes that take place in transmutation and manifestation, and of which we will hear more later. The alchemical circuit is established by linking with the highest level of light vibration and redirecting the circuit back through physicality. Invocation provides not only the circuitry but the power source. We are merely a vehicle, a co-creator with God, lending, embellishing, collaborating and blessing life with our will to love, which is our service. Greater and greater intensities of energy become available to us and will be drawn to us the more we use the alchemical circuit through invocation and the application of the law of light.

Primary to the practice of Inner Alchemy is the use of the violet frequency of transmutation – the healing frequency. Together with the colour and substance of gold, the violet fire has come to symbolise and embody the alchemical process of transmutation from the lower into the higher, and inversely of drawing cosmic light down into the deepest recesses of matter.

Choice

The vacuum created by the systematic dissolution of density has a compelling force to it, demanding the refinement of consciousness and discernment. As we attract light we also attract that which is not light. Freedom, consciousness, awareness and responsibility all come together. We open to light and we open to darkness. We are the openers, the choosers and the doers. There must be no secrets from the Self. From the onset we must know this.

It is important to understand the nature of darkness. There are two distinct kinds of darkness: the darkness which contains the light and the darkness which shuts it out. The first is a phenomenon of cosmic nature, the second is man-made. Lies, secrecy, trickery and manipulation belong to the second kind of darkness. This is a negativity which is not a polarity to light but is a negation of it. Most people are confused, in the belief that darkness is a necessary part of life. Anger, fear, doubt, insecurity, disease and old age are *not* a necessary part of life. They are miscreations of the self, animated and augmented by thousands of years of spiritual and psychological ignorance.

Once the choice for higher consciousness has been made we need to stand firm. This determination is necessary as long as we are in a physical body and subject to the laws of matter which veil our perceptions. The greatest practice that ensures our adherence to the light is the practice of *gratitude*, the acknowledgement of the divine partnership. For this reason, all practices of Inner Alchemy end with a *benediction*, an expression of thankfulness to God for life, for light, for love. This benediction should be a verbal affirmation of the acceptance of the condition which has been called for. In other words we thank God for the healing that has taken place, we thank God for the supply that has come, now as always, never absent and never late. This acceptance seals the call and actually pulls the picture we have created at an earlier stage into manifestation. The alchemical circuitry provides the energy and the substance which will attract what we are calling for by the use of the three powers mentioned earlier, propelled into the ethers by the right use of will, in alignment with the law of light: GOD IS THE ONLY PRESENCE, THE ONLY INTELLIGENCE, THE ONLY ENERGY AND SUBSTANCE ACTING EVERYWHERE.

Implications

The human energetic anatomy is the perfect playground for the God-forces. It is built, on the inside as on the outside, for optimal expressions of both earthly and cosmic modalities. The five fingers of the hand, the pairs of eyes, nostrils, feet, hands and so forth, the cavities within organs, the skull, the resonating chambers within the trunk of the body . . . We take so much for granted! Within our very own bodies lie the keys to godliness and mastery, particularly as revealed through the mechanism of the breath. Especially in the last twenty years, much has been written about the art of breathing. Breathing is synonymous with life. Rebirthing, for example, is as ancient as alchemy. The East remembers but a fraction of the powers generated by the practices of breath as taught by Taoism and the yogic system of *pranayama*, that is, controlled breathing. We are relearning now that breathing is not only a physical phenomenon. Within the human instrument reverberates the breath of God, the cosmic breath of electromagnetic forces that dance around us in an ocean of pulsation.

Breathing activates the properties within our lower faculties and provides the substance for transmutation as well. Depending upon the breath used, we activate the water, air, earth or fire elements and draw from those elements whatever powers need to be had, applied or modified. Breath is a catalyst, with infinite applications. Through certain patterns of breath we may also find the harmony so necessary on the spiritual path. Unless we lead a balanced life, and this includes a good dosage of *humour* and *play*, the intensified practices on the spiritual path take their toll on the physical organism. The attitude of determination and dedication must never be distorted into fanaticism and spiritual greed. We must adopt a relaxed attitude. In a sense there is plenty of time, because time is mind and truth lies beyond the realms of time and mind.

Inner Alchemy is a far cry from the alchemy of the Middle Ages coated with fear and mystification, in dark and darkening powers and lurid self-obsessed manifestations. At this time there is no more place for fear and destruction. The forces of light must prevail and light our way towards inner truths which are irrefutable and irreversible, once experienced. But there is no outer proof that can be offered to the sceptic. If we dare to experience it, being itself, is ample proof that there is but one energy, one substance, one light, one source – God within. Once touched, everything turns into gold. Gold and crystal are to alchemy as God is to life: they stand alone, incapable of contamination, with the purity of wholeness, essence and integrity.

The soul of Inner Alchemy is the fire of spirit. And fire, like man, is not of this earth, although earth is a part of him. Inner Alchemy is a process that leads to the very source of all processes: GOD HIMSELF.

Opening Meditation

Here are a few suggestions that help to set the tone within you for the practice of Inner Alchemy and affirm the divinity within you at the physical level.

Create a physical sacred space according to your nature. Take time to arrange it and establish this space as one for prayer and communication with the highest intelligence. As you are doing this, become aware of the feeling of reverence being generated within you. You are preparing to communicate with the godhead.

Dress for the occasion. Give your body and your appearance the attention that you would if you were going to visit someone very special – which indeed you are! This stage is often neglected and yet your body is the abode of the most high living God! Simplicity and cleanliness are the keys here. And don't forget the inside of your body too. You might like to qualify a glass of water with the power of light and sense, as you drink it, that this light is coursing through your insides.

Establish a harmonious atmosphere. Frankincense and sandalwood are great psychic cleansers. Peppermint oil is the fragrance of purity. Clear the atmosphere of your space by burning incense, with the intention of drawing out all negative vibrations and inviting the protection of the forces of light. I suggest you hold the container where you are burning the incense on the right palm and make counterclockwise circles around the entire space (and house or apartment). Follow the smoke and imagine it reaching into every nook and cranny. You may select a piece of music that is especially soothing. You might want to light a white, violet or blue candle.

Become still. It is best to meditate alone, at least part of the time. If you are with someone, create the feeling of being alone. Withdraw your energy into yourself. (If you are aware of the presence of the other, you are not in your own energy.) Settle within yourself, physically and mentally, and allow the sensations of the physical body and the thoughts in the mind to slide away. When you are no longer aware of distractions or individual thoughts, you are ready to begin.

If you have difficulty reaching stillness, seek to express the restlessness in a creative way that enhances the tone of what you are wanting to do. Dancing to flowing music is one of the ways that you might want to use.

Violet Flame Shaking Practice

One of the most effective ways of stilling the body and the mind is the practice of what I have come to call Violet Flame Shaking. This is a method inspired by a Rajneesh practice, which I use with beginners and old-timers alike. It should be a once-a-week practice for everyone on the path of alchemy.

Call for and then visualise violet flames coursing through your body, from the soles of the feet, sweeping upwards through the body. Vividly imagine these flames. Create the sensation of them entering through the feet and spiralling around and within your body, just as they would around a log of wood in the fireplace. Feel them working their way upwards, and as you begin to sense this, start to shake gently.

Start by shaking the legs from the hips, loosening the muscular hold at the genital area and the belly. When you feel comfortable and there is no tension in the shoulders, face or hands, when you can let it run on automatically so to speak, then you can allow the shaking to spread and include the shoulders, arms and ultimately the head and face. Finally the entire body is gently shaking – like a rag doll – limp and yet held firmly by the sense of an aligned spinal column.

Simultaneously, you are visualising the flames coursing through your body. As you become more proficient in the awareness of both activities at the same time, you will be able to direct the flames into specific areas of density and heal yourself. In time you will notice that these flames are real, especially when you see how they burn away and dissolve impurities at the cellular level and perhaps notice, too, how they seem to clear away thoughtforms and emotions almost magically. You will have a sense of lightness and weight, of greater vision and agility. When healing, or clearing happens, the colour may change from deep violet to pale ultraviolet, pink and white.

Stop when you feel like it. I usually stop when the flames turn white, or when I sense a unification in the body. Three to five minutes is about average. In cases where the person is disconnected from awareness of his body, I suggest ten minutes daily for a period of about two weeks. This particular process serves to unify the body, to relax and yet to redistribute the energies that collect in tension spots.

I now suggest that you sit or lie down and feel the energies coursing through your body. Feel what you have set into motion. Feel the streams and eddies, the circles and bubbles of light energy within your physical body. Feel the universe of vibrating, pulsating life within your body.

End by visualising a stream of golden light flowing like a river through you, coming from above and coursing down to beneath your feet. Absorb this golden light substance into the brain, the spine, the nerve endings and into every cell of your body.

Tune in. Feel Life within and around you. Be in the stillness and in the silence, in the tremendous inner activity and in the soundless sound of infinity. Stay there as long as you like. Allow your inner senses to open. Be receptive. There is nothing to do here. Just Be.

Come back to your ordinary reality. Bring back the experience of your own energetic anatomy and determine to integrate this into your everyday reality. As you return, become aware of the physical form of your body. Delineate with your mind the area that your body occupies. Do it several times and be sure to include the width and breadth of your body.

When you have clearly drawn the container of your body, feel the energies contained within it. In others words, pull in the energies that had expanded to surround your body and to give you the experience of your aura, and beyond. Sense the security within the physical form, the solidity of the compacted energies.

Deliberately breathe into the belly. Open and close the hands, move the feet . . . stretch. . . .

You might want to move around, dance, flow with beautiful music and celebrate the godliness of your physical body. You have just visited the macrocosm through the microcosm of your own physical being. Returning to the real meaning of prayer: Praise the God in you!

I Human Energetic Anatomy

Overview

The study of ourselves – our humanity, our mechanisms, our abilities and our perception – is the study of myriad permutations of energy. Besides a physical anatomy, we possess a very complex and subtle energetic anatomy that regulates our mind, our emotions, our psychic and spiritual faculties. Although this is not the only system, here we will explore the human dynamics in terms of seven bodies, each run by seven faculties and conditioned by seven rays.

Each person may be seen to function in seven different ways, which are called seven bodies or levels of consciousness. Beyond these seven bodies are five more dimensions which from our level of understanding pertain to pure spirit or cosmic force.

Each of our basic seven bodies corresponds loosely to a perception and is made up of substance which for our purpose we will see as particles in different degrees of density or condensation. Each body vibrates at a specific rate or frequency. The whole, or composite, of the seven functions pretty much like an orchestra. The quality of the orchestration will depend on the performance of each of its parts.

We've had few accurate guidelines to explain how we react, respond and are the way we are. Seeing ourselves as a composite of energies is new. What we don't yet fully grasp is that this energetic network which we are is wholly programmable. Our mind has already been programmed to believe and feel in certain ways, by our society, our parents, our environment, our culture and our age. We in fact condition, decondition and recondition ourselves. Our immediate world is a creation, a direct result of mind over matter. And although human behaviour has been viewed in terms of mental patterning, we understand very little of what MIND really is. We are only now beginning to realise that we use but a fraction of the brain.

Physically too we know little. When medicine divorces itself from mind it becomes fragmentary and ineffectual. Even the study of psychosomatic disease offers a superficial view. Science does not really know what makes man 'tick' physically, psychologically and spiritually; primarily because it does not embrace the realms of art and metaphysics. However reluctantly, we need to believe in miracles. Inner Alchemy is the study of miracles, of laws of Light, those laws that govern inner reality and in turn affect the outer.

I know a woman who cured herself of an illness by applying mental focusing and meditation techniques. She intuitively invoked the substance of light, or of sacred fire, available through inner dynamics. She produced the transmutation through an act of faith generated by feeling and the application of will or first ray power and thought. There are many cases like this in recorded history. What has been relegated to the realm of superstition is in effect a direct result of the application of universal laws of energy.

We have lost our connection to essence and as such our direct knowledge of it. Inner Alchemy is the rebirth of essence, clean, clear, simple and practical. When you know the universal laws you know that there are no miracles, or that everything in fact is a miracle.

Everything is energy. Energy is the interaction of substance and space. This substance through space has intelligence (something which Itzhak Bentov dealt with in his book *Stalking the Wild Pendulum*, Destiny Books, 1988), and is responsive to mental direction. Viewed simply this intelligence is Light or God. This primary unit of activity is what the ancients referred to as *prana*, the breath of life. We are currently discovering smaller and smaller building blocks than the atom which are pure light-substance and constitute the essence of all substance.

The fact that Life is Light has been observed by surgeons in the area of the pituitary and pineal glands within a live person. There is no light within the body of a dead person; and a dead person also weighs more. Light as Life seems to be an uplifting influence. Man's essence is pure consciousness expressing itself as a body of spirit through a body of physical matter. The body in which we exist has its own intelligence, its own messages, its own responses, but our real consciousness is of a higher order, of Light. Our body, and the consciousness or intelligence connected with it, is akin to the house we live in. It reflects us, but is not us.

We only think that we are physical entities because three-dimensional reality is so all-consuming. Our faculties are dual however: we have the faculty of cosmic consciousness and also of planetary consciousness. And we are subject to the laws of both matter and light, both planetary substance and Cosmic Light. We are subject to the laws of energy at the two levels.

At the level of the personality our responses follow very clear and decipherable laws. Everywhere we turn, we exist in some kind of relationship with living things. Feelings are constantly being triggered from and towards us. There is a certain pattern that elicits a response and a certain feeling which we identify as good or not-so-good. But THIS ACTIVITY IS NOT WHO WE ARE.

Now, the personality, because it is of planetary substance, responds with the planet. The planet has its own emotional and mental fields just as we do, because the planet is also an intelligence, an entity. At the level of planetary substance there is *polarisation*, or duality. In order for matter to hold, there needs to be negative and positive polarity, there needs to be a holding tension. Man as part of the planet is subject to these polarities. POLARITIES EXIST ONLY IN RELATION TO PLANETARY SUBSTANCE OR MATTER, AND NOT AT THE HIGHER LEVELS OF CONSCIOUSNESS. These physical, mental and emotional polarities, these conglomerations of opposites, rule our lower bodies and our actions and reactions with one another. It is extremely important to our liberation to understand that our planetary experiences apply to the vehicle, not to our consciousness or who we really are at the level of Being.

The way to mastery at the level of personality lies in the understanding of the dualities operating within us, and in the detached observation of them. Our polarised reactions such as joy and sadness, love and hate, harmony and discord, giving and taking, happiness and misery are natural motions of polarity. The moment we try to stay in one pole without taking into consideration the other, we create imbalance. Instead of trying not to feel sad or angry, you can understand that although your nature is blissful you are experiencing sadness at the moment. This process requires that we identify with ourselves at the level of Being (beyond duality), while

49

accepting the activity of the laws of matter. This is *not* repression as some may have it but a *requalification* of the energy, which we are then able to integrate into our totality.

The feeling of helplessness stems from believing that we are matter. It also stems from the belief that we are subject to duality at every level. The only way to transcend this vicious circle is by locating ourselves as Beings of Light; in other words, being one with our higher selves. When you are sad, notice the sadness. You are not sad, the body is sad, the chemistry of the emotional body is going through sadness, experiencing separation or disappointment. Don't deny the experience and fragment yourself further. Embrace it. Integrate it within your totality, whereby it gains power or momentum, while also increasing your tolerance levels for greater energy. Instead of shutting energy out, transform its quality and add its energy to the total system.

There are different kinds of energies that impinge upon and stimulate reactions in us. Perhaps the most difficult to master are those aroused through intimacy, particularly sexual closeness; hence the fear of intimacy in our times. At this level all energies converge with one another at the most intense and dense vibratory rate of the human anatomy. The base chakra has the greatest force for a very specific purpose: it draws energy in and converts it into a life form. Its power is enormous.

When you have been sharing your energies with someone in close physical, emotional and mental proximity and that someone leaves for one reason or another, you are going to feel the withdrawal of that energetic interaction. The energy alchemy of relationships is absolutely basic to the life process, to the process of transformation, transmutation, requalification and expansion of consciousness. Emotional withdrawal symptoms are as painful as those experienced by someone who has been addicted to drugs. In fact, addiction (adherence) is basic to the laws of matter, but *not* to the laws of Light.

How many of you have experienced the feeling of being ripped apart on the inside during separation from a loved one? You don't feel whole. You are in pain; you cannot sleep at night. . . . You are at that moment experiencing the action of the law of matter, of the merging that took place, of the separation that is happening, of the healing and of the wholeness; just as when you rip a plant apart, it suffers. It may wilt for a day or two and then it will adapt itself and grow strong again. Even though it was half, now it is whole. Energy alchemy in relationship will be a chapter in itself later on in the book.

The personality we have is a result of how we respond to the polarities within us. We will have a happy personality, or a sad and heavy one. We will have a nervous or lethargic disposition. Our personalities reveal how we deal with our polarities and the collection of responses we have programmed into our human computer. If, through habit or fear, I stress misery in my life, I cannot be happy. Instead I will be dark and heavy. If I emphasise sunshine instead of darkness, I will be light. I create myself by how I choose to qualify the energy of my responses to life, and these responses act as a magnet to like qualities (which accounts for all kinds of effects, both constructive and destructive).

We project what we feel and we also come to feel what we project. We all know that when we are in love everything looks beautiful. We can do anything. Everything is going our way, and therefore everything is possible. But the moment something crosses our way, we become angry, sulky, irritable.... And if someone says something nasty, we will tend to believe it and the world that was beautiful suddenly turns black. Nothing works; nothing is right. We are grumpy and it seems everybody is grumpy at us.

What happened? *You* created an emotional chain reaction which reflected back upon you and even upon events in our environment. You lost your vision, you lost the power to identify with yourself as a conscious presence within the sea of cause and effect around you.

Your world is actually a reflection of your mastery or lack of it, mirrored through your relationships, successes or failures, health, finances and so forth. If mastery is not showing up in your world, you have not integrated some aspects of yourself that relate to that. If you are still having problems in your world, and even if you feel it is someone else's fault, it is a clear indication that something about you is attracting this. This goes on at the highest as well as at the lowest energetic levels of life. Mastery is revealed through physical acts.

The consciousness of the alchemist, as the essential ingredient, must express a harmonious control and management of the three lower bodies: the physical, the mental and the emotional, in order to offer choice and determine direction. He chooses where he is going to go, what he is going to do, how he is going to manifest his world.

Nothing is impossible when the individual is in wise control over his emotional body. There must be no tension involved in this kind of control. The control that I am speaking about here comes from mastery – the absorption and requalification of energy. This mastery gives us an ability to contain and transcend the energy within us. At the mental level it is a form of knowing.

In embracing energy, be it physical, mental or emotional, we gain not only control but clarity, and a capacity to express ourselves creatively. This is what real choice is all about.

Our Original Purpose

Drawing from an analogy, let's consider briefly how we might have arrived at who and what we are. How did we take on this 'robe of many colours', these seven coatings?

If you can imagine God as an immense sea of fire, consider yourself a tiny spark of flame that has taken on an individual existence from the fire. Assume at this point that you want to experience for yourself, and you might even want to create universes by yourself. As a spark, you take on life the moment that you desire it. You become energised.

This spark has its own cohesiveness, but as it whirls through space at great speed substance adheres to it during its journey through lower and lower rates of vibration. At each level, the collected substance creates a body or vehicle of expression that reflects its activity there. At each stage the vibrations are so engrossing that in time, the essence of the spark as Light is forgotten. As the spark experiences the most dense and grossest of the new vibrations, it begins to express aspects of density that cause pain, such as possessiveness and jealousy (which are qualities of matter, not of light).

Now, when the pain becomes so great, that no outer recourse is enough, the attention (as longing) again goes to the still small voice, or memory of light within. When the little spark turns back to its nature as light, the light expands more and more and the process of irradiatory ascension, the dispelling of the density, begins. And this was its very purpose to begin with: to create universes by expanding the light, and to gain mastery through experiencing for itself.

As the little spark learns to transmute the density, it also learns how to control energy, it learns to co-create with what is in fact itself (at a higher frequency of being). It does this at every level of consciousness, at each of the vehicles or bodies of expression.

What does this mean for us right here in the three-dimensional existence? Within each atom of physical substance is a point of light reminiscent of the original spark. These points of light are in fact part of our Cosmic Selves, of our body of light. As we grow in awareness and consciousness we become lighter in every sense of the word. Some of the saints have even looked luminous, there is a radiance that emanates from the flesh. This process happens automatically. What Inner Alchemy does is accelerate the process by consciously expanding the points of light right from the very centre of the atoms of our cellular bodies. I call these processes 'calibrations' and have developed audiotapes that facilitate individual recalibration.

At a simultaneous angle of development, we seek to understand our psychological make-up as a process of energetic activity. Seven ray psychology provides such an outlook. Unfortunately there are not enough people who understand this psychology and who are either clairvoyant or pure enough to translate the data into common parlance. In understanding our own seven ray make-up we come to understand others. We come to comprehend the particular filters through which we operate.

Life's purpose is to bring down that light and raise or bless matter at each level of consciousness. We do this through our conscious experiencing of all that there is to experience, and through integrating the energy from each act, each emotion, each thought into our totality. This light is embedded within us at three-dimensional existence at the centre of each of the cells in our physical body. As the process of illumination happens it affects all the layers which are overlaid around the primary body or body of light.

Each of our bodies of expression and the psychological constitution of our personalities is determined, as we shall see, by the seven rays. The rays determine our attitudes, aspirations and even our modus operandi, creating the environment for the individual expression of the very quality of our life in its uncontaminated potency.

Your life task is actually decontaminating or purifying yourself at all levels in order to produce or emerge as pure individualised (alchemical) elixir. The combination of the rays were determined for the specific purpose of completing experience and relate closely to the structure of your body's cellular history as well.

Seven ray psychology even more than astrology can help you to discover your make-up, thereby cutting short painful years of hit-and-miss. You come to understand that you can't do what your neighbour does, but you can do something that he can't. It eliminates competitiveness and comparison, which are the root cause of conflict and discord in relationships, and fear and guilt at the inner levels. Knowing your strengths and limits brings a deep relaxation, a peace that leads to mastery.

Will you ask yourselves what it is that you can be and do? Which is your best positive trait? Which are your areas of difficulty? Here are some questions for self-exploration. In addition, formulate your own. Dare to go deeper and deeper, asking more and more questions. Answers don't come unless you ask.

Questions for Self-Observation

You may want to review them every ten days or so, to identify and accelerate whatever learning process life is providing you with.

1. Who am I? Physically. Emotionally. Mentally. (Describe how you feel and function in each.)
2. What is my relationship to the different parts of myself? To my body (awareness, weight management, etc.) To my mind (ability to concentrate, focus, direct or empty the mind). To my emotions (note identifications, attachments, loss of power, etc.)
3. Who am I to myself? Do I feel like different people, different personalities? (Identify these and give them specific names.)
4. Who am I in relation to others? Note relationships, types, duration, capacity for intimacy (karmic trends and changes, if any).
5. How do others see me? (See yourself through others' eyes.)
6. Who am I in relation to God, to my higher self? My grasp over cause and effect? Over dream states?
7. How do I perceive reality? Note changes and subtleties.
8. How intuitive am I? With people. Events. Myself.
9. What are my habits? (Become aware of patterns and changes.) How is my capacity for spontaneity increased? In what areas? Note obsessive behaviour: sex, food, thoughts, etc.
10. What is my relationship to work and outer events? Describe how you feel and function.
11. Where in my life am I out of control or find it difficult to manage? With whom?

12. What do I repress/suppress in myself, in my environment, or in others in my environment?
13. What do I fear? Be honest. What is at stake?
14. What do I dislike in others? (Notice at least three characteristics in three people. See if these are also in you or in someone close.)
15. How may I improve myself? (Be specific. Find an activity or action that will create that improvement.)
16. What steps have I already taken to improve myself? (Notice your progress and allow yourself the feeling of satisfaction.)
17. What are my ambitions, desires, plans for the immediate future? For the remote future? How well am I manifesting my desires?
18. How sensitive am I to others and how does that make me feel?

Formulate a clear plan with a clear picture of yourself, happy, healthy, creative, productive . . . and hold that picture. Walk into the picture (or let the picture descend and enfold you). Absorb it into the cellular structure. Create the feeling of already having it. Allow that feeling its fullness. Let it go. Accept the feeling of acceptance (as if you've already had this for a long time) and allow it to surround you. Bring yourself back to the present. Do not question or discuss this with *anyone*. Thank the God-presence within.

The Seven Rays

The Seven Rays are the building blocks of creation, the main frequencies or ingredients. Each one of the rays represents not only a colour but a musical note and a quality. The rays project a force rather than an energy. A force is different from an energy in that it is directional and specific. As these forces enter into the atmosphere of a planet, be it large such as the Earth itself, or small such as an individual human energy field, it colours that atmosphere.

Everything that exists in manifestation has been imbued by rays, in particular by the seven primary rays. The rays then serve to create the mould for a particular life form's character, so to speak. This is why I say that the study of the rays can serve to promote a deep understanding of the human personality and body types, since the rays condition the astrological influence themselves as well as affect us directly.

Our planetary system is built on the scale of twelve, but our visible spectrum consists presently of only seven. Although we speak of seven primary rays, even at the time of writing, the influence of more recently discovered rays is apparent. I speak about the gold and silver rays which serve to quicken the atomic structure for interdimensional purposes. The rays themselves are forces which are expressed as qualities and are only symbolically associated with a colour. Hence you may notice that the colours themselves have changed with planetary needs.

Everything is in relationship with everything else and all of life is, in fact, interrelated. The seven rays colour the seven bodies and are also outlined in the seven chakras. The remaining five bodies, or dimensions, and five out-of-the-body chakras will be discussed later in the section pertaining to interdimensional activity. At that level too exist cosmic rays which have nothing to do with planetary life at the human levels. As there are permanent rays to the Earth so there are also rays that are directed by interplanetary intelligence for specific purposes over certain periods of time. There exists in fact a planetary, galactic and intergalactic hierarchy of advanced intelligences, who direct the course of life and oversee its evolution.

For the purpose of Inner Alchemy what we need to understand is ourselves, our own composition or anatomy, how our parts work, and how to achieve mastery over ourselves and our inherent creative powers. In other words: how to consciously partake of all of life.

The seven rays originate through the primary module of three forces: the basic trinity of the father-mother aspect, the son aspect and the aspect of the spirit. The father-mother force, or *first ray* serves to impel life (activity) forward. It is pure will which is later depicted as strength, determination and leadership, instilling protection, power, initiative and faith. The colour for this force is blue: strong, cool, penetrating, primordial and infinite. From the deepest to the palest shades blue will inspire determination and confidence, as will the corresponding musical notes.

The *second ray* represents illumination, which is wisdom through love. It is seen in the relationship of a son to the father-mother as, freed from the need to propel itself forward, it reconsiders itself, evaluating, assessing, enlightening and teaching. This ray has been exemplified in history by Lord Buddha and by Master Jesus, both of whom provided blueprints (the basic thoughtform) for humanity. Its colour is the colour for intelligence, peace and illumination: yellow. It is also the colour for the sun, which not only nourishes but illumines.

The *third ray* recalls the aspect of spirit, or divine love. Freed of the need to create and comprehend, the third aspect concerns itself with pure play, the luxury of radiating its fullness, of infinite creativity which stems from a self-sustained wholeness and cohesiveness. It is the pure force of feeling-thought which, as you will remember, provides the motor activity for all manifestation and, in fact, gives birth to the remaining four rays. This is the true intelligence of the heart. The colour of this ray is pink from the palest hues to the deepest magenta. Historical figures on this ray generate the benevolence of goodwill. Saint Francis of Assisi is a good example. This ray also governs all animal and plant life on the planet and all energy distribution.

The following four rays emanate from the activity of the third. They are creative forces generated from the central pool of spiritual energy, which can, now that it has been launched into life, have a form and, animated by the force of feeling, express itself down to the minutest life.

The *fourth ray* has been named the ray of harmony through conflict, not because it fosters adversity or conflict but because it promotes a stability which can only be achieved through experimentation. Once the ideas have come forth, in the course of applying them to life situations we create the form through a process of trial and error. The fourth ray will seek to preserve the purity of the original impulse while generating implementation and expansion. It will deal with all aspects of expansion and contraction, in fact, as contraction brings forth further expansion. This particular ray is embodied in the concept of purity, and its colour is white or crystal.

The *fifth ray* is coloured green and represents truth in all its aspects, including its systematic applications through scientific endeavour. It denotes precision, justice and dedication to service. It is represented symbolically by the all-seeing eye of God, depicted in the old Masonic order and printed on the US dollar bill. It is the main ray responsible for healing and the working of the law in both its exoteric and esoteric expressions.

Whereas the fourth ray establishes solidity and the fifth ray systematic application, the *sixth ray* returns to the source through the aspect of devotion. Its activity relates to the holding of the peace and is closely linked to human emotionality, its refinement and its spiritualisation. The Eastern protectress Kwan Yin, is an excellent example of forgiveness and God's mercy, which she inspires.

Just as the Earth has its cycles, the rays dominate in cyclical manner over certain periods of time. At the time of the ministry of Jesus, the prevailing ray was the sixth. That was a time of great emotional intensity and the need for refinement was imminent. Master Jesus addressed the energy of the time, the aspect of devotional surrender to the Father or Godhead, and raised it to the aspect of transcendence, to such an extent that Christianity has come to call him the Prince of Peace. This ray is closely linked to the second major ray, Master Jesus' own ray. As the needs of the time have changed and this particular cycle towards the twenty-first century requires less emotional force and more clarity of mind and the functioning of the higher mind, the need for this ray's activity has diminished somewhat and has been supplanted by the second ray activity.

The prevailing ray of the present era is the *seventh ray*, a return to higher order represented by the concept of freedom and ceremony. Ritualistic, or rhythmic activity, as stated previously, generates momentum or the greater energy needed at present for the process of cosmic spring cleaning which characterises this cycle. The violet ray is the transmuting fire, the purifying, healing, regenerating force, leading to the qualitatively different life style emerging upon the planet. The transcendence here is from the individual to the global, from the personal to the impersonal, from the mundane to the spiritual. The violet ray is represented by the influx of ascended master teaching, headed by the Count of Saint Germain, the celebrated alchemist of European history. It is also characterised by the upsurge of ritual and ancient practices, particularly those of Druidic or earth quality.

Individual Application

Each of us is ruled by a certain soul ray, which is the ray of the interdimensional or higher self. This will be one of the three major rays and the hallmark of our essence. It is not always easy to identify this ray, which is usually obscured by the personality.

The personality ray shapes the temperament that we have as a result of a previous embodiment, or that we choose to have in order to learn what we came to learn. This ray will determine our individual life purpose, the aspirations that compel us into activity.

Then we have the rays that colour our emotional body, our mental body and our physical body, lending the attributes that we choose (or inherit) to work through. These rays determine how we complete our life purpose.

Feel free to identify with the characteristics within each of the rays and see which are the most prominent in your personality, in your body, in your mind, in your heart's longings. Do you yearn for beauty as an expression of the ultimate? Or is it love? Maybe it is supreme truth?

The rays manifest differently in the different vehicles. Bend the definitions a little to determine, for example, what your body ray might be. A first ray body will be generally wiry and strong, whereas a third ray body will be soft and giving. Dare to explore and experiment. Also know that you know. As you advance in the book you will learn how to enlist the help of your higher self to instruct you and to help you discover and understand yourself. Your higher self is constantly thinking, feeling, speaking through you. Trust it.

Examine your talents and your aspirations, your actions and your inspirations. Discover yourself as an energetic quality rather than as a psychology. Enter into each of the colours and experience for yourself the quality within each. You can buy large sheets of the appropriate colours at the local art supply store and tack them on the wall. Be sure that the colours are pure. Sit in front of each colour and imbibe it: project yourself into it or close your eyes and feel it surrounding you.

What colours do you have an affinity with and what colours seem to repel you? At what levels? How do they affect you? Make a chart of your reactions and later on repeat the process to see if the same variances apply before you try to determine what your individual ray combinations might be.

Two charts follow outlining the characteristics of the rays and also their use through visualisation, particularly for alchemical or transmutation work. Throughout the book I will propose practices and suggestions for their use.

Fig. 1.1 The Seven Rays

I. WILL OF GOD – Blue

The force that makes the decision to draw life to a purpose. Usually rules executives and rulers. It instils protection, power, initiative and faith.

II. ILLUMINATION – Yellow

The directing intelligence. The generated force that cognises and enlightens. Used in all perception, comprehension and education, where ideas need to be made practical. Rules teachers, educators and students wherever there is need for understanding and *wisdom through love*. Used in discrimation, discretion and direction in the use of one's life.

III. INTELLIGENCE OF THE HEART OR DIVINE LOVE – Pink

The harmoniser. Raises, purifies and perfects the feeling world. Gives rise to the development of ideas, i.e. the *actions* by which God-ideas are made manifest through the following four rays. Draws forth the good in people. Rules arbitrators, artists and peacemakers. Its nature is cohesive power, instilling a sense of brotherhood, goodwill, tolerance, unity, culture and tact.

IV. HARMONY THROUGH CONFLICT – White or Crystal

The purifier of ideas. It holds the original divine plan, without distortion. Instils integrity and purity through all of life's activities (or testing grounds). Represents impersonal service, and rules builders, architects, engineers, musicians and artists of all sorts.

V. SCIENCE – TRUTH – Green

Generates scientific presentation and the systematic action of the cosmic law; understanding of the exactitude and mathematical accuracy of the laws of creation. Instils concentration and consecration to serving the Light. Creates selflessness and outer surrender and rules such professions as doctors, nurses, healers, inventors and scientists. Is responsible for all science, precipitation, etherealisation, levitation, all vocations and healing in general. This ray represented the old Mosaic law.

VI. DEVOTION – Gold/Ruby

Imparts spiritual nourishment and the radiating of spiritual vitality, peace, tranquillity, healing and ministration. Provides the sustaining power of peace needed to make manifestation permanent. Rules ministers, priests, healers and all professions where devotion, forgiveness, mercy, grace and ministration are called for. Was the prevailing ray at the time of Jesus.

VII. FREEDOM, CEREMONY – Violet

Represents conscious invocation by which energy is transformed. Also purification of existing forms and the redemption of their energies. As such it facilitates sublimation and transmutation. Works through rhythm (rhythmic invocation, decrees and chants utilising sound or the spoken word). Rules gentlemen and gentlewomen and all fields utilising diplomacy, refinement and ordered service.

Fig. 1.2 Use of the Seven Rays in Purification,
Transmutation and Manifestation

FIRST RAY – Blue

Invokes power, will, abundance, opulence. Is used to crack, shatter, break up substance at the different densities. It is visualised with tremendous power, swordlike, seen as blue flame, as a bolt of lightning, or as electricity. It may be also be used as a strong protective shield over people, places or things, and even parts of the body (particularly around the throat chakra, its home base on the physical body). Its force is most imminent at the level of the causal body.

SECOND RAY – Yellow

Pertains to the sun (or son aspect in the Trinity). It colours the Christ which in the physical body is outlined at the level of the cosmic heart. It provides the balance between the first and third rays, between power and love. This ray refines the mind and clarifies the consciousness. It is the colour of peace and invoking this colour will soothe human activity, particularly the nervous system. It may be visualised as pale golden or brilliant yellow gold, the latter serving to accelerate the vibratory activity of the brain to give access to higher dimensions. It is seen as golden liquid light, as sunshine, as golden oil (over the nervous system) or as a golden seal (as over the solar plexus). It is the colour of both Master Jesus and Lord Gautama and of their service to this planet.

THIRD RAY – Pink

Signifies love and the activity of the Holy Spirit. This ray provides the primary substance for all activity, as love is sufficient unto itself and its nature is cohesiveness. From this force, the other four emanate to qualify the activity of the force of Love. Pink, in its various shades from the palest to magenta, is used to penetrate where sheer power would shatter the individual. It shatters patterns obstructing inner or self-love. It is best used around angry or hate-filled people, to induce the activity of the higher self which is love.

FOURTH RAY – White

This ray is actually crystal coloured. It may be visualised as fluidity, the colour of water, or silvery as in the silver cord that connects the etheric to the physical vehicle. It is the colour of the ascension flame, that process that surrounds the physical body during the transmutation transition. As it holds the divine pattern in the body, it also loosens it. It is the colour of purity and is seen around angelic apparitions. One of its wonderful uses is as a stream through the brain, linking our thinking to the higher self visualised in front and slightly above. Its seat is at the base of the spine in the human body.

FIFTH RAY – Green

It is the ray governing healing and scientific endeavours. As a flame it is used in transmuting limitation and developing inner vision. Its seat is at the level of the third eye: it rules the lower mental body and as such may be directed into substance that blocks the manifestation of the God Idea.

SIXTH RAY – Ruby/Gold

This ray promotes impersonal love and devotion in the individual. As a laser it is used to penetrate and shatter thoughtforms. It is especially effective in opening up the world beneath our feet where many satanic and demonic forms exist, bringing the substances up for transmutation. It is a very intense ray, particularly as it affects the emotional body and its activities through the solar plexus. Its use was prevalent in biblical times and during the time of Jesus's life. As a form of protection it seals off negative aspects of the lower world until one can handle them. Seen as boiling ruby oil (opens up the subconscious), a growling ruby ray (dislodges, opens and explodes substance which is difficult to move) and the ruby cylinder (which protects from projections and negative influences). Its use has been largely de-emphasised and transferred to the third (primary) ray (gold).

SEVENTH RAY – Violet

This is the most active ray at this time and promotes divine alchemy. It is the ray governing all ceremonial magic, as in the Druidic tradition (remnant of the Atlantean heritage). It provokes freedom and a sense of forgiveness, purification and redemption – conscious transmutation or requalification of substance. It is the colour for mastery over the physical plane, visualised as violet flame, which is the grace of Christianity. Its realm is at the etheric (4th body), working through the second centre and affecting all levels of physicality, facilitating the collaboration with the higher self and the merger therein.

The Seven Bodies

The number seven plays an important part in this system of worlds and characterises all manifested reality. Seven rays. Seven bodies. Seven chakras. . . . Beyond these are five more dimensions that pertain to planetary experience, but not at the level of personal evolution, as we shall see later.

We've conceived of the real you as a spark from Spirit which takes on different coatings. These coatings at the varying stages are the seven bodies. The first body created is of the finest energetic frequencies of Light. We call this body the seventh body as we view it from the perspective of physicality. The last body to be created is the physical body. For our purposes this is the first body.

We shall call the original spark the individual God-Self. Its attributes are of the Godhead and it is in fact the individualised presence of the Godhead, as pristine, pure and fully powerful as it ever was, though obscured and largely dormant. This presence resides in the uppermost regions of the planetary vibrational scale; the twelfth dimension. It represents the hallmark of your individuality and your Life force at the electronic level. It is the source which you draw from: It is Life, It is intelligence, It is Love. It *is* God – the God-Self.

This electronic source projects itself through the different dimensions until it reaches the third plane, which is where we are in a physical form. Midway between the third and twelfth dimensions is the seventh. The seventh, as we shall explore more deeply within the chapters on interdimensionality, is the region of the Akashic records and the higher self. It is the intermediary station, the bridge between our personal and Cosmic Selves.

For now, let's view the process of the creation of the bodies and how they relate to us in the here and now. Each body, from the seventh to the first is a kind of step-down transformer, channelling the Life force in degrees and varieties of expression. The electronic vibration of the seventh body is absolute. Like the Godhead it is all that is, without attributes. In order to express it needs to fragment its powers, abilities and energies. If the electronic vibration were to be directed into the physical it would literally electrocute you and blow all your circuits.

Each one of the seven bodies acts as a protective shield for the other. Each is a vehicle of awareness which senses a specific realm of vibration and activity constantly, whether we are conscious of it or not. In the path of Inner Alchemy we endeavour to detect and function within each of these levels consciously.

Although all seven bodies as faculties of consciousness are expressed within third-dimensional reality, the first three bodies – the physical, the emotional and the mental – are what we term the personality.

The fourth body is a bridge between the upper and the lower three. It is a messenger body and a record keeper which actually links up with the blueprint for each of the lower three bodies in embodiment. The upper three bodies are spiritual by nature and serve as interdimensional and cosmic receptors and transmitters.

The physical body is in reality a conglomerate of all the others, with the addition of planetary substance or matter. (All the other bodies are made up of light-substance.) This explains why everything, mental, emotional, psychic and spiritual, is outlined in the physical body.

Below are the general characteristics of the seven bodies as experienced in the physical plane, in order of their creation around the descent of Light into matter:

The Seventh Body

This is what we call the electronic body. It is cylindrically shaped and enfolds all the other bodies within itself. The substance of the electronic body, although permeating all the bodies right into the cellular, is found in its purest form at the outermost ridges of the cylinder. This is the finest grade of light-substance, which can appear as threads of silvery-golden light.

In our dreaming or meditative states, when we feel very

expanded and uplifted, we are often in touch with the formless and pure reality of our electronic body. It is in fact a cosmic presence with no relation to physicality.

Visually, this body perceives infinity. The sense is one of huge spaces and light, diaphanous substance and large lightforms. Auditorially, the sound heard is like white noise, or a deep throbbing humming. Sensorially, it experiences tremendous peace and stillness, inexplicable and without content; also power, as if one were a sun of majestic proportions and commensurate luminosity.

When one is able to maintain consciousness at this level, which is done only through meditation in environments that are removed from external (urban) stimulation, the experience is what the East has called one of 'seedless-Samadhi', ('seedless' because there is no perspective from which to observe reality, just pure being-ness.)

Buddhas of the past and Enlightened Ones who still watch over this planet, as well as our own God-Selves, reside at this level. In order to teach and reach us they must lower their vibration to meet us at one of the lower planes.

The Sixth Body

This is the causal body. Its shape is egglike and it occupies a slightly smaller sphere within the cylinder. It has been perceived as a form made up of rays of iridescent pastel light around the aura. This body is loosely associated with activities at the seventh and higher dimensions.

Visually, one sees tremendous light and lightforms, but viewed from a centralised perspective. Auditorially, it is similar to the seventh body perception. Sensorially, one experiences a feeling of majesty and mastery of spiritual ecstasy and fulfilment. It is the emotional (feeling) level of the spiritual plane.

When a person's consciousness is stationed at the level of vibration of the causal body, we say that they have merged with their Christ-like or higher self, that repository of completed or perfected experience over all embodiments.

Whereas the electronic body was the essence or source, the God-Self, the causal is the individualised expression at the level of essence. It is our perfect self; what Christians call the Son in relation to the Father. In the East it is called the experience of Samadhi-with-seed (the 'seed' referring to a central vantage point through which one perceives reality).

The Fifth Body

This is the higher mental body. Its range is more compacted, circular in shape. At this level there is a distinct intelligence, capable of dealing with all levels of reality.

Visually, we perceive our own and others' guides and spirits of high development, very beautiful and radiant, godlike. Auditorially, we sense the inner voice and inner knowing from partnership with our own higher self. These are the moments of inspiration and prophecy, where we might see and hear voices and infer meaning. Sensorially, we experience a sense of mastery over the physical vehicle, a unitary experience of the three lower bodies and a direct connection to higher forces. Strength and certainty are its hallmarks.

The higher mental body acts as a communication bridge between all bodies. It has a distinct existence, quite different from the other bodies. Its form within the aura has been described as made of electric blue webbing.

As a consciousness, the higher mental body is a function of intelligence that goes beyond dualism and which has access to all we have ever known or been, and all that has ever existed in this planet. This body understands the karmic forces behind actions. It is the divine discerner, the proverbial watcher, the superconscious.

Let's take the time for a moment to understand that all our bodies or levels of consciousness operate separately and also simultaneously. Right now you are here, in all of your bodies. Your consciousness, like a TV station, is arrowed at one channel, so you can't fully grasp that you are also tuning into other levels of reality.

Right now you are understanding me through your lower mental body, but your physical and emotional bodies are also responding. Take a moment to notice what your physical body is sensing and what your feelings are about what you are reading. Take notice of how your higher mental body comprehends holistically. Become aware of how your spiritual bodies are humming ... in a kind of remembrance.

You are in fact in touch with some feeling-knowing-sensing faculties at the causal level, and with the grace or ecstasy of your electronic self. As you are experiencing all of these things while reading, you can imagine how much you are also experiencing while talking, dancing, loving and sleeping!

The Fourth Body

This is what I call etheric body.

This body is closer to the physical. Its substance is of the fourth ether and consists of an exact replica of the physical body. The colour of the body itself is silvery-blue. In every way it is closer to the physical existence and serves as a messenger between dimensions, particularly from the third to the seventh. It is also linked to the emotional and mental bodies of consciousness in out-of-the-body projection. It is attached to the physical by the silver cord.

This vehicle contains traces of the experience accumulated over the past. All the karma that you have gathered (good and bad) is impressed on this body, as are the chakras and the astrological programming (the imprints of planetary influences). The astrological programmings will correlate to the seven ray make-up. All of these shape and mould the etheric body, which in turn shapes and moulds the physical, lower mental and emotional bodies.

Visually, this body perceives more keenly and sharply than the physical faculties. Etheric vision includes auric vision and the ability to see through the body and through physical objects. Auditorially, telepathy is possible at the level of the etheric body, and an overall keen sense of hearing. Sensorially, this body feels extremely intensely and is responsible for the feeling-memory associated with amputated limbs. As a body of light, however, it can be refined to exclude painful stimuli. Sex distinctions (which are absent in the higher bodies) start at the level of the etheric.

The Third Body

This is the lower mental body complex. It is more like a frequency of consciousness, although some healers perceive it as a body shape made of pale golden lines of force.

The seat of the lower mental body is the physical brain. The functioning of the brain, as we know, affects all the parts of the body. The frequency of this body is much easier to detect when engaged in deep thought. It is a linear energy and rather cold. It reflects the consensus of facts and knowledge of the ages.

The lower mental body is closely connected to the solar plexus chakra. The lower mind, like the mass mind that it reflects, operates through emotionally charged belief, judgements, superstitions and assessment with tremendous righteousness, directness and personal will. Business ethics, the stock market in particular, have been run in their entirety by solar plexus, lower mental body power energy.

This collectively based personal consciousness builds the thoughtforms that the emotional body animates and brings into manifestation, but it is devoid of feeling or sensation, and even sensitivity. It is locked into its own programming. We will discuss this body in greater depth within the section on the power of thought.

The Second Body

This is the emotional body, a multicoloured, easily agitated, water-like energy surrounding and interpenetrating the physical body, which is capable of expanding to reach quite a large circumference. Everyone knows how a highly emotional, volatile person is capable of filling up an entire room with his or her energy.

This body has the same properties of water, with currents, whorls, vortices and eddies of energy within itself; and like water, it can be refreshing, cool, nourishing, or heavy, stormy and disturbing.

The nature of this particular energy is tremendously dynamic. The energy of feeling within this body moves and gathers sub-stance. It is the energy that agitates thought into manifestation.

This body has been called by some the astral (or star-like) body. You use it every time that you project your emotions. Feelings can become so intense that before you know it you are swept away by them, pulled into some emotional whirlpool which is difficult to subdue or control, especially as it will tend to travel towards the object of its desire. Emotions are experienced at the second and solar plexus centres. The mechanism that projects the emotions is at the solar plexus. The feelings themselves are born at the second centre.

The emotional body has been the target of massive experimentation, particularly during the encounter and growth groups of the 60s and 70s. It is the body through which we experience ourselves as an emotional agent experiencing others: we feel ourselves feeling others.

The emotional body is not limited to time and space. It moves with ease and agility. Lovers know the feeling when their loved one is thinking of them, or when their loved one has been unfaithful. They know this intuitively through the workings of the emotional body.

A person who is emotionally addicted is easily bored and needs to create drama after drama to remain interested in life. On the other hand, a harmonised emotional body is a delight to be with. It is the intuitive vessel that feels with the heart of the God-Self and transmits that love emotionally to all of creation upon the earth.

This body and the dynamics of feeling and emotion will be discussed in the chapter on the power of feeling, and also in discussing the second chakra within the section on chakras.

The First Body

This is our ordinary physical body. By the very fact that we have drawn from the planetary substance in building this body, we are committed to the evolution and safekeeping of the earth. What we do to our bodies we do to the planet, and vice versa.

The physical body outlines karmic impressions and also reflects the planetary status at the moment. Not everything that is manifested on the physical body has its origins in personal past history. Our embodiments, or the quality of our life, can help transmute much of the pollution that has been generated throughout time.

The physical does reveal your emotional and mental attitudes. Therapies such as Reichian and neo-Reichian, bioenergetics and others will concern themselves with the reading of body types. You can tell a person's character structure by the way their shoulder lies, by the slant of the hips, by the angles of the legs, by the way they hold their feet or the shape of their toes, by the set of the jaw, the face. The body is a map that can be read by anybody who is trained. Everything shows up.

The physical body exists only in three-dimensional time and space. It can only be here. When a person is fixed on physicality,

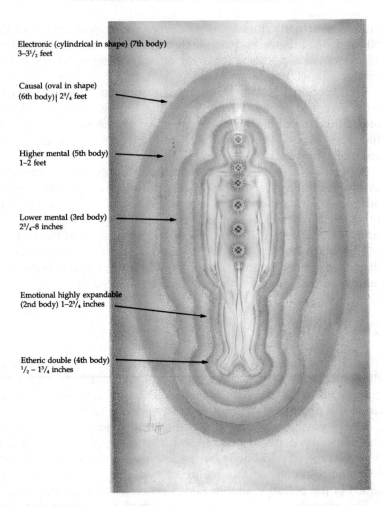

Electronic (cylindrical in shape) (7th body)
3–3½ feet

Causal (oval in shape)
(6th body)| 2¾ feet

Higher mental (5th body)
1–2 feet

Lower mental (3rd body)
2¾–8 inches

Emotional highly expandable
(2nd body) 1–2¾ inches

Etheric double (4th body)
½ – 1¾ inches

Notice that the etheric (4th) is closest to the body.
The 2nd and 3rd extend out further.

Fig. 1.3 Layers of the Aura

he cannot perceive other realms of activity. His vibration is slow
and his sensation is restricted to dense stimulation.

Inner Alchemy concerns itself with the consciousness of light
within matter and with the Light Body, its awakening and its

integration within all aspects of living. The seven bodies outlined here apply to levels of consciousness and not to physical structure, as some of the more scientifically oriented healing practices describe.

The seven bodies are closely connected to the seven chakras. Whereas the chakras are focuses of energy, the seven bodies are the consciousness formed by the interplay of these focuses of energy in planetary life. For this reason the chakras are the subject of our next chapter.

Fig. 1.4 The Seven Bodies

1st: THE PHYSICAL	Repository of the substance of all the bodies. Outlines all the bodies and transmits all the energies from the rays through the chakras (represented by the endocrine system here). The densest sheath. Exists in three-dimensional time and space only. Its seat is the base of the spine.
2nd: THE EMOTIONAL	Not limited to time and space. Responds more rapidly. Its sensors reach out. Enjoys intensity and change. Respond to finer vibrations. Its feeling capacity ranges from animal passions to unselfish love. In conjunction with the Third Body it translates feelings into actions on the physical plane, drawing the necessary substance for manifestation. Its mechanism operates from the solar plexus.
3rd: THE LOWER MENTAL	The logical or concrete mind. Receives thoughts from a higher plane for the purpose of implementation on the physical. Subject to illusion and control. Builds thought-forms largely from the mass-mind. Is separated into sub-planes, or compartments. It seat is the physical brain.
4th: THE ETHERIC	The 'refined' physical. Contains the etheric records and the Light pattern body, the astrological energies and the chakras (source of vitality. Providing an opportunity to learn mastery over impacts. This body is the bridge between the upper and lower vibratory frequencies. It is the vehicle for out-of-the-body travel, linked to the mental and emotional consciousness. It is connected through a silver cord to the physical.
5th: THE HIGHER MENTAL	Beyond dualistic thinking. Intuition. Knowing. Frees us from the vibrations of the material plane. Can be subject to illusion. Acts as the go-between for the Christ consciousness and the personality, or human. The discrimination of the super-conscious. Its seat is in the third eye area.

71

6th: THE CAUSAL

Also known as the Christ consciousness. The storehouse of treasures and talents from the source. The perfected self. Its seat is in the third eye and extends out of the body over the head and just in front of the forehead.

7th: THE ELECTRONIC

The individualised God-presence or source of all energy. Radiates pure unqualified energy for use in all the bodies. Its field extends at least thirty feet over the top of the head.

The Chakras

The chakras are spherical vortices on the etheric body that act as receivers and transmitters for the rays, and colour our activity on the physical plane through the function of the endocrine glands. These glands affect physical substance at the level of body functions, mental balance and emotional integrity.

There is much talk nowadays about the chakras. There are chakra workers, chakra balancers, chakra readers and so on. It might appear that the chakras are the wherewithal of consciousness and life upon the planet. They aren't. They express the results of complex dynamics rather than act as the cause of behaviour. Sometimes they are overactive; sometimes they are underactive, as are the glands that they rule. They are never entirely blocked or closed.

Consciousness is a function of the entire life stream as it expresses itself in the bodies, through the coloration of the rays, which in turn impress or map out a potential plan for the life. The chakras reflect the workings of this consciousness, as they themselves are used by the life stream. The chakras, like energy, are neutral. It is the use that we make of their activity and of our energies that is either constructive or discordant. Of course, the chakras will also reflect the atmospheric conditions of the time, and if we are being impinged upon by a certain ray or astrological configuration which hosts a particular combination of rays, we will be affected accordingly.

The chakras are many in number. Systems have been built on as few as three major chakras and on as many as three hundred or more foci of energy, such as the system of acupuncture and shiatsu. The customary number used to understand the subtle energetic network in the body is seven.

The seven basic chakras are loosely related to the seven body

73

sheaths in that they seem to plug into the consciousness of the different bodies at the centre involved. In any event their activity is primarily concerned with earth life and development. The lowest chakra will pertain to the embodiment into matter and the highest or seventh will represent the leap from material to cosmic dimensions.

There are different chakra maps or systems, according to tradition and historical time frame. The energetic anatomy of man has evolved with planetary consciousness and the needs of the time. The Vedic or Hindu map will differ from the Theosophical map and all will differ from the contemporary Western maps.

Sexuality is a function of the whole being: physical, mental, emotional, psychic and spiritual. The human being experiences sexuality (the meeting of negative and positive polarities) at each of the chakras. Everything pertaining to our physical embodiment *must* be polarised: the seven bodies are polarised from each other on both men and women, as are the chakras on both sexes. What is positive for one sex will be negative for the other. This facilitates merger and intensification of energy at each level for purposes of growth and expansion.

Unfortunately, at present our body centres are negative absorbers, accepting and taking on the qualities about us, instead of being positive and radiating focuses, accepting only that which is desired. Chakras are meant to be magnetic and irradiatory.

There is no 'good' or 'bad' chakra. There is no higher or lower chakra in terms of spirituality. *All* chakras are in fact needed for earthly experience and the spiritualisation process itself. There are only higher and lower frequencies, like musical notes or shades of coloration, each equal, each beautiful, each necessary.

There is a double directional flow in operation through the chakras, depending upon the degree of individual experience and mastery. In previous cycles the kundalini* force, a spiral movement that drives the physical energy upwards towards greater and greater consciousness, more refinement and finer degrees of perception, was stressed. Whereas *in physical terms only* there is an upward-moving current, consciousness actually makes three journeys

---

* Kundalini is a Sanskrit word that literally means serpent-like. It has been used to describe the wavelike movement of energy in different parts of the body, but is best known as the yoga of the ascending current of force through the spinal column, or Kundalini Yoga.

through physicality: ascending towards spirit, redescending again into matter and finally ascending again with the full integration, acceptance and power of each centre mastered. At this particular phase of planetary development, much of humanity is at the redescending stage, consciously embodying Light at cellular levels, lending itself to the activity of cosmic forces upon matter.

Understand that although each chakra function will be described separately, they function as a whole, and our consciousness will lock itself into any one, or group of them, over a period of time. Each chakra also has a dual function. With the exception of the seventh, each chakra will involve a frontal or extroverted (worldly) and inner or introverted (spiritual) activity.

The First or Base Chakra

The functioning of this chakra will determine our connection to the earth and matter. It is the anchor of the spirit, so to speak. Along the spine there is a particular kind of tissue which seems to be responsible for holding the body in shape. This tissue appears to be tied into the base chakra's operational activity. When not working properly, disease takes over and the body begins a process of deterioration, which would indicate some connection to the immunological system as well.

This is the chakra commonly associated with sex. It is also the seat of the most intense energy in the human body, that energy that draws substance together to create a life form. This particular chakra, as do all chakras, will ignite to the stimulus of spiritual intent. When highly activated by desire, the individual will immediately seek to satisfy the craving felt at the level experienced. Once experienced or satisfied, or course, the energy level recedes. With consistent drainage, it will never rise beyond its initial intensity, operating pretty much on what I call the 'itch' syndrome. This is what happens at the instinctual or animal level of experience.

When, however, the individual is activated at higher aspirational levels of being, such as at the levels of emotion, power or unconditional love, he will choose to delay the satisfaction at the lower frequency levels until the higher need is quelled. The satisfaction may even be transferred to another dimension altogether, whereby

75

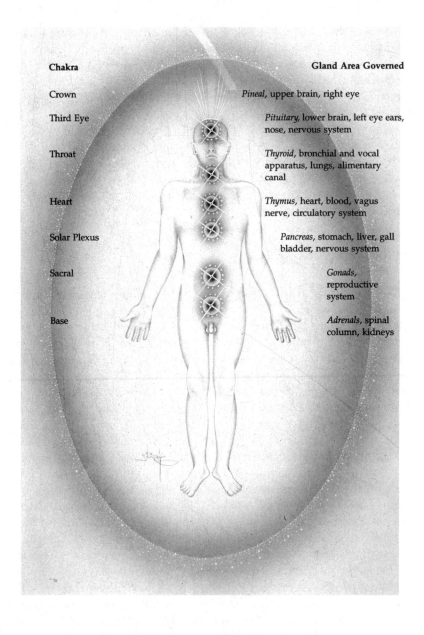

Chakra	Gland Area Governed
Crown	*Pineal*, upper brain, right eye
Third Eye	*Pituitary,* lower brain, left eye ears, nose, nervous system
Throat	*Thyroid*, bronchial and vocal apparatus, lungs, alimentary canal
Heart	*Thymus*, heart, blood, vagus nerve, circulatory system
Solar Plexus	*Pancreas*, stomach, liver, gall bladder, nervous system
Sacral	*Gonads*, reproductive system
Base	*Adrenals*, spinal column, kidneys

Fig. 1.5 The Seven Major Spinal Chakras

the initially sexual stimulus would not even be acknowledged as such.

Sexuality as well as any activity at the level of the base chakra is animal lust, passion devoid of individuality and tenderness. It is the drive for instant gratification, focused on the self and not on the other. The main objective at this level is survival, where self-needs such as food, sex, security and sensation are imminent.

As the centre that is responsible for invoking and creating a life form, its uncontaminated power is one of extreme purity. Mastery over this centre can only be had through purity and the acknowledgement of responsibility that comes with the perception of oneself in embodiment (through partnership with Earth and its forces).

It works pretty much like this. The consciousness nose-dives, so to speak, into matter at the densest level. It requires heavy stimulation to feel itself alive. It also requires heavy foods and much sleep. Aesthetics is not a priority, and neither is social behaviour or spirituality. The individual is entirely involved in the experience of the element earth. The chakra activates the adrenals (the fight or flight mechanisms), the kidneys (fear), and the spinal column, while embodying fourth ray activities, which involve the form and processes such as purification and refinement. In other words, the fourth ray projects its force through the etheric dimension and creates the glandular activity at the physical levels as mentioned above.

The colour that has been connected to the base chakra is red. Red activates the motor mechanism at the densest levels, propelling it forward to experience. The purified chakra, however, will appear white, or ultraviolet white, the colour of its respective ray. The coloration at each of the chakras will be pure. In between, the colours will appear in varying stages of muddiness and distortion. The activity of the chakras is mastered once the individual is able to use energy purely, accessing it freely and placing it, as well as all the others in the service of the highest values, without repression or indulgence.

The individual will need the purified activity of an integrated, healthy base chakra for all his earth plane activity, much as a tree will need its roots to soar higher into the heavens. Consciousness will descend into the base level, flush through and then rise again according to the focusing mechanism of the individual. Should he choose to focus it primarily at the first level, his attitudes, appearance, tastes and habits will reflect the characteristics of this centre, including the need for violent relationships to provoke the feeling of life.

It will be interesting, and in fact necessary, for the aspiring alchemist to notice his physical and emotional tendencies and their variations from day to day, to determine which chakra is most active or which chakra is seeking to be awakened further, where the consciousness has been focused, and whether positive or negative attributes are being expressed. He will then have the choice of clearing, refining and expanding beyond his own unconsciousness.

The wilful misuse of this chakra will result in numerous spinal and haemorrhoidal problems on the physical, loss of resources or control on the emotional and social levels, and a sense of alienation on the spiritual. The problems on this level will involve the lessons surrounding the correct use of the will.

The experiences of the base chakra will concern physicality, security, strength and solidity.

The Second Chakra

This chakra is centred in the physical body around the reproductive organs, or the gonads. At this level the indwelling spirit seeks to experience another. To do this he must experience himself as a sensing, emotional being. Sensuality is associated with consciousness at the level of this centre, involving the play of male and female.

The emotional training will involve expanding the capacity to receive and to give. When that is blocked the experience sought will be the intensities of pleasure or of pain. The caricature of an individual stuck at this level would depict the hysterical and the emotional addict; those individuals who seek to assault the senses by over-indulgence in emotional interactions and intensities. The usual amount of sleep required to restore the organism from this kind of existence would be about ten hours.

At the level of mastery, the individual's attention at the second chakra integrates with both social and personal identity and equilibrium. His energy feels stable, balanced, present and available to the other in a very physical and emotionally responsive way.

The nature of this centre is waterlike, from the raging oceans to the placid mirror-like aspects of water. The tendency of the individual will be more oriented towards preservation. In other words planning for the future. This chakra is ruled by the forces of the seventh ray: that activity which generates and restructures matter itself. The colour that energises this centre is orange; the colour of the purified chakra will reflect the pink tones of its ray.

The Third Chakra

Now the individual is ready to learn the lessons of control through the experience of domination and submission. Many experiences may pass before he can master this activity at the level of the solar plexus, which affects the entire nervous system, the liver, the gall bladder, the pancreas and the stomach.

The individual must learn how to manage his own power in the world and in himself; in other words a sense of cooperation, or a balance between activity and passivity. He learns through power struggles for sensation and security, through jealousy and possessiveness, which often results in heart attacks and ulcers.

In the end, the individual at the level of the solar plexus learns to express himself physically in an appropriate manner and gains access to a sense of sight or foresight. At the solar plexus, in fact, there are primitive brain cells. The sense of clairsentience, of being able to 'tune in' to people, places and things, comes from the intensified use of this centre, as does the ability to project the body (and maintain the memory of it) through the etheric. This will include time travel.

In its inactive phase, the organism seeking to expand the activity of this center will crave fast energy foods such as sugar, coffee, tea, alcohol and drugs, with an average sleep requirement of eight hours.

The element associated with this chakra is fire. It is fire-like in its drive and its totality. The main ray operating through it is the sixth, promoting the refinement of emotional generation. The sixth ray through its previous uses is also linked with the mobilisation faculty of all lower world phenomena and the subconscious. In our time the sixth ray and the solar plexus will tend to generate power and its misuse, such as cut-throat competitiveness, and its neglect,

79

such as the naïveté and veneration of authority that is manifest today.

The vitalising colour for this centre is yellow. The rays which feed it are ruby and gold, the coloration of the sixth ray.

The Fourth Chakra

This chakra is responsible for all compassion and selfless love, a transcendence of judgmentalism, prejudice and dualistic thinking. This centre is in fact the seat of the higher self, promoting unconditionality and release of attachments. At this level the emotions have become empathy and deep understanding. The individual will generate a sense of impeccability and creativity, feeling a nurturing and nourishment within himself and irradiating that quality to others.

The consciousness has moved beyond the self-involvement of the second chakra and the ambitiousness of the third and now finds itself in a relationship with its environment and spirit. This is why the East emphasises the qualities of this chakra. The ego, that sense of separation from others, begins to dissolve.

The representative element here is air, its lightness and its spaciousness. The ray is the third major ray of divine love. The colour for this ray and the purified functions of the heart centre is pink, but the vitalising, balancing force for its functioning is green, the colour of harmony and balance. At this level the self seeks to integrate the upper and lower force within itself, and also the right and left brain functions. This is a meeting place for all dualities, represented in some systems as the Star of David: joining both upright and downward triangular forces.

The energies generated here affect the heart, blood and circulatory system, the vagus nerve and also the thymus, which is responsible for the proper functioning of the immune system. We might venture to say here that perhaps one of the causes of Aids is the limited functioning of the heart chakra, and its cure might lie in opening and generating the forces inherent in the fourth chakra.

The positive attributes at this level include tolerance and trust in the higher aspects of the self in action everywhere, whereas the negative reactions are a sense of emptiness which is often expressed as suicide, falsity and superficiality.

You may recognise individuals at this level of consciousness by their taste, particularly in foods. They will be simple and aesthetic. Sleep patterns vary from nine to sixteen hours, depending on time needed for out-of-body activity and regeneration of the physical organism. At the fourth level, one is often immersed in a sense of timelessness as the spirit blends occasionally with the electronic body. Perhaps this is why there is such a need for physical expression through touch here.

The Fifth Chakra

This chakra is centred around the throat, influencing expression and communication, hearing, telepathy and all esoteric uses of sound and of the word – one might say, creativity through sound vibrations, including telekinesis. As the originator and modulator of sound frequencies, it is the most used centre in the practice of alchemy, through invocation and the use of power words, mantras, decrees and formulas.

This centre is particularly important because it is also the meeting place for the three upper chakras. It is what the ancients called the 'Bindu' or 'Jade Gate', the vehicle for higher faculties. At this level, the powers collect at the base of the brain (looping from the centre of the throat, through the third eye, the crown and back down to the base of the skull).

When this centre has been integrated, the voice takes on a melodious tone, harmonious and beautiful, conveying the range of human emotions and aspiration and evoking higher truths. The energy at this level becomes nurture through sound, much like a mother's gentle lullaby. In fact this centre is symbolised by the mother and child, as the individual receives from above, enabling him not only to survive at the higher vibratory levels, but to recreate himself. In this way, this centre has also been called the 'cornucopia' centre: what you voice becomes a wish-come-true.

The fifth chakra rules the thyroid, the bronchial and vocal apparatus, the lungs and the alimentary canal as well as inner hearing (clairaudience). At this level the individual is able to transmute all foods and sleep patterns vary sharply. Because the vibratory impulses of this centre are so high, one cannot sustain awareness here unless one has mastered the lower vibratory impulses. A great

81

degree of purity is needed. Not only is the individual able to move interdimensionally, recreate himself and manifest his highest intentions, he is able to lengthen his life. It is the centre responsible for rejuvenation and longevity, connected directly with the activities of the causal body.

Two elements have been associated with this centre. One is wood and the other is light. The first conveys the sense of inner sound and the second the awakening of higher powers relating to the base of the skull. Whatever the expression, this centre is ruled, coloured and activated by the first ray: blue.

When the energy runs through this centre and the individual for one reason or another is unable to integrate himself with it, he may go through periods of intense confusion between inner and outer reality, to the extent of tuning others out of his awareness, appearing self-obsessed and introspective. As temporary as this might be, for the individual this would be experienced as worldly failure. He just can't seem to pull things together as he used to.

On the purely physical level, dysfunctions of this centre include vertigo, anaemia, allergies, fatigue and asthma, as well as all improper oxidation and processes of calcium metabolism.

The Sixth Chakra

This is the third eye, the 'all-seeing-eye', the centre of visionary foresight and clairvoyance. In its worldly aspect, this centre rules the intellect; in its spiritual aspect it rules inner vision and intuitional inspiration.

Here the individual is faced with higher forms of order and will, including the projection of his thoughtforms and psychic balance, as well as with the integration of the right and left aspects of his personality. It is at this point that the leap from lower mind to higher mind manifests itself. The Christ mind becomes operational when the heart, throat and third eye energies have been mastered. The individual enters the realms of causality beyond time. He also steps beyond his own individual karma.

In the physical body, the third eye rules the pituitary gland, the left brain, the left eye, ears, nose and the nervous system in general. The third eye is the centre of the integrated personality and the master-controlling gland of the endocrine system. The element associated with the third eye is alpha, a primordial substance of light.

When integration at this level is not possible, expression becomes illogical or over-intellectual. The individual seems 'spaced out', forgetful, fearful, particularly of the future (which involves planning and ordering). Avoidance of the lessons of this centre will further manifest itself as introversion.

The ray which rules this centre is the fifth ray of science and concentration. Its primary colour is green. The spiritual colour of this centre, however, is indigo. Indigo will heal, activate and stimulate the faculties at the level of the third eye.

The Seventh Chakra

Although this chakra feeds cosmic life into the individual, this happens in a natural way that does not require conscious evoking. The full potency of this chakra is not usually operating unless the individual has done conscious spiritual work or unless he has damaged the otherwise protective shield through accident or wilful misuse of his power.

Understand that the energies operating here are extremely sensitive and delicate, of very high frequency and requiring a high degree of personal integrity, purity and harmlessness. If a person who does not possess these requirements should happen to hyperactivate this centre, his experience will be one of fantasy, of feeling controlled or possessed. In this way too, the negative reactions at this level will echo a faithlessness.

This chakra rules the pineal gland, the upper brain and the right eye. It is connected to the causal and electronic bodies and is activated by the second primary ray, the ray of wisdom, perception and action at the highest levels. It is interesting to note that the pineal contains vestigial retinal tissue, as well as a replica of each chakra, or the pattern of the total man. This is the master control panel for the initiate.

When the individual's evolution brings him to the crown centre, he gives life to his Being (apart from the personality). He has synthesised the concepts of self and other beyond duality and now partakes of the sense of Life's oneness – a genuine at-one-ment with creation, knowing beyond knowledge the true source of all

Life. He understands for the first time that there are no limits to creation and that he is one with this potentiality. At this point he knows once and for all that he has the power of transmutation. Mastery at this level will involve the eventual transcendence of the causal body itself.

Minor Chakras

As mentioned previously, there are hundreds and perhaps thousands of energy points within the physical body and around it, including points within the mental, emotional and spiritual vehicles. These points have been used by both spiritual disciplines (in the various Vedic and yogic practices) and by physical scientists (including ancient healers). These centres are created by the criss-crossing of energy lines. The major chakras are created by the crossing of 21 energy lines, the minor ones by 14 and the lesser ones by 7. The most widely accepted map of these points would be the acupuncture and shiatsu map showing the centres and the energy meridians upon which they are situated.

From the alchemical point of view, perhaps the most important of these minor chakras would be at the hands and at the feet. The hands serve to bless and to transmute and are the most important tool for the alchemist. It is here where the five elements express themselves through the five fingers. Transmutation of physical substance can occur only through the sense of touch, where intentionality and substance converge. The feet in turn bless the earth upon which we walk and carry out the act of transference into the lower kingdoms.

Protection

Ancient occult literature points to three 'psychic gates' through which energy enters the physical body: (1) the coccyx, (2) the kidneys, (3) the back of the head. Each of these acts as a passageway for interdimensional energies to flow into us, but each passageway can also let in undesirable energies from the environment.

Psychic self-defence practices teach us to guard these areas through the use of protective visualisations. Christianity and spiri-

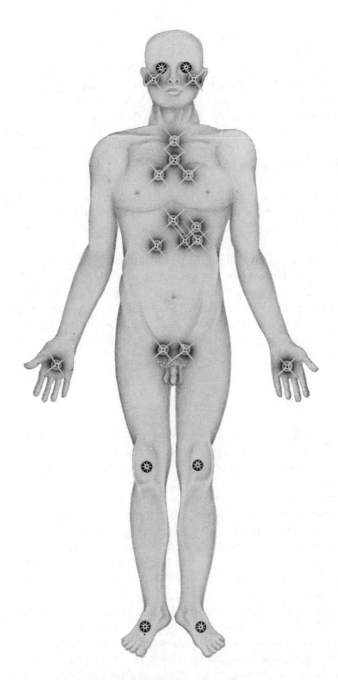

Fig. 1.6 The 21 Minor Chakras

tualism have long upheld the power of creating a thoughtform of a cross of light closed by a circle. This picture may be placed at the desired location, or you may use water (or 'holy' water).

A favourite visualisation of mine is that of a revolving disc of golden light placed behind the solar plexus. This covers the area of the kidneys and is not only protective but soothing to otherwise disturbed emotional energies.

The human organism is such that it protects itself automatically in most cases. Where the individual himself is through his personality over-activating a particular centre, such as misuse of the sex chakra or of the power centres or even of the third eye centre, there is little that protection techniques can do.

For the times when you might feel undue pressure, or hyperactivity usually at the level of the pituitary, heal yourself with the use of colour. This is the safest and easiest. There are many books on the use of colour healing, but primarily green-, indigo- and magenta-coloured lamps are wonderful. And then of course there is the earth (the healing green of nature), which is the best and richest harmoniser of all!

Conclusions

As I mentioned earlier, the pathways through the chakras involve the upward as well as downward journeys of consciousness. In describing the various chakras I've portrayed the upward movement.

When the individual has completed the first part towards spiritualisation, he is then ready to apply the higher frequencies to the management of matter in a conscious way. He then makes the return journey through the upper chakras down into the lower ones. Now begins the painful journey into density which causes so much anguish to the spirit who has flown with the angels and travelled with the gods.

When the individual, for example, descends from the consciousness of the third eye into the throat and heart centres, he must relearn trust without the use of clear sight. As he moves into progressive density, he must bring with him the peace, the knowingness of the upper centres in the midst of chaos and the cacophony of discordant stimuli. Once he integrates at the lowest levels, he regains the clarity of his higher power, magnifying the energies at the level of substance (base chakra) with the amplitude of the spirit.

On the re-ascending journey, the individual will once again face the temptations of the first cycle and fall many many times before he gains the courage to rise, finally, to the Creator. At this stage it may seem to him that he needs to forgo the pleasures of physicality, of earthly existence, until he comes to understand the real meaning of transcendence and sublimation. This stage cannot be rushed. At each level there is an offering of the self and a surrendering to the Godhead. The ultimate death (the unconsciousness of personality) leads here to the ultimate rebirth and the process of ascension.

Polarity, Pairs and Meeting Points

The base chakra on a male is positive and on a female is negative. This polarity continues all the way up, the heart centre being positive on a female and negative on a male, reversing at the throat centre, to become positive again at the level of the third eye for a female and negative on a male. The crown centre will be positive for a male and negative for a female.

What does this mean? Simply stated at the level of the crown centre a man will express himself through a positive polarity or activity, whereas a female will express herself in a more receptive, negative modality. A woman is capable of emotionally nourishing a man at the third eye and heart and at the second centre, a man is capable of vitally nourishing a female at the sex, power and throat levels. We should understand the need to experience life through both male and female bodies. Each person carries within himself the memory of all possible experience.

The chakras also work in pairs. For example, the activity of the second and throat chakras, the solar plexus and the third eye, the heart and crown centre work together towards a common goal. Both the second and throat chakras pertain to creativity. Both the solar plexus and third eye relate to vision and intelligence. Both the heart and crown centres express cosmic dimensions. One centre will express the same function on a lower frequency level.

As the centres (besides the crown and base) have a dual function in matter and in spirit, they also embrace opposites (dualities)

87

within themselves, the major meetings being at the level of the third eye and at the heart, where all the energies converge to facilitate the experience of the electronic body in physical expression. It is in the domain of the heart, integrated, full, potent and pure, that the electronic energies of the God-Self may abide. It is within the heart where we may hear the voice of our higher self and see its light, where we may receive insights, vision and gain a deeper understanding of that which is. It is in the heart that we are present to both our physical and personal selves and our cosmic, interdimensional potential. All bodies, all chakras, all powers converge. The secret art of alchemy is seated within the realm of the heart. The highest powers are reserved only for the very pure in heart. The powers of Light transcend all darkness.

Dysfunctions

The chakras are, in effect, a conglomerate of energies proceeding from cosmic sources, from the collective unconscious, and from the physical, mental and emotional worlds. As incoming energies they affect our chemistry at the personality and psychic levels. Once we have mastered the lessons and the energies at each level, we actually transmute the substance associated with them and release the energies into subtle energetic pathways along the spine, which spiral in two directions simultaneously. These two pathways (called 'nadis' in the East) feed into the nervous system in general, affecting the endocrine system and eventually the blood itself.

Disease is caused by the inability to absorb, transmute or integrate energetic frequencies. When an energy comes into a chakra and is blocked in some way, it will seek expression through psychological dysfunction. When an energy is already within a centre but expressing itself negatively (in other words being sent out with discordant qualification), this energy will eventually manifest itself through physical problems. This happens unconsciously.

Energy Circulation

The practice of transmutation in alchemy involves generating energy through the vehicle of the alchemist himself. In traditional

Taoist alchemy, this was done by circulating energy through the various circuits in the body in a systematic way. Here, the energy is also circulated, but save for the training given in advanced alchemy practices, it is not done so through physical channels.

In Taoism the energy circulation was based on physical body points. Here it is done through etheric counterparts, moved by will, animated by feeling and generated by spirit. Taoism used a microcosmic orbit. Here we create an alchemical circuit and draw the cosmic energy downward into the planet itself via the individual organism. Taoist alchemy, like its medieval cousin, and Inner Alchemy seek to transmute the lower into the higher and to embody the higher.

The practice of Inner Alchemy is absolutely safe. One step leads to another. Each step is a safeguard in itself. You cannot proceed unless you have mastered the first step. You cannot partake of the powers of Light unless you yourself have become Light. The individual is linked to the sources of cosmic energy. It is a journey from self to Self through the exploration of:

I. Time, space and personality development
II. Simultaneous dimensionality with the Now
III. Spiritual reality and identity

Interdimensional Chakras

This chapter on chakras would not be complete without mention of the five out-of-body energy centres and the superconscious powers generated by them.

Since we live in a three-dimensional reality, we must define other dimensionality in three-dimensional terms. The out-of-body chakras are located in other dimensions of being. It is as if they existed within the present, which indeed they do, and yet were invisible or inaccessible to us through our three-dimensional senses. Once we raise our vibration, however, we are able to perceive, sense and gain access to them. They become as familiar to us as our three-dimensional power of thought, feeling and speech.

In order to explain the chakras in a vertical way, as I've done with the basic seven which pertain to Earth life in the third dimension, we would have to say that these chakras appear in pairs. The

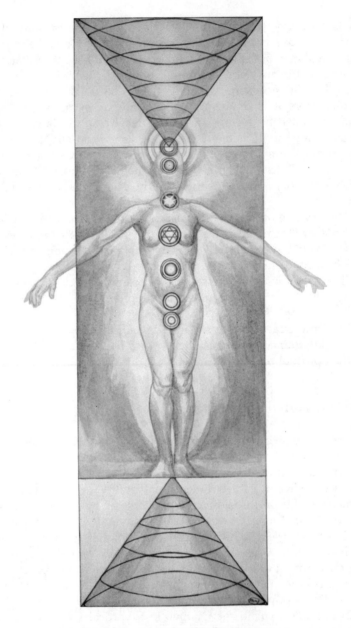

Fig. 1.7 Chakras and Psychological States
including the rings situated outside the body (the unity rings)

first set would be located about a foot above the head and a foot under the feet, the second set about three feet in both directions, and the third set about four feet. The fourth and fifth set would surpass even our three-dimensional concepts and extend into infinity above and below.

According to Petey Stevens in her book, *Opening up to your Psychic Self*, the eighth chakra filters and purifies cosmic and earth energies and regulates them for our use. At this level the individual feels his oneness with both the planet Earth and with the cosmos, and in touch with the properties from both dimensions above and below the third, such as the elemental kingdom and non-physical expressions of Self.

The ninth chakra opens into a kind of laboratory dimension for creating and manifesting personal reality. At this level the individual may experiment with different ways of being and having. These images are created in non-physical dimensions and then pulled into manifestation by first and second dimensional frequency. This chakra might be named the probability chakra, giving access to a never-ending pool of probabilities by generating a nurturing magnetic quality.

The tenth chakra might be termed the possibility chakra and taps into the creative matter of the planet as well as the creative ideas of the cosmos. At this frequency we create wholly new ideas for personal reality, much like a future thinker or sage might, with the added advantage of extracting new combinations of matter for creating this personal reality.

The eleventh chakra relates to group creative thoughts, combined with physical matter to create the Universe. It might be termed the universal chakra.

The twelfth chakra could be said to contain all that Is and the One at the same time.

It should be understood at this point that these chakras operate with or without our conscious participation. They are located above and below the body for purposes of simplification, but exist in reality coincidentally with our physicality and non-directionally. Like the other chakras, these are focuses of energy and functions of consciousness. It is not within the scope of this present work to enter into detailed description of them, but to familiarise the reader with their reality and the wider scope of Divine Alchemy – the arena of the totality of the Self.

Fig 1.8 The Seven Chakras
Functions of consciousness (at the physical level)

	Attributes	Rays	Negative Reactions/Needs (When the pure attributes are not integrated)	Bodies Affected/Senses
1st	Use of personal will. Purity. Commitment to the planet. Responsibility. Security. Grounding (base of spine and legs).	4th	Alienation and jumpiness. Needs 12 hrs sleep, heavy foods, violence.	Kidneys, adrenals, spinal column. Physical. Sense of smell and sensations.
2nd	Invocation. Sensitivity to vibration (supersensitivity). Individuality. Balance between the social and the personal.	7th	Hysteria. Sensuality (pleasure/pain). Acting now for the future, loud music, spices, 10 hrs sleep.	Etheric. Sense of Taste. Gonads, reproductive system.
3rd	Mobility. Personal control. Peace. Fearlessness. Generosity. Balance. Ability to set limits. Time. Travel. Orderliness and cooperation.	6th	Untogetherness, inability to say 'no'. Tendency to power-trip: control through domination or submission. Jealousy. Needs sugars and 8 hrs sleep	Emotional. The nervous system. Sight. Gall bladder. Pancreas. Stomach.
4th	Divine Love. Tolerance Forbearance. Trust. Being 'in touch with self'. Unconditional Love. Timelessness. Joining consciousness and matter.	3rd	Sense of emptiness. Suicidal. Acting 'nice'. Judgmental. Craves simple foods and 9 to 16 hrs sleep.	Electronic and higher mental. Thymus & circulatory system. Heart, Blood, Vagus nerve. Touching.

5th	Divine will. Power to create. Expression and communication. Hearing, telepathy, time and space travel. Cornucopia.	1st	Confusion. Alienating others. Putting the self down. Can transmute all foods and may partake of any sleep pattern.	Causal. Sense of hearing, the thyroid and the vocals. Bronchials, lungs and alimentary canal.
6th	The All-seeing eye. Concentration and consecration. Clairvoyance. Order and will. The Future.	5th	Illogical, over-intellectual. Spaced-out. Introversion, forgetfulness, fearful of the future.	Lower mental and higher mental bodies. Left brain, left eye, ears, nose and the nervous system. Pituitary.
7th	Invocation. Knowing. The Christ Self. No limits. Cosmic consciousness. Oneness. Power of transmutation.	2nd	No faith. A sense of being controlled or possessed.	Causal and Electronic and dimensions beyond. The upper brain and the right eye. Pineal.

Note: The upper three chakras, i.e. the 5th, 6th, 7th join at the base of the brain and function as a unit at the level of interdimensional activity. In ancient times this part of the brain was called the Bindu, Jade Gate or Bliss Pool.

93

Below are two charts outlining the characteristics of the different chakras in their pure, positive attributes and in their reactive states, with correlations to the rays involved at the level of each chakra and the bodies affected.

Take the time to study each chakra and examine yourself in the light of the information given. Get to know yourself in your reactive as well as positive generating state. Use the chart as a self-diagnostic tool and to help you understand others' reactions as well. Once you have a better understanding of the energy dynamics at the level of the chakras, rays and bodies, you can begin to project healing love and energy to harmonise the imbalance and establish the atmosphere of peace and cooperation that we are all seeking.

Please notice that the functions of consciousness are never fixed. You always have free will, while inner or other circumstances create upheavals, reversals or accelerations of energy. Watch the rhythm of your sleep and the foods that you crave (without judgement), and you will be able to flow more easily with the natural cycles and needs that your body dictates. Your physical, mental and emotional bodies speak to you. You would do well to learn their language and see to these needs as tenderly as you would to a child.

The information given here is meant to assist and not to confuse. Ultimately you are your best friend and your intuition is your best guide.

Fig. 1.9 The Relation of the Rays to the Centres

Inner Alchemy	Chakras	The Arcane School
Second: Love-wisdom	7	First: Willpower
Fifth: Concrete knowledge	6	Same
First: Willpower	5	Third: Active intelligence
Third: Love	4	Second: Love-wisdom
Sixth: Devotion	3	Same
Seventh: Ceremonial magic	2	Same
Fourth: Harmony	1	Same

Lines of Force

Lines of force are located on the etheric body but manifest themselves identically on the physical body as energy pathways that link different points within the organism and also connect the organism to like points within the planet or the heavens.

The Grounding Circuit

Here too (as with the chakras) we are talking about different systems that have been used through the ages. In the meditative traditions of the East, particularly India and Tibet, the physical energy was grounded (or earthed) through the base chakra into the body of the planet. The physical posture used was crossed legs. The purpose was to achieve total inner silence and emptiness. Inactivity. In the Egyptian tradition, on the other hand, as well as in the martial arts, grounding is done through the soles of the feet.

In the first case the grounding sought is for purpose of inner work – the body is located in time and space to secure re-entry, identification and stability. In the second case, that of the Western hermetic and Egyptian tradition and of the Eastern martial arts, the entire body is involved. Grounding here enables the individual to use his body in motion or activity in the world. In this second case, his service to the world depends on linking inner and outer reality.

Both modalities involve service, or the application of spiritual principles to the uplifting of humanity in some way or other. In the first case the service given consists of prayer and thought formation, and the generation of Light-substance (goodwill, which the Buddhists called 'Bodhicitta'). In the second case the service is one

95

of physical action in the world, an action that involves physical transformation as well as spirituality.

Grounding Practices

Inner Alchemy is based on the principle that we are constructing a body of light, an immortal vehicle, right here in the physical plane while in embodiment. We are doing this by transmuting the body of physical density and awakening the core, or body of light.

Most of us are never grounded enough, and if we think we are it is usually the wrong kind of grounding. The substance of the earth itself is so polluted by physical and energetic toxins that it is hardly refreshing to 'surrender to the earth', as some new age practices suggest.

If we can get it through our heads that the earth is just as we are, we can come to understand that it too has a light body, a Light Being. When I propose grounding, I do not advocate linking to the physical substance of the planet as much as I do to its heart core. Now, of course we are speaking of anchoring the light within a vehicle of matter, and this matter acts as a container and an emitter of the frequencies that we are receiving and conveying. This vehicle of matter is not your body of density: it is your body of light, your etheric.

It is my firm belief that we are evolving into a new frequency of life. This life will happen at etheric levels of activity, just as it does in other planets within our own solar system. The earth is, in fact, the *only* planet in this system that has three-dimensional (i.e. physical) existence. In preparation for this new vibration, our bodies and the body of the planet itself is being recalibrated.

Grounding Visualisations

You will need to activate the energy flow within the first and second chakras and the lines of force coursing through your legs. One of my favourite ways of doing this is through soft stimulation such as T'ai Chi and Aikido. Running and hard physical exercise, while strengthening the muscles of the legs, do not provide the delicate awareness needed really to avail yourself of the energy flow coming from the heart of the earth.

You might simply like to hold the 'horse posture' used as a preliminary in the martial arts for as long as necessary to feel the awakening of the 'hara' – which is the Japanese name for the energies pooled at the navel center (see drawing at p. 94).

The Taoist alchemist in fact considered the martial arts an essential practice for the creation of the immortal vehicle, the maintenance of vigour and youth and the generation of vital power needed to effect the practices of alchemy.

After holding the posture for a while, you will begin to sense a trembling in the legs. This is the same trembling that is induced in Western bioenergetic stances and serves to generate the life form which is the source of the orgasmic reflex. You may sense a feeling of burning heat within the legs and will be tempted again and again to stop. The awakening of this energy, as Willhelm Reich knew, triggers off the locked imprints within the survival and emotional centres.

If you can hold the posture through the trembling, you will begin to sense an upsurge of energy flooding through you. At that point I suggest that you consciously visualise your 'hara' connected to the centre of the Earth. Do this by visualising your legs as the two sides of an upright triangle whose apex marks the location of the chakra. Extend the lines of force beneath your legs into a second, inverted triangle, whose apex is located in the centre of the earth.

Another visualisation that is helpful, particularly if you are unable to use the physical means of generating the vital energy flow, is to use the image of a grounding cord. This is an almost standard grounding procedure in the West. Some advocate connecting to the centre of the Earth through the visualisation of arcs of light anchored at the pelvic area. Others will suggest mentally reaching into the core of the planet by projecting an actual cord (usually golden) and tying it securely around an imaginary ring there.

One technique uses the same light particles as in the centre of the atomic structure of the body. This grounding cord resembles a tail and is an extension of the central energy circuitry within the body itself. You may like to imagine that your light body is connecting with the light body of the Earth via the grounding cord.

As your body grows in luminescence (upon sustaining the visual-

97

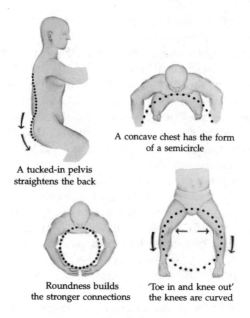

A concave chest has the form
of a semicircle

A tucked-in pelvis
straightens the back

Roundness builds
the stronger connections

'Toe in and knee out'
the knees are curved

Fig. 1.10 Horse Posture

isation of the points of light in the centre of each atom of your body), so does the body of the Earth. See the core of the planet as a radiant, golden, crystal-like heart centre, emanating a soft pink glow. Draw from it as a child does from its mother. Feel it rising up your grounding cord and nourishing you at the level of every atom and molecule of your body. Feel the solidity and the security of being anchored there. Let your body rest in that feeling.

The grounding technique that we use at the Center for Inner Alchemy is the Figure of Light, based on practices which were used by the Essenes, including Master Jesus himself, or so I was led to believe. The full set of practices is contained in a little booklet by Olive Pixley, called *Armour of Light*. The basis is a light-double of the physical at the level of the feet. This serves to anchor physicality directly into light and acts as a natural protection against the absorption of negative particles from the earth and the environment. It is tremendously powerful. Try it.

Begin by lying down. Sense a figure of light at your feet, an exact replica of your physical form, only in brilliant light. Sense the contact with the feet and allow that contact to energise your feet.

Then draw from it upwards through your body. End by sealing the connection by projecting a circular beam of light from the right side over your head, around and over the head of the figure of light and back to close the circle over your own head.

This visualisation should be done quickly. Its purpose is not only to energise the physical body in light, but to expand the capacity of our mind so that we become able to register instantaneous contact with Light. It is a quickening process and should be done in a flash. I find the relationship with my own body of light expressed this way to be comforting. It also serves the purpose of creating the balance or tension necessary for the creation of the alchemical circuit, of which we will speak of soon.

Healing and the Healing Circuit

The healing circuit is formed by lines of force linking the heart chakra with the minor chakras at the palm of the hands. One system may utilise the entire body energy, while another will utilise pure Light-substance directed through out-of-body means and thought projection. One system will advocate radiating love through the heart chakra, another through the solar plexus. One uses physical touch, another auric* and yet another thought projected through distance in the form of absent healing.

The actual healing energy comes from Spirit. It descends through the upper chakras into the Bindu at the base of the skull. From there it proceeds to the heart chakra. If the healer uses the laying-on-of-hands technique, his shoulder and hand chakras will be especially open. If he is the silent, invisible yogi, he will radiate through his aura.

The healing circuit may involve the use of the wrist chakras, the soles of the feet chakras and any number of centres. The most important for purposes of everyday life are the centres at the palm of the hands. Just as the feet are an extension of the base of the spine, the hands are an extension of the heart.

Everyone's touch, everyone's footsteps imprint energy upon living things; and everyone is a potential healer because everyone is a battery, a conduit for energetic frequencies. The hands and feet

* Auric: pertaining to the aura.

99

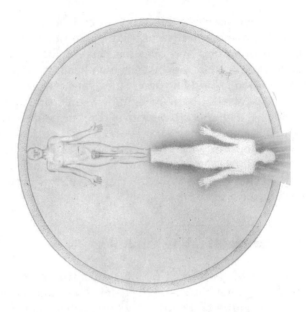

Fig. 1.11 Grounding with the Earth: Figure of Light

are particularly important. All of the elements are reflected in the hands and in the feet.

The ancient alchemists created their lodestone (the magical alchemical stone) by charging it with energy invoked from other dimensions, requalified with the help of elemental energies and channelled into the substance through physical touch (via the five fingers of the hand). This is how a material substance such as coal can be refined into diamond, or how lead can be turned into gold. The molecular structure is altered by the expert manipulation of the alchemist's vibratory frequency. The vibratory rate of the atomic structure is raised through the medium of the alchemist's body and channelled through the hands. And then this lodestone can be used to recalibrate other substances as well.

Think of the implications of this on rejuvenation, on healing. The energy balancing system called polarity has profound insight into the human energetic structure, including right-left and inner-outer polarities. Another such system is the Alexander Technique. The organs themselves, as well as the bodies, have positive or negative polarities. By matching poles one affects balance. Harmony is the magical ingredient responsible for all healing.

A hug is one of the most healing acts. Particularly one given out of an overflow of love and an abundance of physical (vital) energy. The energy simply leaps over into the depleted person. Energy always seeks balance.

It is important to know your strength, your constitution, your energetic make-up. Know what your healing abilities are. Not everybody is a healer at physical levels.

When I put my hands on somebody, I am in touch with their higher self. Within this state of mind, I am aware of my connection to my god-self. I allow that force to come through me in whatever way is needed. By virtue of having a body, I am in authority over physicality. Whereas energy balancing will happen spontaneously and in certain instances bring about healing, healing itself cannot happen without intentionality, without some form of prayer or invocation (to be discussed in a subsequent chapter). The forces of Light need to be invited. They have no authority at the level of physical matter. We do. Healing happens out of the partnership between matter and light.

When an individual is not able to receive touch (either physical or auric), the energy can be projected through thought. Whereas the physical substance is not approached directly, the emotional body is. That can trigger a certain restructuring at the physical level. By the time such an individual leaves a session, he feels relaxed, uplifted.

Whenever I do energy balancing work, I never know how long the hands will remain in a certain place. Usually the person falls asleep, which is the most sought-after state, as the mind (which is what normally interferes in the healing process) is laid aside. The brainwave activity is slowed down and at that point the forces that work through me are able to bring about the balancing, aligning, vitalising, recalibrating or relaxing activity called for, right at the level of the physical body. The process of harmonising prior to transmutation has begun.

By the very fact that I am in alignment with the forces of Light through my living and through my conscious invocation, when someone comes through the door they will be affected by the vibrations of Light.

Everyone can do this.

101

Fig. 1.12 Meditation: Star of David
The six-pointed star

Healing Visualisations

To heal yourself:

Visualise a large golden Star of David, made of bright yellow gold, just before you. See this star made of brilliant golden fire. Notice the aura of brilliant white surrounding it.
Notice in the centre of this star a brilliant sphere of white . . . a pulsating white sun . . . which seems to be far, far away . . . into infinity.
Walk towards the star (in your mind) and through it and into the Central Sun. Merge into it . . . absorb it, let it absorb you . . . your body . . . your aura.
Be still and know that 'I am God'.

To heal another:

Bring the symbol of the star within your own heart chakra. Be with it. Sustain its intensity.

Visualise the physical form of the person you wish to see healed . . . and place it within the Central Sun.

There are many, many beautiful and powerful visualisations that may be used to attract the light force needed to effect spiritual healing and alignment, and even physical restructuring.

Explore the forms and colours that inspire and uplift you.

The lines of force provide the basic frame. They create the pathways that enable the alchemical work to occur by uniting the polarities of light and matter. This work is usually divided into:

Transmutation: all healing and recalibration
Precipitation: physical or non-physical manifestations
Etherealisation: the purification of density and its restructuring into lightforms

There are two more basic circuits that I would like to mention, though briefly, as they delineate more clearly the aspects of physicality and spirituality inherent in work of this nature.

The kundalini circuit is basically what was used by ancient Taoist alchemists and by Indian yogis. It consists of the circulation of energy through the chakras in a continuous looping motion which serves to activate the chakras, ignite each progressive one with the energy of the first and amplify continually that energy by building up the momentum through circulation.

The increasing intensity of this visualisation stimulates the kundalini circuit into activity and often forces a passageway. This can be dangerous to physical, mental and emotional health. I know one person who was particularly frightened by the premature awakening of his kundalini. He had been assiduously practising the teachings of Gopi Krishna and almost went mad in the process. He became fearful of contacting the spiritual energies again. It set him back for years.

The most direct and safest circuitry is the spiritual circuit, formed by linking the personal self to the God-Self through feeling, visualisation and affirmation. It connects the cosmic lines of force with the planetary to create what I have come to call the Alchemical Circuit. This consists of collecting the energies of the lower chakras at the heart centre, where they are transmuted from fire into light.

From the heart, the force generated proceeds to pass through the throat, third eye and pineal centres, and beyond that through the soul centre towards the higher self, ultimately connecting the God-Self at the twelfth dimension. And the God-Self returns the force in a loop to the point of origin.

The approach of Inner Alchemy does not restrict itself to the circulation of energy within the body itself. It draws from the heart of the earth and connects with the heavens. The Alchemical Circuit will be discussed in detail in the next section.

Breath

The practice of alchemy, as well as of many other esoteric and metaphysical disciplines, involves the conscious use of breath. Studies have been made confirming that breath carries life force throughout the body. The better, more deeply and more fully we breathe, the better, more vital and healthy we feel. Breath quickens the blood and energises the system.

In the processes that I have used within the context of Inner Alchemy, breath has also played a very important part. It is perhaps the simplest way to change emotional states and body tension. One deep breath will serve to oxygenate the blood to such a degree that fatigue is minimised, even in the midst of urban polluted life.

The ancients knew the function of breath. Part of the yogic system of *pranayama* consists in varying forms of breathing. The standard balanced breath – equal counts on the inbreath as on the outbreath – was a practice equally important for the Western traditions, including Egyptian and Druidic. The use of mantras and chants, both in East and West, is one of the most enjoyable ways of extending and prolonging the breath.

Why is it important to breathe in a balanced way, and why is it advisable to extend the count in certain cases? A balanced breath will create or maintain a balanced physical vehicle by equalising the right and left sides of the body, of the brain and of the nervous system. The steady flow of oxygen in and out will flush out any obstruction, fixation or block that may be in the mind, the feeling and the body itself, and change the overall frequency. After a few minutes of balanced breathing, you feel more relaxed, therefore more receptive to finer perceptions.

Chants, mantras and most forms of singing and recitation will force the organism to take deeper breaths, thus increasing oxygen intake, retention and exhalation. Singing, particularly of devotional songs, is one of the easiest ways of opening the door to spiritual forces.

Another of the practices advised in the yogic system is the retention of the breath, both on the intake and on the outbreath. Upon practising it on yourself, you will notice that as you hold your breath with full lungs, not only will you have a feeling of bursting, you will begin tingling immediately from the increase of oxygen in the lungs. When you hold your breath on the downside of the breath, that is when the lungs are emptied of your ordinary breath, you will experience the feeling of collapse bordering on fear, and yet the end result will also lead to the feeling of tingling. The emptied lungs force one to breathe in more air. The full breath might be construed as the fullness of Life or birth: the empty breath might be seen as the emptiness or night, the aspect of dying. Notice for yourself which aspects of life frighten you the most: the inbreath or the outbreath. Examine your own breathing patterns. We are constantly dying and being reborn.

These breathing patterns and other variations are the basis not only of yoga but also of Tao. The esoteric practices of Shinto – called *shugindo* – have come to be known to us as rebirthing. Breath is absolutely central to all transformation work. Breath acts upon the blood that carries life force and cosmic coloration through the physical organism, affecting body, mind and emotions.

Notice for yourself. It is not possible to breathe fully and be angry or sad. Become aware of how you breathe when you are in one of your moods and you will see that you are holding your breath. Some emotions require that you breathe more air in than out; in others the reverse will be true. In some emotional states you will be breathing more through the mouth, in others through the nose.

There is a purpose for both nose and mouth breathing. The Sufis have a system of breathing according to the elements. Each breath will provoke the feeling and integration of that element within the body. For example: the process of breathing in and out through the nose will intensify the purification of the earth element. The mouth breath will intensify the experience of the element of air. Breathing in through the nose and out through the mouth will produce a feeling of water, and breathing in through the mouth and out through the nose will intensify the fire flow through the body. In this manner one is able to balance one's body and transmute the emotional states into balanced positive states of harmony and creativity.

The ancient Eastern practices, particularly yoga, advocated the use of breathing through the nose exclusively. This has led modern followers to believe that this is still a necessity. Our body physiology has changed, and so have our needs. All breathing patterns will be necessary for a balanced, grounded spirituality.

Inner Alchemy will draw from all disciplines and will adapt these to the individual need, rather than try to fit the individual within one system. Breath, for us, is the fuel which will catalyse the energy process that culminates in transmutation.

Just as the lines of force serve to construct vehicles for energy and Light, so does the breath serve as a conductor for the sacred fire breath of the Godhead. Breath contains Life – fire and Light. It also carries the qualities of the individual. Breath is a conductor that serves to transfer energies of all sorts, as well as to seal and to awaken. In the hands of a skilled energy tactician, breath can be used to disperse or ignite energies within the aura. When the breath is further qualified with sound and consciously directed, its scope is even greater. This is another reason why the spoken word is such a powerful tool.

Suffice it to say that alchemically a kiss is not just a kiss. What happens in kissing involves an energy plus a vitality transfer through the medium of the breath and through saliva. Saliva carries the physical life force, or etheric records of the individual. Many sacred acts, particularly related to the exchange of breath and body fluids in intimacy and sexuality, were initially performed with great reverence, discernment and deliberation. A kiss is a powerful act of energy transference at many levels, intended to create a bond of love.

I want to mention briefly that all of the body's fluids, particularly semen and vaginal fluids, carry the individual's life force. A woman's power over a male, for example, is amplified by her retention of his semen within her. The energetic effects of this bond last months. This understanding is enough to make one stop and reconsider one's intentions in face of the sanctity of Life manifest everywhere as the power of the life force and the magnificence of the greater Life of Spirit pervading all.

Brain Waves, Breath and the Spiritual Faculties

Brain waves are a reflection of neural activity in the brain. The greater, or faster, the brain activity, the more logical and rational the state of mind. The slower the brain activity, the more elusive and other-worldly is the experience at the level of mind.

At the level called *beta*, the neural activity is 14 to 22 cycles per second. This is our ordinary alert waking consciousness, which also corresponds, according to studies made, to about 18 breaths per minute. This is the average three-dimensional awareness.

At the level called *alpha*, at a rate of 7 to 14 cycles per second, we have the state of light trance, an ordinary ability seldom recognised as such. Computer electronics and television create a state of alpha naturally, which opens the psyche up to subliminal programming and hypnotic control. This is the state of daydreaming, which at its deepest becomes psychic ability and colour vision in dreams. Body sensations during this pattern are light and tingly. It is the natural state for animals, who function on a heightened sense of perception and are able to see further into the colour spectrum and hear sounds imperceptible to the human ear. The corresponding breathing pattern for this state is ten breaths per minute.

Next comes the *theta* pattern of brain wave activity at 4 to 7 cycles per second. This state is usually present in sleep or in meditative trance, where the lower mind is quelled and the activity of the physical body itself is silenced or numbed. This rhythm is the natural state for plants. When humans are consciously present at this state, they are able to see auras, travel in space, out of time and interdimensionally. The breathing pattern here is six breaths per minute.

Last in the varieties of known brain wave patterns is the *delta* state, with 1/3 to 4 cycles per second of neural activity. This is the state of deep dreamless sleep. I believe that this is the space the physical body falls into when we are in the highest state of interdimensional and spiritual activity. It is claimed that this is the pattern prevalent in teleportation and body transference. There is no access to or from this state other than through inner means such as meditation and transcendental spiritual experience.

Breath regulation is one of the fastest ways of regulating brain patterns and entering higher states of consciousness. The method that I use requires that you breathe through the mouth in greater and greater quantities, much as in rebirthing or in the Shugindo practices. These are powerful methods of reaching energies and forces which may be used in alchemical work. A good rebirther will guide you into deeper states by changing your breathing pattern and gently coaxing you into higher and higher states of consciousness, particularly through the levels of unconsciousness encountered in the *theta* and *delta* stages. He or she will also know when it is advisable to take you through the initial emotional release stages and into reality beyond.

The journey through intensified and directed breathing practices is the journey of yourself through the different states of consciousness, from the intensely physical and emotional to the mental, higher mental, psychic and spiritual states. This is possible because you are accelerating the level of vibrations of your entire being, from the blood, through the cells, the brain and the entire energetic circuitry. Open mouth breathing facilitates this better than nostril breathing because it affects the entire cellular structure. Nostril breathing was used in the past, but in many it tends to induce out-of-the-body states which disconnect us from the physical recalibration process.

As brain waves decrease higher faculties of perception increase. Eventually you are in partnership, however momentarily, with your higher self. You can enter into realms of Light ordinarily unavailable in waking states. With proper guidance through those periods where you would normally lose consciousness, you can perceive other realities.

Suggested Practices

As an initial practice, I suggest that you become aware of how you breathe. Decide to change the pattern. Take deeper, fuller breaths. Try breathing in and out through the nose at even counts – the same number of counts in and out. Then try mouth breathing in the same way. Try holding the breath . . . on the inbreath . . . on the outbreath.

Review

We have outlined the basic energetic anatomy of the human being. It seems a highly delicate apparatus, much too complex to be monitored consciously. Relax. You don't need to. You are your own generator and bookkeeper in one. You are in this three-dimensional existence to explore and master detail. You are here to live fully at all the levels of being possible in this dimension. You partake of the highest and of the lowest forms of life. Within you the elements live and multiply and in turn create and evolve. To them too you appear as vast and infinite as the concept of the twelfth dimension appears to you now.

The only thing you need to do is to be present to yourself and to your faculties as they evolve and expand. And, if you want to work overtime, you may do so out of your own free will. When you remember to play too some of the time, life becomes an exciting adventure, where bigger and greater things are forever within reach.

Let's review. You have seven vehicles or bodies. Your physical life revolves around three-dimensional reality and corresponds to the activity of the first three bodies: the physical, the emotional and the lower mental body. At this level your physical apparatus is run by the endocrine system which affects all its parts. This endocrine system is fed by the activity of the chakras.

The chakras exist in a body of light which is a blueprint of your physical body. These chakras are created by the activity of cosmic rays, emanating from dimensions other than the physical, as well as from environmental and internal responses. The activity of these chakras is created by your own higher self, heightened, distorted or attenuated by your personal self.

Now, the chakras facilitate functions at the third dimension but also act as antennae for the other dimensions of our being. Our chakras are located in our fourth body, which is the etheric, the blueprint for the physical. The first three chakras permit access to information pertaining to earth life. Through the four upper chakras we may, when clear and ready, contact other dimensions and decode that information into three-dimensional terminology. The eighth, ninth and tenth out-of-the-body chakras will relate to fourth-, fifth- and sixth-dimensional existence. The eleventh and twelfth chakras will relate directly to eleventh- and twelfth-dimensional reality.

But the chakras are not the only way of experiencing other dimensions. We may also experience interdimensional life through our other bodies. These other bodies, in this case the fifth, sixth and seventh, are reached through spiritual means: they are bodies of light and respond directly to the laws of Light. In these bodies, which are in fact states of consciousness, we experience ourselves in varying degrees of awareness, from the spiritual to the cosmic.

The alchemist knows himself and knows that his reach is infinite, particularly at the level of spiritual evolution. The alchemist knows the supremacy of Light over technology, over matter and ultimately over lower mind itself. The alchemist has intuited the Creator in the deepest recesses of his being. The alchemist has chosen to partner with the Creator in the service of the Light. The alchemist uses all these aspects of himself (his entire 'family of Self' so to speak) to help him co-create, transmute, heal and bless his immediate world, his environment and his planet.

How Does the Alchemist Work?

The first step, while becoming aware of the personality blocks, is to work on flexibilising or destructuring the personality. The second stage, which may be coincidental to the first, is exploration of the personal self through time and space. As a person purifies his personality he is able to reach memories from the register of other lives. This happens naturally, but can be enhanced by the knowledge of the energetic anatomy. At this point the aspiring alchemist will begin the conscious journey of identifying with his divine heritage. He will deliberately ignite the fire within the heart and begin the arduous path of taming the instinctual responses of the three lower bodies. As this progresses, he will penetrate the higher chakras and through them other realities, other dimensions of being.

111

Then begins the third stage of exploration into multidimensional existence.

You may ask: 'What is the difference between this path and that trod by masses of adepts, alchemists and metaphysicians of the past?' There may not be any difference. In many cases, however, the aim was the love of power. Here, in Inner Alchemy, the aim is the power of love and the profound understanding that this is, in fact, the greatest power. All of the stages outlined above are made possible only through the activity of Spirit. As we grow in awareness of this fact, in deep humility and gratitude, the power of Spirit intensifies, much as a friendly companion does to the response of love. For the God-Self is, in fact, the only presence acting in all things. This is the secret to the art of Inner Alchemy.

II The Human Faculties

The Power of Feeling

Have you ever asked yourself: 'What are feelings?', 'Where do they come from?', 'Where do they go?', 'What is the dynamic behind them?', and finally 'What are they for?' Perhaps you haven't asked these questions in quite the same way, and yet we have all wondered where anger, fear or sadness come from. Not satisfied with the usual explanations that these states just happen, that they are moods and that we all have them (although some people are more moody than others), we begin to explore the cause of feelings.

In the course of this exploration, we come to discern good from bad feelings, motivations, intentionality and the whole relation of activity to a sense of evolving values. What we don't understand at the outset, however, is that emotion is a collective phenomenon. We are, as a matter of fact, moving within an ocean of feeling and emotion, generated by millions of people who have gone before us, millions who are surrounding us and millions who are waiting to carry on the experience of emotionality, or the workings of the laws of cause and effect at the lower levels of matter.

Feeling and Emotion

Feeling is the energy of love, creative and self-generated. Emotion is the human motions of feeling, the myriad permutations and distortions of love, and also its absence. Feeling is the faculty of experiencing and the energy generated by that experience. Emotion is a human phenomenon, whereas feeling is a capacity, a potency, a power that originates from beyond – one of the three basic powers in man.

There is a world of difference between feeling and sensation.

113

Sensation refers to the physical senses. Feeling is non-physical. Feeling is actually a function of the heart, translated into irritation, anger and greed, fear, possessiveness or pride by the individual whose consciousness may be lodged in one of the lower chakras. By the individual whose consciousness is being expressed through one of the higher chakras, this feeling gets translated into humanitarianism, joy, generosity, fulfilment and a vast array of aesthetic satisfactions.

Mechanics

We are a consciousness, an intelligence within a vehicle of matter. Matter is composed of different ingredients in different kinds of activity (atomic and molecular, electric, magnetic, electronic, sonic, etc.). We are also in a body of feeling which as far as substance is concerned, has nothing to do with physical matter but resonates in synchronicity with it. This is the second body. The third body, or the lower mental body, has a different kind of substance and resonates in synchronicity with the first and second bodies. The first three bodies actually move as one. They are interwoven together in what we call the personality.

What this means is that whatever happens physically, mentally or emotionally will have either originated or caused ripples in one of the other two bodies. Psychology is all about understanding this interrelation, but to date has not fully embraced the mechanisms underlying the interrelationship or the dynamics operating within each body. Psychology has largely entrenched itself in linearity, which is a property of the lower mental body. Feeling is non-linear; it is concentric.

We could liken the activity of the three lower bodies to that of the elements of earth, water, air and fire. The physical body would correspond to the density, stability and solidity of earth. The emotional body would correspond to water, its fluidity, its properties of congealing and evaporating, of streaming, rolling, mirroring and contouring. The mental body would correspond to the properties of air, cool, dry, cutting or refreshing and inspiring. Fire pertains to consciousness, or Spirit, and ignites whatever it directs itself to; it is the spark of the higher life within the bodies.

These three bodies and their properties are part of the experience of the planet. Everybody has them, although in different degrees and qualifications. It is as if each of us had been entrusted by this great entity, the planet Earth, with a part of itself in the form of these three bodies. How we care for them will reflect back to the Earth itself.

This is where the concept of qualification, which I mentioned briefly in the introduction, comes in. Feeling amplifies energy. As an intelligence we have the ability to envision something and give it energy through our feeling. When we view something as beautiful, this thing actually becomes beautiful; when we view something as ugly or fearful, the reverse becomes true. What we behold creates a feeling in us, either through repetition from the past, novelty of the present or constructive intentionality – an act of will.

We 'qualify' whatever we look at. We are constantly qualifying everything in our environment by the way we view it through our feelings. The more people see something in a certain light, the more this thing will conform to the way people see it. If enough people, for example, see sex as evil, then sex will manifest itself as evil. If enough people see death as fearful, then death will be dreaded. What we feel magnifies what is, and the more the feeling, the greater the magnification. There are many shared conceptions such as these, including the process of ageing and decay. Our life span is so short at this time (as compared to the ancients), not only because of pollutants and stress, but also because of the consensus that we deteriorate with age.

When enough people in a locality think and feel the same way, cultural idiosyncrasies are formed. When the entire population of the Earth feels the same way, we have a mighty, deep-rooted belief. This mass feeling creates emotional trends and vortices of energy that act with tremendous impact upon the individual, impinging upon his own energies through superstition, suggestion or hypnotic control.

The energy of the emotional body, in its pure and uncontaminated state, looks and feels like a scintillating mist of fine colours, pretty much as they would look on a soap bubble. When this energy is qualified – modified, intensified or frozen – by the individual, it takes on a different density and coloration. It becomes deeper in colour and muddier. The colours no longer operate through spirit as they do in their pure state. They now reflect the selfishness or wilfulness of the individual will. At this point, through the agitation

115

of the energy currents inherent within the emotional body, vortices form. Every time that the individual feels in the same way, he deepens the groove, creating a more powerful vortex which acts like a whirlpool magnetically to draw like energies into itself, colour those energies and then radiate its properties, affecting everything in its circumference. The feeling, now become an emotion, sucks you in and you feel helpless. Before you know it you are projecting anger, fear, sadness through the power of momentum. You lose control over yourself. The vortex serves to stimulate, agitate, seduce or otherwise engulf you in negative feeling such as irritation, dissatisfaction, frustration, lust, greed, pride or domination out of habitual and unconscious stimulation.

When the vortices created by the individual are different from those of his locality or of the age, the individual feels out of sorts. When they correspond to the surroundings they are, of course, intensified even further.

The emotional, mental and physical bodies, as I said earlier, are created from an etheric blueprint, the fourth body. This etheric blueprint contains the record (known as the *akashic** record) of all actions, feelings and trends set in your cellular history, including emotional vortices. You have the cellular history of your ancestors to work through; your likes, your dislikes, your fears, doubts, pride and limitations. These records do not change unless *you* (who alone hold the key, as they are *part* of you) change them through consciousness, deliberate re-qualification. Unchecked, these impulses or compulsions will continue to intensify similar characteristics in you and add to the profusion of impulses generated by the age, culture, the individual life plan and the seeds of past behaviour.

You can see how important it is to work through your emotions, to understand, face and conquer them so that the power of feeling may be freed to animate and enhance conscious creation. It is important to extricate yourself from the mass influence of energies and your own unconscious habits, which coerce and sway you into unauthentic behaviour patterns or which feed a past momentum which may no longer be your goal in this lifetime. In the past we have attempted to master our emotionality by retreating in some way; in the East through meditation and esoteric science, in the

---

* Akasha: a Sanskrit term for the ether or vibration upon which human and other experiences or events are recorded as memory.

West through linear forms of control through philosophy and introspective thought, or through some forms of psychology.

The cause of our present-day ills stems from a lack of understanding of the mechanics of the personality as an emotional body. This body has a mind of its own, so to speak, that of habits, impulses and unchecked or unexpressed desires, longings and aspirations from the grossest to the sublime. In some psychological schools of thought these impulses have been termed the ego, the id, the four-year-old, the child, the libido, etc. In the East it is simply called the ego, that which separates you from the Source.

It is becoming increasingly obvious that the way through and out of the pull of the emotions is not through philosophy or ordinary thinking, but through another, higher frequency, that of the activity of spirit as pure mind. This is the hidden agent in the power of transmutation referred to by alchemists, indirectly recognising the occult power of feeling in the creation of universes, from the personal to the cosmic.

Before we can speak about the creation of universes we must understand our personal universe, particularly the interrelation of body, mind and feeling. I said that feeling was a function of the heart and that it is a power that comes from beyond. The heart, you will remember, is 'The abode of the most high living God': the God 'I AM'. It is our direct link to our individualised God-Self which lies at the level of the twelfth plane, the source of our Life and our Light. This God-Self speaks through stirrings of the heart. Many ancient scriptures agree on the need to 'be born again' into the attributes of the heart – innocence, purity, humility and brotherhood.

This voice of the heart is 'the will of God' or divine will. *Feeling, then, is a function of the will.* When we listen to the heart we are attuned to the Source; when we listen to our thoughts against the heart we operate on personal will. This is perhaps what Master Jesus meant when He said, 'Father, your will, not mine, be done!' And here is a primal key to the art of transmutation; the power of feeling is amplified through a pure heart that expresses the will (pure mind) of the Godhead.

At this point we might answer for ourselves the question, 'What are feelings *for?*' They are to generate the will of God, to create through the power of spirit, to transform the whirlpool of feeling into the generating activity for transmutation. We do it through

117

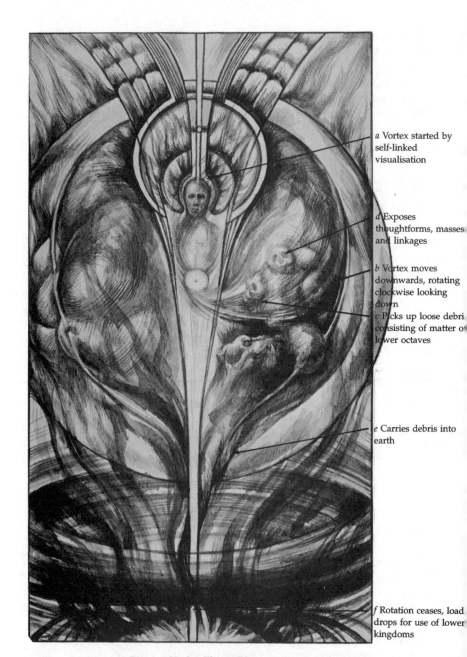

a Vortex started by self-linked visualisation

d Exposes thoughtforms, masses and linkages

b Vortex moves downwards, rotating clockwise looking down

c Picks up loose debris consisting of matter of lower octaves

e Carries debris into earth

f Rotation ceases, load drops for use of lower kingdoms

Fig. 2.1 Violet Flame Vortex

understanding who and what we are. We do it by conscious deliberate choice, by an act of will. We do it by choosing to identify with our divine heritage, to assume our unity with all that is, rather than to identify with the physical laws of matter and temporality. Our determination stakes our claim as beings of Light to bring us the dominion and mastery that come from oneness with the Godhead.

The practices recommended here initiate the transmutation process. They begin with sealing the self from impinging energies through the formation of a thoughtform, which resembles a cylinder of light. Within this cylinder we invite the fire of spirit through the activity of the seventh ray of transmutation: the violet flame. Exerting our divine will we choose to identify with Light and determine to make every action a conscious act in the service of that Light.

We then need to face humanity's mis-creations through our own lives by confronting that which we have probably avoided. Some of us will have more to work through than others. For all, the first step will consist in mastering the activity of the vortices of energy within the emotional body, in bringing the emotions under control and sustaining that control (which at times might seem like taming a bronco), until we choose, as Francis of Assisi said, to console rather than to be consoled, to understand rather than to be understood, to love rather than to seek to be loved: 'For it is in giving that we receive, it is in pardoning that we are pardoned, and it is in dying that we are born to eternal life.'

Spirituality and science are one, loving and knowing are one and matter and spirit are but the two faces of one godliness. We are born anew every moment of conscious Life.

Meditation to Harmonise the Emotions and Generate Feeling

(Also serves to clear accumulated 'misqualified' substance that has adhered at the level of all three lower bodies.)

Determine to put aside all mental conjectures about what your feelings are, where they come from, whose fault they are, etc. Get ready to nose-dive into the ocean of emotions within and around you. Take it as an energetic experience that has nothing to do with you as a personality.

This is a vigorous process. I suggest that you do it fully. The substance of the emotional body is thick and dense. Particularly if there are strong imprints, it is sticky and rather murky. You would do well to generate as much physical energy as you can to dislodge the negativity from the cellular structure.

Begin by the violet flame-shaking practice outlined in the opening pages. Sustain that visualisation as you intensify the shaking to include your entire body.

Amplify the activity of the violet flame to extend to well over three feet around you in all directions.

Stop after three to five minutes and freeze in place. Remain standing. If you have problems in keeping your balance, practise one of the grounding visualisations suggested earlier. (You might like to imagine actual roots extending from the navel, through the soles of your feet and anchoring you deeply into the earth.)

Continue with the visualisation of the violet flames and intensify their activity. Watch them begin to swirl until they create a spinning vortex around you. The physical spinal column and an imaginary line extending through you, from over your head to below your feet, serves as the central axis around which this column of spinning violet flame revolves.

If your hearing is at all sensitive, at this point you might pick up a deep vacuous humming, like a huge oceanic space enfolding you.

Sustain the activity for another two minutes. The momentum of the spinning violet flame enlarges the column to about ten feet around you now.

Notice all density, like ashes, fall down unto the ground. Imagine the ground absorbing and transmuting this substance. Notice, too, a darkish smoke rising up over the column to be absorbed and transmuted by the heavens.

Return to this reality and sit silently. Become aware of the feeling of lightness within you.

As you sit silently now, bring your attention to the centre of your chest, to the heart chakra.

Notice a focus of light there, like a small sun. Feel the pulsing irradiation from this sun, swelling up within you ... and extend it ... like heat-waves ... out from you in all directions.

Continue to observe the radiant light generated from the sun within your heart until it surrounds you totally. Be a sun-presence of your God-Self within your physical body. Generate this feeling of energy further and further and further. Let it reach everyone and everything. (You can modify this later on, and embrace someone you may be having difficulty with, someone who may be ill or someone that you may simply want to help.)

In coming back, take time to wind down the vibratory activity that you have set into motion through the power of feeling.

You may like to lie down and rest to soft music.

Notice now where your feelings are!

The Emotional Body

The physical interface for the emotional body is the entire nervous system. However, the emotional brain might be said to be lodged in the mid-brain. It includes the limbic system, a circuit which serves to carry messages and memories. The cerebral cortex here has a line to the hypothalamus, the immune system and the automatic nervous system. The emotional circuitry affects our entire body.

The emotional body has also been called the astral or desire body. The consciousness within this body is one of desire. It longs for creativity through interaction with other energies; its nature is to reach, intermingle and express. Its original yearning was to embrace creation and through merging with it, raise its vibration and return it to the Source.

We must remember that the emotional body is part of the body of the planet. Because of the largely selfish, adhesive nature of misqualified feeling upon that planet, the initially flowing liquidity of this body grew dense and sticky. (Chris Griscom calls it the 'stickum'.) This substance expands and adheres to like substances, creating a sense of heaviness.

The emotional body has also been associated with astral projection. Emotions, especially strong feelings such as anger, fear, sexual desire and curiosity, will cause you to project a form of yourself animated with your own vitality on to the object of your desire.

These projections, be they conscious or unconscious, deplete the physical body because the astral, or emotional, body is more a state of activity than an actual body itself. It draws from the vitality of the physical. Desire coats the etheric double in density, which is experienced as a heavy, slow vibration, magnetically attracted to the earth. Anyone who has had astral projection experiences will describe the sensations of moving as if through water, sometimes

121

at a tilt, going through walls and floating, as if swimming, flying, walking on split-levelled surfaces . . .

The 'lower' astral, a term which was coined by the Theosophists, refers to the collective desires of humanity at the level of the lower chakras. The emotional body itself is dictated by the activity (the attractions, repulsions and karmic lessons) of the first three chakras. By the time a feeling reaches the level of the heart chakra, the activity has been transferred to one of the higher bodies.

The emotional body thrives on excitement and interprets the lack of this kind of titillation as boredom. Like the second chakra which it parallels, the emotional body has all the properties of water and is easily stirred and agitated. An individual who is locked into the consciousness of this body has intense likes and dislikes and is somewhat addicted to the stimulation of the second and third chakras (emotive sensitivity and action).

This is the prime body involved in all kinds of relationships. The etheric imprints activate the vortices on this body in such a way that its intensity perpetuates karma. All issues related to contractual and conditional giving, expectations and the many forms of manipulation operating in relationships are a direct result of the activity of this body.

Because the tendency of this energy is to project itself, our emotional thinking goes onto the environment in the form of judgements and accusations. We hate, dislike and are irritated by people and situations that mirror something within ourselves or from our emotional history that we have not come to terms with. In other words we are still fighting it.

This can be observed in the perfectionist who demands that others be as perfect as he pretends to be. He will be intolerant and petulant. He will be unkind and unloving, despite the fact that he may want to be kind and loving. Since he is intolerant and demanding with himself, his self-denial is the antithesis of what he holds as virtue. The same applies to forgiveness. Unforgiving people find it hard to forgive themselves. The key is always loving ourselves.

Most of the bonding that goes on in the name of love is extremely destructive. It may be seen as thick murky lines of force that tie people's emotional bodies together in a reciprocal swapping of power, attitudes and beliefs, to the extent that individual identity and feeling are largely lost.

Notice how doubt and fear are the primary gateway for negativity. If you examine both mechanisms you will see that they are predicted upon the notion that we are alone in an alien world. When we cannot trust in God, the higher self or in forces of Light, we are vulnerable, frightened. That fear is expressed as doubt on the mental level. You can't trust yourself, you can't trust another. These two mechanisms lower the frequency of our vibrations and invite negative forces. All negative emotions in fact proceed from doubt and fear, including those of our classic perfectionist whose inner fear is committing mistakes and being indulgent.

It is especially important to keep an emotional body harmonious uninterruptedly. Only in this way can we build a positive momentum. Emotional energy builds through momentum.

Watch your expectations. Everyone is caught within the mirages of his or her own emotional body. Be sensitive not only to yourself, but to the fact that others by virtue of their own projections may not be able to see themselves – *or you.*

The work of Inner Alchemy at this level is to understand and experience our own attractions and repulsions, our reactive as well as our responsive behaviour. We need to observe our 'qualifications' (i.e. the way in which we view reality through the projection of our own emotions) and redirect the misqualifications into positive motions.

Ask yourself:

How am I feeling?

Am I reacting automatically, or am I responding genuinely to my environment?

How am I coming across? Am I successfully conveying my feeling, or am I being interpreted differently?

How can I change the way that I perceive myself?

How can I change the way that others perceive me?

How am I in my innermost privacy? And how is that different from how I am in public?

How am I with my closest friends? With a stranger?

What are my likes and dislikes? How addicted am I to them and to certain emotional patterns?

Whom do I dislike and why? Do these people have traits that I am not acknowledging within myself?

Once these questions have been answered in deepest honesty, we need to act on what we have noted, particularly in regard to people and characteristics that we dislike even mildly. Those vibrations, like the sound waves which they are, travel to the object of our dislike and return to us with the same quality amplified. And then they lodge in our aura and add to the 'stickum'.

The material of the emotional body especially, like all substance from the finest to the grossest, responds to rhythm, particularly music. It loves art, nature and the excitement of the entire range of human emotions. Emotional intensity moves in cyclical activity. Understanding this, we can counterbalance the 'crash' that usually follows peak activity, and avert the manic-depressive syndrome that characterises so much of our social behaviour. In this way we begin to exert a certain mastery over the energies within the emotional body, thereby establishing that equilibrium that brings harmony.

Interdependence and Loss of Power

Interdependence is perhaps the most difficult lesson of three-dimensional existence, where we co-exist with beings at all levels of consciousness, where the attractions and repulsions are constantly being projected; where manipulation is used by authority figures, by our parents, lovers and best friends, by the media and by our educational institutions; where hypnotic control in the form of friendly advice from friends or astrologers and from masses of 'readers' persuade and impinge upon our own feelings, creating fear, doubt and dependence, especially dependence upon authority and outside figures. When our attention goes away from the innermost self, we relinquish or give away our power.

The human aura is a most distressing sight, which is perhaps why it is merciful that most people do not have clairvoyant sight. Where the three lower bodies rule through the amplification faculties of the emotional body, the reddish and brownish blobs of stubbornness, selfishness and deceit predominate, and the tears and wounds of past catastrophes indicate the places where we gave away our power sexually, emotionally, intellectually. Here are lodged other people's energies (usually beliefs), which we have adopted as our own, which our energies are dispersed in the auras of other people, whom we have manipulated in some way and who have empowered us instead of themselves.

Extricating ourselves from this entanglement is like peeling our own skin. This is the long and painful path of emotional mastery through relationship, critical, intense and unavoidable for our spiritual evolution.

Methods for Loosening and Facing Emotions

Loosening Emotional Energies

(This method resembles gibberish and bypasses the mind's hold over our emotions, allowing them to be expressed without intellectual content or meaning.)

Sit yourself very comfortably. Alone.

Disconnect the phone and ensure that you can be as free as possible to express yourself. This may include raising your voice.

Start to rock yourself back and forth. Loose the mental hold over your thoughts.

Begin to make faces. Be sure to include your tongue.

Start flapping your tongue and making noises, nonsense sounds like the sound of an engine. 'Brrrrmmmmmmm . . . la la la prrrrtto o offa . . . la . . . la . . . mmmuuu . . . laggga. . . .'

Continue making these nonsense sounds and slowly build into a nonsense language.

Dramatise. Pretend that you are communicating with someone in this nonsense language and that you are telling a dynamic story. (Note: If any of the words that you say have a meaning, it shows that your own mind has got in the way.)

Exaggerate even further by including gestures and your whole body. Overlook any sense of looking silly or acting in a ridiculous way. Stand up when the energy calls for it. You will notice the increase in energy throughout your body.)

Continue the monologue, becoming more and more dramatic, allowing for the waxing and waning and gently building up again.

Become aware of the desire to communicate. Feel the energy swelling up within you and give it a voice and gesture. Let the energy itself direct you.

Do this for about ten minutes and then stop. Rest.

Become aware of the emotions expressed. If you have used an audiocassette or a home video, you might like to see how you looked and sounded before you sheepishly destroy all evidence!

Facing Emotions

(You may use anger, fear, sadness or any other emotion that comes up naturally or that you have difficulty with.)

Suppose that you are facing the emotion of anger. Whether you are angry at someone in the present or in the past is irrelevant.

Summon up that feeling. Notice how it is triggered by a thought. Intensify that feeling. Dramatise it. Exaggerate it. Become aware of the energy within it.

When you have tapped into the quality of this emotion, find a positive expression for that very same energy.

Observing the Effect of Emotions

(This is done with a partner, someone you feel comfortable with and can trust with your emotions. There should be no inhibitions here.)

Sit facing your partner. Acknowledge and give thanks to each other for lending yourselves to this experiment.

Pick an emotion or a negative characteristic, such as anger, greed, terror, deceit.

Each of you is going to play out this emotion before the other. There must be no physical interaction but complete freedom of expression. Decide who will be active first. The non-active person is to observe the other carefully while also observing himself – his own bodily reactions and his own feelings – but he must not react outwardly to the other in any way (including laughing, trying to stop, assuage or comfort the other).

The active person should begin by eliciting a memory of a time or incident in which he was exposed to the particular feeling. If it is anger, then remember a time when he or she felt this anger . . . rage . . . indignation. . . . If a memory doesn't come easily, then imagine a character in a book or in a movie who had that experience. Do this with closed eyes.

Think of the images and events that triggered or could trigger off this anger. Perhaps the injustice. . . . Intensify this anger within. (The partner might want to guide the person, if they are having difficulty getting into it.)

Keep building. When ready, open the eyes and give yourself

complete freedom to express it verbally and through gestures before the other person.

(The non-active partner has agreed *not* to react but to observe.) After three minutes of intense expression, stop.

Simultaneously, the non-active partner has been attempting to shield himself or herself from this energy. He may have turned around, thought of something else . . . whatever he feels inclined to do *not to become involved* with the emotional energy coming at him.

Second phase: The active partner continues to project sexual energy but the non-active partner now prepares himself to receive the energy. Visually and emotionally, the partner now accepts the energy *into the heart*. Both the active and non-active partner take note of their experience without discussing it with the other yet.

Notice the effects of this emotion on your physical body. Allow whatever emotional reaction (crying, trembling, etc.) to subside before switching roles with your partner.

The non-active partner has also taken note of his or her reaction before this emotional display. He or she should ask the following questions:

Who does this remind me of?
What is my habitual defensive tactic? To run, to hide, to attack?
What is my body feeling?
How do I feel now?

Switch roles. Repeat the whole procedure, with the same emotion.

When both partners have had their turn, only then may you share *out loud* the experiences you have had in doing the exercise.

You might want to hum gently, breathe deeply, or practise the sun-presence meditation of the previous section to bring yourself back to a state of balance and heartfulness; or you might want to do the following meditation for spiritual balance.

Balance and the Three Primary Rays or Forces

The rays, as you will remember, are pure cosmic qualities that originate from the central sun. They are the constituent ingredients for all creation. Light emanates as beams or rays, but when it reaches the surface of earth's physical density and acts upon matter itself, it becomes etheric flame, such as the violet flame which you are already familiar with.

At the heart of our being, in the form of three flames, is the foundation of our Spirit form and the seed power for our every activity. This is an exact replica of the heart of creation. Within our physical form, at the heart chakra, we find a miniature reproduction of this triune activity of the sacred fire. It is an etheric phenomenon which can be easily sensed and readily approached to charge, heal and balance ourselves, strengthen our aura and irradiate qualities of perfection to everyone around.

In the remote past, at a time when the physical density of the human body was not so compacted but more translucent, this triune flame was much larger and surrounded the body. With the deceleration in vibration, the flame shrank to its actual size. This meditation expands the flame back to its original size and brings about the harmony which is ours as beings of Light.

Meditation for Spiritual Balance

Sit down in a quiet, safe environment.

Bring yourself to a state of stillness: physical, mental and emotional.

Sense a small flame within the centre of your chest. (If you have been a Christian, you might remember the phenomenon of the Sacred Heart of Jesus, or Mary.)

Feel the activity of this energetic focus of inner light and allow your whole attention to dwell within it. Go inside it. Notice that at the very centre of this brilliant core is a threefold flame.

The first colour that strikes you is the bright yellow golden central flame: be in it, feel it.

To the left is a deep pink flame with a magenta-coloured centre. Let your heart embrace that pink flame.

Now, to the right, is a blue flame, pale with electric blue ribbons of flame. Let your heart expand to contain that flame as well.

Be with this three-tongued flame and notice it intertwine within itself, forming one magnificent flame.

Become aware of a crystal sphere that seems to cover the flame and cause it to give off a flow of multi-coloured pastel light.

Now, as you focus within that flame, sense and see it glow

brighter and brighter and expand larger and larger. Continue the process until it completely surrounds your body and your aura.

Remain with this threefold flame as it brings peace and balance to every part of you.

When you are ready to return to your ordinary world, allow the flame to return to its usual size.

Take a few deep breaths and ground yourself.

Express your gratitude for this Light in acknowledgement to your own essence, your God-Self. Having felt the magnitude of its power, let your feelings bow in humble reverence.

Review

Where *do* emotions come from, and where do they go? They originate within you. They reflect where you are as a personality, how finely attuned you are to yourself as Spirit. Individual emotional patterns are as varied as snowflakes.

Have you examined your behaviour from the physical point of view? Do you take the time to feel your body from within? I don't mean the tension and stress of athletic performance. I mean the gentle stirring of the breath inside you or the way your stomach feels when you overeat or drug it with alcohol and other poisons. Have you stopped to really feel what you are doing to your body when you smoke? What intentionality do you operate under when you are in close proximity to other bodies? Do you feel exploitative, or are you in awe at the majesty of the life within?

What about your emotional patterns of behaviour? How much are you out for yourself (even if it is *your* enlightenment)? How realistically and thoroughly do you initiate a reversal of your negative energy patterns? Do you really care about the life that beats within each individual? Are you more concerned with great causes such as feeding the poor or housing the homeless, but cringe at the thought of facing a beggar? Or touching a victim of Aids?

As three-dimensional beings, we exist within an ocean of energy waves that continually animate recurrent thoughtforms. Within this reality we have the powers to direct and recreate energy and substance through the conscious application of the law of Light, or through the unconscious mechanism of this very same law. The law works whether we are avail ourselves of it or not. The choice is for consciousness or unconsciousness. In consciousness we create positive forms. In unconsciousness we perpetuate misery, lack and limitation, disease and strife.

Inner Alchemy advocates the deliberate and conscious application of the precepts of Light into ordinary daily life, beginning with our emotional life. Our emotional life in fact sets the foundation for everything that happens upon the planet. We need not only to understand the principles underlying the unconscious mechanisms of the emotional body but also to apply them constructively.

I can't emphasise enough the tremendous power of the feeling faculty of man, especially as it applies to projection of energy. We need but look at our moment-to-moment actions, thoughts and feelings to see the prevalence of automatic subhuman behaviour patterns. We look, think and act out of fear. Fear is the seed feeling for all negativity, including the anger and violence that clouds our times.

We are constantly gossiping in the name of conversation. We are forever giving away our power through a misguided sense of loving and sharing. And when we behold one another, we do so with greed and lust, possessiveness, jealousy and exploitation, instead of as unique beings of Light and Love and spiritual power. When faced with injustice we belligerently retaliate with more injustice. In an era where so much lip service is paid to the virtues of surrender and 'turning the other cheek', of peace and brotherhood, we ignorantly misconstrue the messages by giving away even more of our power to newer forms of political and religious authority.

And yet somewhere, somehow, we are 'getting it'. Here and there friends of the Light are emerging who are embodying the teachings of Light, who are holding to the vision of Light, who with great courage, gently, but with unyielding firmness, hold the torch that is lighting the world. Look for them. But I warn you, these are deceptive times. Things are not what they appear to be. You will know and see the 'real' only when you know and see the truth of the god within. The shortest path to truth is a leap into the dimensions beyond the known of your very own self. There are no teachers or guides, and there is no teaching. There is only YOU, in your aloneness. When you rejoice in fullness (*not* emptiness) of your aloneness, you have arrived home and everywhere at the same time. Only then will you recognise the same in others, beyond the landmarks of the known. Only then will you know the real meaning of power, that of the power of Light.

The Power of Thought

Thought is vision with meaning. The power of thought is just as important as the power of feeling in every aspect of creation. The two work together. Every time you have a feeling about something, there is a visual counterpart – a memory, a desire – that ignites it. A thought, or idea, occurs when there is a picture, or a series of pictures that convey a meaning. This meaning will then strike a responsive cord in the individual, a response or reaction (depending on the degree of consciousness present), which leads to action.

Thought is tangible. Clairvoyants and psychics know this well, as do parapsychologists who are constantly researching ESP and telepathy. Governments know it too when they indulge in psychic propaganda and psychotronic (using psychic faculties or powers to obtain information) warfare. And of course the media know it, when they create images, jingles and feelings that linger in the minds and feelings of the public. Everyone is, in fact, using thoughts as tangibles without acknowledging it.

The truth is that not only are thoughts a tangible reality, they are part and parcel of our contemporary model, which is, through lack of its acknowledgement, creating negative, confusing imprints. There is a massive traffic jam of thoughts polluting our atmosphere from people who believe that just because they have not voiced their thoughts, these thoughts are somehow non-existent. We hold secrets not only from our loved ones but from ourselves. At the higher levels of consciousness there are no secrets. There is no need for secrets because there where Light prevails is Love – honesty, integrity and purity. Secrets are a phenomenon directly related to third-dimensional life, where the coating of density allows for a uniformity of appearance and where the din of heavier frequencies obstructs or distracts the seer from Truth.

Thoughts have definite form, occupy space and have the quality of the feeling associated with them. They will continue to surround the aura of an individual until they dissolve through some kind of resolution. Thought is held as long as a feeling animates it. It dissolves either when it is enacted or when it disperses through lack of energy or attention. There are many thoughtforms around each person, some stronger than others, some as old as lifetimes.

In the energy field surrounding an individual will be housed, not only the vortices created by the habitual motion of feeling, but also the profusion of thoughtforms created through humanity's embodiments. Anyone with proper training can come to read these images and feelings and know not only the personal history of the person, but the present intentions and future trends. It is a well known esoteric fact that in the courts of ancient rulers, from Egyptian pharaohs to Russian czars, high priests and psychics held power through their ability to read people and conditions.

Just as the emotional body is a field of energy vibrating at a particular frequency and a Light substance that ignites and revolves in a certain way, the mental body has its own field, its own frequency, its own modus operandi. Just as there are emotions within the emotional body, whose capacity is expressed through feeling, there are thoughtforms within the mental body, whose faculty is expressed through thought. The mental body, then, is not so much the collectivity of thoughtforms as it is the substance within which thoughts are stored.

Now the power behind thought originates from the mind. Mind is the vehicle of consciousness that cognises, organises, understands, focuses and projects form and meaning through the use of intelligence. Intellect, as interesting and useful as it is, is a very basic form of intelligence used at the level of the third dimension. It tends to be as myopic as things can be at this level.

Intelligence expressed at the level of detail, of course, relates to the laws of physicality. There is a regularity to it. It is definable. It can be set into rules. It can be learned by rote. It does not demand either flexibility or spontaneity. Intelligence at this level is what I will define as the lower mental body (LMB). At the higher, more intuitive levels of perception and organisation, the mind will operate through the lower mental body aligned to a similar though vibrationally higher body of consciousness called the higher mental body (HMB). The higher mental body is a higher consciousness that comprehends intelligence interdimensionally.

At the level of the lower mental body mental energy manifests itself in a linear, direct way and is experienced at times as aggression; at the level of the higher mental body it shows up as creative and regenerative, embracing holistic concepts.

The mind builds moulds or blueprints through its faculty of visualisation. These forms appear as attitudes that set off emotional patterns. These attitudes take on different connotations at the lower and higher levels. For example, belief, so necessary at the lower levels to inspire and redirect energy, becomes faith. Dogma, so necessary to tame unbridled instincts, becomes the experience of knowing. Faith, seen in its proper light is an irrefutable inner knowingness. And knowing surpasses its counterpart in the lower levels, knowledge.

The lower mental body and the higher mental body operate on different circuits.

The lower mental body uses the solar plexus as its power centre and governs activities relating to mobility at the level of everyday actions. It deals with the outer reality: events, facts and chronology. For our purposes, the higher mental body uses the throat centre as well as the third eye as its source of power, but its primary energy comes from the heart. It deals with inner experience and with the bridging aspects of that experience to the outer world. Both vehicles will use the throat centre, through the spoken word, to precipitate animated thoughtforms into materialisation.

Fig. 2.2 The Three Creative Powers as Expressed Through the Chakras

Powers	Chakra	Manifestation
Thought	6	HMB Higher frequency manifestation
Spoken word	5	Light-substance, thoughtforms
Feeling	4	
Action/Power	3	LMB Lower manifestation
Feeling	2	Physical substance, matter
Thought	1	

The Lower Mental Body

The lower mental body, or third body, expresses mind at the level of physical substance. Together with the emotional and physical bodies it constitutes the personality or human self. This body utilises all the chakras, but will express itself through the energy generated at the solar plexus. It draws from the higher intelligence that filters in from the Godhead at the level of the third eye and reassembles it for concrete reality within the physical brain.

Whereas the driving energy originates from the solar plexus, the brain itself serves as the physical interface with the lower mental body. The brain receives the stimuli from the environment and responds by sending stimuli to the emotional body and to the physical body, whereby action is initiated. The memory circuit in the brain will interpret the stimuli according to historical precedent. The entire system operates automatically, for purposes of protecting the organism, until the consciousness of the individual aligns with the higher principles operating within the laws of Light.

For purposes of simplification we will speak about the lower mental body as if it were an entity of its own. The lower mental body receives the God-ideas generated at the twelfth dimensional level after they have been decoded by the higher self at the seventh dimension, and implements them in the physical world through a logical or rational approach. We need to understand here that linear thinking is another effect of three-dimensional life, of mind operating in detail and in sequence. Higher mind does not work linearly, it intuits the whole; it is visionary and also sees beyond time and space.

The lower mental body works in sequential logic and comes to pride itself on its smooth-running efficiency. This pride leads to certain arrogance and a feeling of self-sufficiency, which is illusory. It is as if the manager of a corporation were to set himself up as president of the board. (This happens all the time literally and symbolically). In this way the lower mental body sets itself up as the controller.

Because its vision is functionally myopic or three-dimensional, it divides its perceptions into categories and pairs and forgets the unity behind these apparent opposites. Remember that duality is a product of physicality which operates through polarity, or tension, in order to hold a form. Duality is a reflection of polarity. This division is the mind's way of embodying duality and polarity. In this way morality arises. The lower mental body builds systems upon these divisions, upon concepts of good or evil, right or wrong. In its attempt to organise thinking, the lower mental body distorts Truth and becomes narrow, pointing in one direction.

Having built upon a faulty foundation, the lower mental body needs to justify its tenets, much as a liar does when he must defend his position. Like the liar, the lower mental body comes to believe its lies. Its priority then is to protect itself and not to express the God-Self impartially.

The lower mental body possesses a skilled data-managing system. It segments or compartmentalises parts of itself, much as a file clerk will to facilitate recovery of facts. The hidden files of the lower mental body will be those thoughts and memories which least serve its current purposes or which threaten to sabotage immediate plans. This is how the sub-conscious and superconscious aspects of the mind come to be.

These hidden portions of the lower mental body are not only out of mind, they are effectively disconnected from the whole organism, particularly from the emotional body. They have to be. When connected to feeling, these thoughts could prove dangerous, even life-threatening. Those thoughts that are considered 'bad' are stuffed into the subconscious; those thoughts that are considered 'good', (which rather than originating from the higher mental body come from culture) are relegated to the superconscious.

You can understand now how we live in a world filled with double and triple meanings. The words will say one thing, the feeling will convey another, and the mind will be concocting yet another 'reality'.

At the sub-planes of the lower mental body we find thoughts of domination and possessiveness, cruelty and sadism. At the higher sub-planes we find thoughts of beauty, art, music and science.

All three, the conscious, sub-conscious and super-conscious aspects of the mind, are part of the lower mental body functions, concerned with linearity, with three-dimensional life, and only partially with the God-ideas. This is the realm of our present-day psychology.

At this point we may see the absurdity of any psychological theory constructed upon three-dimensional laws, which would relegate the entire realm of psychology to a study of the lower mental

135

body. We will never come to understand the real workings of the mind unless we acknowledge the power of the Source; unless in deep humility we understand the Reality beyond the scope of the lower mental body.

In order to reinstate the power of that highest, fullest aspect of ourselves we need to see the lower mental body for what it is – a tool of something higher and greater. Its function is categorising, appraising and implementing ideas. This it can do magnificently. It is a wonderful servant but an arrogant boss, who, left to itself, will sit in judgment and exploitation.

The power of the lower mental body is great. It builds thought-forms. It has the ability to mobilise physical energies. It translates ideas. It scales down energies. It links directly to the emotional body and together with it draws the materials needed for manifestation on the physical plane. The higher mental body does not have direct access to the personal self except through the perception and faculties of the lower mental body. The lower mental body is the doorkeeper and the spokesman for the mass mind. We do well to befriend it.

Stop a moment and examine your attitudes and beliefs. Be especially honest about your prejudices and inclinations. Contrast what you think what you feel in areas which you consider weak or excessive. Are you sending out double messages? An easy way to determine whether you are indeed sending out double messages is to see how the world around you responds to your needs. Are you manifesting what you want? Look at the reality of your immediate world. Does it fit in with your ideas? How often do you act from what you know and choose, rather than from what you think you ought to do?

How realistic are you about yourself and your world? Do you know what you can do and what you can't do? Do you underestimate, or overestimate, yourself? Are you at odds with your emotions? In other words, how connected are you to your feelings and to your physical body? Do you live in your mind? Do you think what you feel and feel what you think? And then, do you *act* on those thoughts and feelings?

Not only do your three lower bodies, or aspects, need to be integrated and harmonised, you need to blend the energy at each level and manifest that integrity through behaviour and cellular activity. Real integrity shows up in actions and in a feeling synchronicity with living things, not just in thoughts, however lofty they may be. At this point you begin to use the faculties of the higher mind.

The Higher Mental Body

The mechanism of both mental bodies implies by its nature remoteness. The difference in higher or lower resides in the scope of consciousness. What at one level appears judgement, at another might be discernment. What might appear as arrogance, on the higher levels could be termed honour, integrity and fearlessness. The essence of the higher mental body expresses itself through the faculties of the lower mental body once the lower mental body and the emotional body have both been transcended and integrated.

There is always some inspirational activity of the higher mental body filtering through all levels of humanity. It reveals itself in thoughts of peace, brotherhood and goodwill, and wherever the whole is considered over the individual will. Its language is primarily symbolic and abstract. Mostly, however, these occurrences are not able to be part of a sustained activity for the individual unless he has taken a significant step in his own evolution.

In order to function at the level of the higher mental body, we need to have comprehended and perceived beyond rationality. We must have separated ourselves from the mass mind. We also need to have integrated the lessons of the emotional body. Now the lower mental body and the emotional body may move in harmony: the brain capacity can expand to both right and left brain and in addition activate the central brain portion, which is responsible for perception beyond duality. Whole brain thinking is a faculty of the higher mental body.

There are many ways of stimulating whole brain thinking and of opening to visions of a higher, fuller life. When whole brain function is arrived at naturally, an entirely different state of being emerges which is qualitatively different. You might say that at this level the higher mental body becomes Christ-like. The direction of the individual's life – his energy and his attention – moves to the level of the sixth or causal body (the repository of all good achieved throughout lifetimes).

The Christed higher mental body is the true intelligence of the heart. Its energy is non-linear. It is the realm of intuition and that 'knowing' which proceeds from accumulated inner experience. At this level the feeling nature has already been refined from the heat of passionate intensity into the coolness of compassion and is ready to serve.

Whereas the higher mental body reflected what we have come to call the superconscious, or the discerning and discriminating impulses of the soul conveyed to the individual, when this body is Christed its actions are inspired by compassion, love, understanding and forgiveness. It will continue to avail itself of the mechanism of the lower mental body in its function as superconsciousness, giving go or no-go decisions, but it does so objectively and impersonally. Its vantage point not only brings about the revelation of the individual's divine plan for life, but every possibility of its fulfilment.

The Christed higher mental body is in effect a partnership with the seventh dimensional self. It is through the grace of the higher self (the higher mental body itself) that we are able to intuit higher principles in the first place. Our partnership will be as strong as our intimacy with the higher self. By having perfected the personal self, the vibrational level of the individual as a whole is higher, which permits a more direct access to higher mental activity as long as the individual can sustain the frequency. It is not possible to live in this frequency on a permanent basis.

In Inner Alchemy we seek to perfect the physical, emotional and mental vehicles to such a degree that we co-exist in very conscious and close proximity to the higher self and the dimensions beyond the seventh, whereby we gain access to the creative ideas, forces and powers that enable us to rebuild the self, the world and the planet in greater perfection. We can only do that if we begin by stilling the emotions and silencing the endless chatter of mass mind.

The control of mind can only be gained after the emotions have been stilled. You must have had the courage not only to face yourself, but to delve into the deepest, ugliest, most volcanic parts of your emotions. Out of a total *experiential* acceptance will emerge mastery. *Emotions serve to train us to tolerate increasing voltages of energy.*

We must understand here that the mind, in its typical lower mental body arrogance will 'think' it has experienced, will 'think' it has forgiven and will proceed to act 'as if', and perpetuate the deceit which serves to confuse humanity. People who are ruled by this kind of thinking lack emotional sensitivity to their environment.

Mind tempered by purified feeling turns self-indulgent reasoning into reciprocity and greater vision of the whole. Mental activity is slowed down and frequency is accelerated. The slowing down creates pockets of silence which convey far greater and higher thoughtforms as well as the regenerative force from Spirit. This is the silence sought and achieved through meditation; the silence that contains the All.

Clarity is a virtue of silence and the ultimate clarity is the experience of the highest frequencies known as the primordial void or the infinite All. In that overwhelming and humbling realisation we come to know that 'I AM' THE ONLY POWER ACTING through feeling, through thought and now through the faculty of the spoken word.

Mind Energetics
Methods of Energy Dynamics

Experiencing Thought Projection

This is done in pairs. It is best with a group of at least six people.

As in the pair exercise at the end of the chapter on the power of feeling, this exercise demands your full participation and the commitment to explore uninhibitedly the energies within thought-forms, which are usually subliminal. The fundamental ingredients of these exercises were created by two dear friends, Wadud and Waduda.

Sit facing your partner. Acknowledge the light within each of you and verbally thank one another for the opportunity to explore the self in a controlled environment of trust and cooperation.

You are now about to explore three basic energies which are commonly projected at you and which you often unconsciously project to others. These constitute the basics of seduction, manipulation and coercion. These particular thoughts are heavily laced with the lower chakra feeling force.

Sexual Energy

Both the opposite sex and the same sex energy should be experienced.

Decide who will be active first. The non-active participant must not react. He or she should endeavour to observe himself, his feelings, his energy fluctuations, his habitual impulse (avoidance or indulgence), etc.

An important addition to this exercise is that *the non-active partner is asked to shield him or herself from the energy that will be coming towards him.* He is to do this in the way that is natural to him. There should be no prior prompting. The whole point of the exercise is to discover *how we protect* and *how we shield,* however appropriate or effective this might be.

The active partner should now elicit the thoughts that trigger off the feelings of sexuality within him or her. (Note: This may be very difficult for some. For this reason it must be done in a safe, supportive setting.) The entire process should be done *without words* and without touching the partner. Sounds, gestures and movements may be used. Continue to intensify those thoughts and feelings. Become aware of which thoughts work best. Notice the breathing pattern and intensify it. Allow yourself to make sounds . . . and when ready, open the eyes and surround your partner with your energy.

Notice if there is any fear there and go past that. You are exploring this energy in a loving environment. You are bringing it out of secrecy and into the light.

Allow the energy to build intensely and continue to project it for about another two minutes.

Stop. Become aware of how you feel physically, mentally, emotionally.

Simultaneously, the non-active partner has been attempting to shield himself or herself from this energy. He may have turned around, thought of something else . . . whatever he feels inclined to do *not to become involved* with the sexual energy coming at him.

Second phase: The active partner continues to project sexual energy but the non-active partner now prepares himself to receive the energy. Visually and emotionally, the partner now accepts the energy *into the heart.* Both the active and non-active partner take note of their experience without discussing it with the other yet.

140

Roles are now reversed.

After both partners have had their turn at projecting, shielding and receiving the energy into the heart, they share their experiences with one another.

Power Energy

The process is identical to the previous one, except that now the energy projected is that of power – the solar plexus energy.

Each partner is to project the drive to get things done: winning in a competition; selling a good thing; speaking up for a cause; promoting a political campaign. . . . Find the ways in which you apply these energies in your life. And if you happen to be a fairly passive individual, then conceive of someone who is like this and act out being that person. Do your best to become this person and to involve the other person in your scenario.

The non-active partner is to try to resist in every way that he or she can.

After about three minutes of this, the non-active partner (at a moment designated by both, or by a third party) accepts the energy into the heart.

Roles are reversed as above.

Intellectual Energy

This time, the energy being projected is directed from the lower mind, such as when persuading or trying to win an argument.

Put yourself in the frame of mind of thinking that you are right and that the other is wrong. Mentally try to convince the other with your reasoning. Try to penetrate through whatever resistance might be there.

The non-active person shields, and at the designated moment, accepts the energy into the heart. This usually requires that you visually bend the energy that is being directed from the frontal part of the third eye and see it entering in the heart.

Roles are reversed.

Conclusions

Each of these exercises not only reveals your own psychology and the working of your mind, but the ways in which you unsuccessfully defend yourself. These exercises are usually not dangerous if done in a supportive environment. If there is any fear, or doubt *don't do them*. If you feel insecure or unsure of your partner, *don't do them*.

This technique provides excellent training in discerning and discriminating among the different qualities of energies which are projected in conjunction with the chakras. Take note of the different sensations.

Notice which of the three was the most difficult to convey, the most difficult to resist, the most difficult to accept. Then notice what you experienced as the sender, when any of these three energies was received in the heart. Herein is the secret to your real self-defence.

Meditation on Wisdom

This visualisation cleans and clears the brain of impurities and accelerates the vibratory rate of the brain itself.

After generating enough energy and when you feel aligned and still, visualise a golden pyramid about three feet on each side, point upwards, several feet above you in the centre of the room.

With your eyes closed, image a singular eye within this pyramid.

See crystal rays of light emanating from the eye in all directions.

Sense the rays entering your own physical brain and opening the all-seeing eye of the Godhead within you.

Rest in the silence of that knowingness.

Meditation Uniting Heart and Mind

This one comes from Olive Pixley and uses sound as well.

Picture a golden upright triangle at a distance in front of you at the level of your third eye.

See the triangle coming closer until is is flush against your forehead. Pull the triangle inside your head to form a three-pointed base – one on each temple, the third toward the back of the head. The upper point is just by your crown centre. As you draw in the triangle, do it to an inbreath and to the inner sound "Pie' . . .

On the outbreath, to the inner sound 'Youuuu', visualise turning the triangle inside out (like a sock) and upside down from the base. See the base of the triangle rising over your head and the point now pointing downwards into the heart.

Do the visualisation again, only now fill the base of the triangle in the upright position with whatever thoughts or problems may be troubling you. As you breathe out, offer these thoughtforms to the Godhead for transmutation. Feel the light that pours through from above into your heart in return.

Meditation to Quicken the Brain

This particular visualisation is especially useful for interdimensional perception.

Visualise a bright golden yellow sun before you, the size of a plum.

Pull that sun inside your head. Sustain the visualisation of the bright golden sun within the brain and visualise it colouring the grey matter of the brain in yellow golden light. See your brain become golden.

Feel the sensation of this sizzling yellow golden sun within your head and see it sending out golden rays in all directions around you.

After a minute or so, follow the golden sun as it rises through the head and poises itself about a foot above it. Relax the head and sustain the picture for as long as you can.

Allow whatever images appear within your mind to be there. Take note of them, without judgement.

Return to your usual reality by stages. Be sure to ground yourself thoroughly by filling the entire container of your body with the presence of yourself.

When you are well in your body, return. You might like to keep a journal of your observations.

Meditation to Clear the Mind

This meditation also forms part of Olive Pixley's series of exercises to build an armour of light.

Begin by connecting with the great central sun source through the awareness of your God-Self. Invoke the forces of central intelli-

143

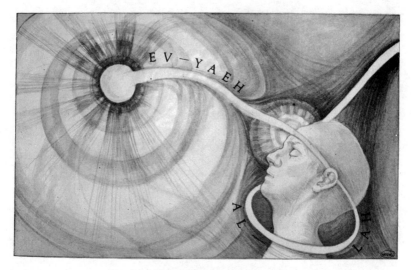

Fig. 2.3 Meditation to Clear the Mind
Allah-he-ay-veh

gence to descend. Call upon the visual image of your own higher self or that of a master, such as Jesus, Buddha, Quan Yin, or of the sun presence, which represents the individualised God force.

Visualise a ray of white light coming from infinity (above and behind you) down in front of the face, piercing the throat and flashing halfway up the back of the head. It rays through the head and out of the middle of the forehead, straight back into the forehead of the image of the inner guide or teacher that you have invoked.

This exercise is done either standing or sitting.

The power of the light pouring through the head washes the mind clean of all dusty thoughts accumulated during the day. Even though this exercise can be done at any time, it is a good practice to do it at night. In the morning the mind should awaken cleared of the previous day's frustrations.

Procedure

On the sound AHLLA (from ancient Aramaic) on a deep inhaling breath, bring the Light down through the throat and up the back of the head.

On the sound HEAY-VE, on a forceful outbreath, flash the light through the head and out through the centre of the forehead, back into the visualised radiance of the mind of the Christ symbol.

The head should be tilted upwards and this exercise should be done three times, whenever the need for clear thinking is urgent.

Pronunciation: HE as in 'see'
AY as in 'day'
VE as in French 'de'

The Power of the Spoken Word

Who has not pondered the meaning behind the biblical statement, 'In the beginning was the Word . . .'. Why and how is the Word 'the beginning'? And what *is* 'the Word' anyway?

Conceive of the primordial source as a nexus of vibration from which all substance and all attributes derive. This Source is One. It has to be. It is the universal sum total of unqualified energy – no-thing. The instant the energy is qualified, its vibratory action is lowered and it becomes something. *The process of qualification occurs through sound.* From an oceanic, all-pervading humming (Om, Aum, I Am . . .) it individuates into notes, or practice resonances. Each resonance will vibrate in a unique way, congealing or breaking up into some kind of form or definition. In other words it acquires substance. Sound is the precipitating activity that creates substance by gathering energy into like clusters, which then mould into a form. Colour is sound substance. We can now begin to understand how the rays build or create all that is. Out of colour and combinations of colour/sound frequency, Light Substance and physical matter emerge as form.

It stands to reason too that as sound creates it can also destroy. This latter activity is one that we are already familiar with in this century, where Caruso's voice could break glass and supersonic jets have penetrated through the sound barrier.

We utilise the same principles in creating ourselves and our worlds. Not knowing how to use sound purely, we use the energy of sound through the spoken word. A word is a sound that has been invested with meaning; it carries a thoughtform and a feeling. Words don't have to make sense to the mind or carry conscious intentionality to have effects. Tone itself will convey feeling and colour the environment appropriately. When, however, tone is injected into a word that carries intentionality, we have a power word. 'Trouble, trouble, toil and trouble . . .' or 'Be still and know . . .' are examples of power phrases, incantations, decrees or affirmations which bring about envisioned results.

We have already established how the throat chakra, a vehicle for first ray activity, is responsible for expressing will, both personal and divine. Will is the propelling force for manifestation and creation. When the throat is a vehicle for the will of the lower chakras it conveys those qualities to the listener, creating the effects of bitter-sweet emotionality, romance and sensuality, or raw power, even violence. When the throat chakra is at the service of the upper chakras, the sound produced inspires, uplifts, lulls and awakens one to inner truths. The throat chakra's function is also one of nourishment, imparting the will to live and conveying the sense of warm folds of sensual security as well as dreamy spaces of Light and Love.

Once the thoughtform has been conceived, the photographic (etheric) imprint produced by the combination of lower mental body and emotional body activity serves to mould it. We now need the material to build the physical three-dimensional counterpart, or create the conditions for it to materialise. We need substance. At this point we follow the exact procedure as the principle of creation previously outlined. We use sound: the word.

All words are invested with cumulative power or momentum. Magical formulas and incantations are invested with the energy from thousands of magicians and adepts from centuries past who created a powerful vortex for manifestation. Although we have retained the knowledge of some formulas, we have lost most, and certainly the deepest understanding of the dynamics involved.

Here, as always, we have to thank the grace of Spirit and of those luminous presences that guard and inspire us, for having sealed off the knowledge of the dynamics of the Law from a civilisation that was not ready to use it wisely, and for again reopening that seal at this time. Now is the time to recreate. We rediscover the workings of the Law out of the awareness of the divine partnership with the Godhead – the 'inner guru', the higher self.

Making the Call

'Making the Call' involves conscious linking with the God-Self through the medium of the higher self and establishing what I call 'the alchemical circuit'. This is done energetically through visualisation and established through prayer or affirmation – the recitation of power words.

The actual alchemical formulas follow the same mechanism as the alchemical circuit and consist of these simple steps:

1. Invocation – Extending your physical life-force (thought or visualisation, feeling and words) up to the God-Self, which serves to reach and connect with that higher frequency in a way that reverberates back upon the physical body. At this stage you voice the 'Call', the desired result, in a clear way.

2. Identification – Owning that frequency as your own and becoming one with it to the extent of allowing the waves of energy to well up and be sustained within the physical and emotional vehicles anchored below. At the same time you speak in affirmation of that identification, as for example: 'I AM all Light'. In this manner you yourself project energy from this highest level down upon physicality. You speak the answer that you invoke at the first stage.

3. Acceptance – Redescending to the consciousness of the physical body and embodying the Light experienced at the higher dimensions. You accept your identity as a God-Self within matter and you accept the fulfilment of the 'Call' you have made at the first stage through the invocation. The acceptance is stated as a fact that has already happened. In this way you set the mental blueprint, or form, within which the condition or activity invoked takes place.

This formula has been used through millennia and was most recently popularised by Leonard Orr (who originated 'rebirthing'), through his manifestation technique and by other schools that joined the bandwagon. It is the fundamental ingredient of prosperity workshops, positive thinking seminars and all kinds of self-improvement. It works.

'Making the Call' follows the same principles as the law of supply and demand. In 'making the Call' you create a demand for the supply (of what you are asking for) to be released. You are in fact reaching for yourself and giving it to yourself; you are coming from a place of centrality and wholeness, with a focus on the heart through the faculties of higher mind.

Affirmations or Decrees

An affirmation, or decree, is a spiritual fiat. All substance, whether Light or matter, must follow the command of the word. This is the Law.

Most of humanity is surrounded by discordant and contradictory imprints that negate one another and disperse in time from inattention. There are also thoughtforms created by the habitual and unconscious use of the word that last over millennia. These form strong imprints that act as magnetic drawing forces which coerce individuals into disturbing patterns of behaviour. The only way to break the seal of these imprints is through the use of the very same mechanism that created it in the first place.

An affirmation has been said with power, that is, repeated *over time* with the adequate degree of feeling intensity and visualisation, to produce a dynamic living force that congeals into a positive image within the aura. A new pattern is set which may be used for physical manifestation, or for feeling or thought behaviour.

Humming

Humming is one of the most powerful ways of balancing yourself, as it affects you at each of your bodies. The vibratory activity set off by your humming redistributes the energy throughout the cellular structure as well. The momentum built up by the humming is important. Once you begin, stay with it for at least ten minutes.

The eyes should be closed.

Sit comfortably in a position that you can remain in, without having to shift or adjust. Loosen your clothing.

Begin to hum. At first you will feel it locally in the throat area and in the head. Allow it to spread throughout your body.

Be inside your body and gently, through the power of your visualisation and feeling, spread the vibration to the toes, the soles of the feet. . . .

Feel your entire body pulsating to each sound.

Now extend your awareness to the space around you and feel the humming like an invisible membrane vibrating there as well. See your physical body as a central cord, giving off resonances that vibrate through the entire room.

(If there is any area of your body that is unwell, direct the sound to it for a few minutes, using your hands to focus the energy if you need to, and then proceed to expand the vibratory activity.)

You may intensify the activity by extending your arms out around you. Palms up helps to give out energy; palms down helps to gather it. Explore both.

Colour the outflow now with your heart's energy. Send out, through sounds and palms, your own individual feeling force to the universe.

Stay as long as you like.

After you stop humming, sit silently (or lie) for as long as you need.

Group Humming

A very powerful process, particularly if you join hands. When humming in a group the momentum builds much more intensely if the sound is held continuously. Be sure that there is always someone humming while others are taking breaths.

A magnificent pillar of blue flame forms naturally in the centre of a circle where people are humming. Within that pillar, you can place people or images of people or places that you would like to heal or bless with this force.

Other Sounds

Vowels are especially powerful. Explore for yourself the quality of energy created by each. Notice how you feel in chanting them. Notice how it feels when someone else chants them.

You might like to investigate the properties of toning with one another. You may do this in pairs. Even better, do it in threes. One or two people can do the actual toning while the receiver lies down, eyes closed, and experiences the effect of sound upon his body.

Chant each vowel softly. When doing it with another, be sure to harmonise the tones. Get really close to one another and to the area in the body that you are focusing on. You might like to start with the area of the belly and move down the grounding circuit, through the legs and feet. . . . And then you might try the healing circuit, from the heart and down the arms and hands. I suggest you do not tone around the head area. At this level the individual can tone himself much better.

Notice the different effects of each of the vowels. 'Ah' will serve to expand. 'Eh' goes a bit deeper and rounder, creating a soft vortex. 'Ee' (or latin 'i') is quite focused and seems to vibrate in a spiral formation. 'Oh' penetrates and reverberates within. 'U' (or 'ooo') goes deepest of all, almost like a laser beam.

Now explore the different pitches.

Whenever you practise toning, be sure to relate verbally to the

151

person who is being toned. Never create discomfort, and always leave them feeling whole. You might like to end with a few minutes of silent laying-on of hands, one person at the head and the other at the feet, gently blending with him in loving intentionality.

The whole purpose of this exercise is to experience the effects of sound upon your physical, mental and emotional bodies. Once you are familiar with them, you may choose to use them to harmonise or energise yourself as needed.

Explore the effects of chanting the powerful combination of vowels which form the sacred word: 'I-A-O-U-E'.

Mantras

Words have an even stronger effect. There are combinations that you can make yourself. I especially like chanting 'I AM' over and over again. The sound and the feeling, together with the visualisation, serve to energize and harmonise me.

Explore. When you have connected with yourself at interdimensional levels (as explained in the next section), you may discover your own sound at different levels of being. When you hear such a sound, or name, with your inner senses, chant it and discover its properties.

Then there are the traditional mantras, which contain centuries of momentum and qualification, such as 'Aum'. Though it produces phenomenal effects, this particular chant belongs to a previous cycle of activity.

Here's an example of an extremely powerful Buddhist chant for the heart. It brings peace and stillness: 'Aditya Hridayam Punyam, Sharu Shastru Bina Shanam'. Get to the point where you can do it all in one breath.

And then there is one of my favourites, the Sufi affirmation, 'Nothing exists but God!' 'La Illa ha, il alla hu!' And many many others. Experiment!

Sound and Movement

This is the very powerful combination used by Sufis in the form of 'zikhrs', which are mantras chanted in combination with movements and dances performed ritualistically, akin to many primitive tribal customs.

The Sufis are perhaps the best practitioners of an earthy esotericism that unites body, mind and spirit. If dance, chant, rhythm and devotion appeal to you, you would do well to investigate Sufi practices, including the whirling dance of the dervishes.

I want to propose a simple practice that allows you to feel for yourself the power of sound and movement, in this case to centre you within both corporeality and spirituality.

It is best to sit cross-legged on the floor or on a flat platform. If this is not possible, then sit on a stool with your feet firmly planted on the ground without tension. You must not have back support for this exercise.

After the initial humming practices suggested earlier, place both your hands at the level of the navel while continuing to hum. Begin to rotate your body in a clockwise fashion from the pelvic cradle. The back must be straight. The axis for the motion is right at the level of the navel centre. Become aware of your shoulders and avoid the tendency to slouch. Also avoid the opposite sway-back rigidity, which would prevent you from connecting with this centre.

You will emerge feeling stronger and more centred in your body. The visual counterpart would be a big-bellied Buddha, or more commonly a roly-poly.

Practise it and see.

Protective Procedures

The Vertical Map

In order for us to connect experientially with higher vibrational frequencies we need to use three-dimensional vocabulary. Although there is, of course, no *real* map for dimensions beyond this one, we may guide ourselves through the use of certain visualisations and feeling, thus translating multi-dimensional reality into three-dimensional linearity. The best consciousness map that I have found is the vertical one. This map is as old as mankind upon the planet, but was reintroduced to the public at the end of last century by the Theosophical movement and popularised in the 1930s by Mr and Mrs Guy W. Ballard.

As we visualise a vertical ascent we actually move the energy interdimensionally and effect a vibrational acceleration. Try it yourself.

Our individualised God-Self is the highest vibrational frequency possible for any intelligence in embodiment who has not dissolved into the primordial source or void. The pure sustained intensity of this twelfth-dimensional frequency is something which is not available, or possible, at this stage of evolution, or within this dimension. Furthermore, it has no reference point for us. It is in effect an interiority. Like the dimensions beyond this one and below the individualised God-Self, it is experienced as coincidental space within the Now.

The fact that it is coincidental and experienced as an energy frequency finer than this one can indicate that we have our being there as well. We would not be able to experience what is not a part of us.

From our perspective of linearity in time and space, it is located

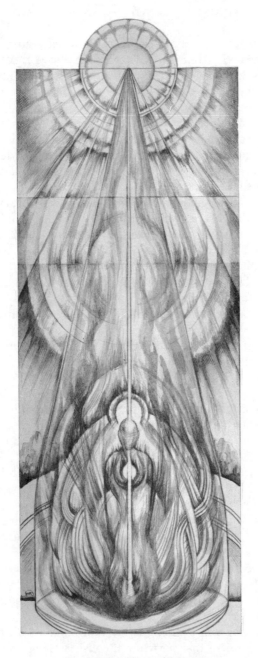

Fig. 2.4 The Vertical Map

155

about thirty feet directly over the head when sitting or standing, and over the body while lying. There is no exact correlation between distance and dimensionality, merely an approximation. (This is given in the chapter on Interdimensionality.) As you ascend there is a sense of riding a supersonic jet during take-off.

Before engaging on the 'take-off', you need to be wholly in your physicality, sensorially, emotionally and mentally. This serves as the anchor. Besides, it is precisely the physical vehicle which we want to charge, so as to be able to transmit the higher frequencies around us in the form of blessing.

Next you locate the heart centre, because it is through the heart that you connect to interdimensionality and to spirit. In esoteric traditions of the past, this is seen as the sacred heart or the abode of the sacred fire, the home of the divine spark. As we know, say in the meditation for spiritual balance given at the end of the chapter on the power of feeling, the first three rays have their base here in the form of a threefold flame. As the three rays meet in the shape of a flame, a multicoloured flame is formed that radiates in all directions in proportion to the intensity of purity and spiritual development of the individual. This flame can be magnified and expanded once again, and sustained according to our ability to abide within Light.

Within the sacred fire in the heart reside all the powers of the Godhead and the faculties of Light. Whereas we might gain certain powers through the development of the upper chakras and the application of energy, *we can never go beyond a certain level without developing spiritually.*

Now, this sacred heart is an exact replica of ourselves as essence at the electronic levels of the twelfth dimension, outlined in the subtle energetic anatomy of the physical body. We might, at this point, consider that we are, in fact, coincidental and understand how our physical self is a projection from the furthest dimensions.

As you follow an energetic line, a beam of light, extending from the heart upwards to the source about thirty feet above, you go through the heart, the throat, the head and the top of the head and continue until you experience a focus of light so intense that you can scarcely contain its energy.

The light appears brilliant white and contains all the different rays and colours of the spectrum. It consists of concentric circles or globes of light giving out emanations of primordial substance, like

156

a sun. (The physical sun, by the way, is an entity to itself, as we are, and outlines physically the form of the Great Central Sun.) Our God-Self is an individualised inner sun. This God-Self is what has been called the 'I AM'.

Considered in our totality of being, we come to understand now the saying: 'I AM' (down here in physical embodiment), THAT 'I AM' (up there in Light-substance). Saying this is an affirmation which establishes the alchemical circuit in etheric form, connecting the matter of your earth body to the substance of your light body.

The way in which we use the spoken word in making a Call is absolutely crucial, as is the visualisation involved. Notice the difference between what some people call prayer and an affirmation such as the one cited above. In the common misconception of prayer there is a suggestion of begging to an outside god. You seek help 'out there'. The implication is that you see yourself as inferior. In this way you inadvertently identify with your limitations, your temporality, your three-dimensionality, and empower an outside source. In the use of the power words 'I AM', you affirm, you make your claim, you establish in word and in deed (visualisation) that you and your source are one.

When you make the Call now, at the third stage of acceptance, you indicate:

I know that you and I are one. I also know that where you are, there is no time and space. There everything exists in pure potentiality. As I speak in calling for the manifestation of your divine gifts and the fulfilment of your divine plan for me on this Earth, *this Call is already fulfilled.*

You are drawing down the seed idea, or affirmation, into physical reality. You are perfectly aware that you exist in two dimensions simultaneously and exert the powers over both the substance of Light and matter.

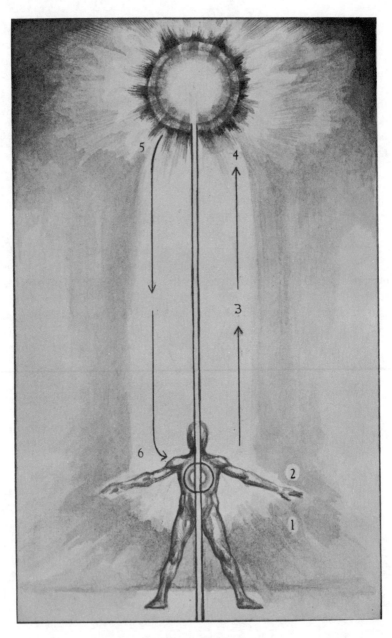

The Alchemical Circuit

Fig. 2.5 The Alchemical Circuit

1 The awakening of the points of light in the centre of the physical atoms of the entire body which as a whole compose the body of light. This is a process through which one becomes aware both of the weight of matter and of the electricity of the subtle body, culminating in the creation of a physical anchor: grounding.

2 The focusing or conscious stimulation of the heart centre as an identity point and a meeting place of cosmic energies constituting a replica of the 12th dimensional 'I AM' in matter.

3 The invocation or directional act of energetic acceleration: the call which evokes the answer.

4 Cosmic identity: the act of feeling oneself one with the fountain of Life or the individual divine essence. Fusion.

5 The conscious projection emanating from the perspective of the 12th dimensional 'I AM' towards the 3rd dimensional 'I' which serves to pierce through realities and complete the circuit initiated at the 3rd step indicated above: the answer.

6 The acceptance. The incorporation of realities both cosmic and physical in simultaneous fusion with the Self which includes the whole family of Self in its multi-dimensionality.

The Protective Tube of Light

The tube of light is an emanation from the God-Self, which results from invoked and sustained contact with it. It is the outpouring from that level, which then surrounds the physical self to look like a tube or cylinder. It contains the seventh body but is quite different. It is consciously constructed and it is protective.

At levels other than that of physical substance, the tube of light is a natural protective activity of the God-Self over its vehicles of expression. (It also serves as a tunnel or passageway which is used in the projection of consciousness and at the moment of death.) At the onset of physical embodiment upon the planet, this tube was an activity that was automatically sustained. As the centuries progressed we turned more and more towards personal and physical satisfaction, without integrating them within spiritual experience. As such we lowered our orientation, damaged the protective shields and relinquished our god-powers. This, understand, happened naturally when the vibratory activity was lessened: the frequencies of light could no longer hold and our access to them dimmed.

We have been operating without protection through these very

159

real 'dark ages' of the soul upon embodiment on the planet. This has made us prey to manipulation and superstition. It is no wonder that we have despaired and even gone as far as to question the existence of the Godhead. Even where protective methods have been taught, they are often practised robotically without inner understanding. We have prayed to an outside god for so long that even if we *say* that we know that we are one within him, we simply do *not* live that way. If we did, even for a day, we would witness miracles.

To regain the protection that we have lost, we need to turn to the Light and consciously rebuild the tube of light through the use of the three creative powers of thought, feeling and the spoken word. The first step entails having faith in the power of the God-Self, identifying with it, trusting the experience, remembering it often enough and applying it. In other words *daring to believe*. Then you *make the Call*.

Everything moves in rhythm. Whatever goes out returns to the sender energetically. A CALL COMPELS AN ANSWER. This is an energetic truth and the meaning behind Master Jesus' statement, 'Knock and the doors shall be opened.' All calls are answered. The problem lies not in the answering process, but the way in which the call is made. If it is projected through fear and a consciousness of limitation, it will return to the sender in like state. If projected in innocence and trust, positive effects are assured. If projected in full consciousness and power, with purity of intention, determined commitment and purpose, no miracle is too big.

To review: the rebuilding process entails calling to the God-Self, or linking with it. At first this will seem as if you were, again, praying to an outside god, but once the space for receiving the energy from the Godhead is created, the experience is unforgettable. Remembering that the projecting energy is that of love, you will invoke it and then extend yourself there through the use of creative visualisation.

In rebuilding the tube of light, the invocation aspect of the call will require addressing the God-Self with words such as these:

Beloved presence of god which 'I AM'! I send my love to you and ask that you enfold me in your light of pure electronic substance that keeps me protected and insulated against all that is not of the Light, and consciously sensitive to you within me.

As you say words such as these (and I suggest you make up your own and stay with them until you experience the build-up of momentum), you need to consciously *feel* what you are saying and experience the power of that very feeling and the circuit that you are creating with it. You will also need to sustain the visualisation and make it so real that you may want to raise your arms and also extend them around you, sensing the thoughtform that you have created through the power of spirit (identification).

Feel and see yourself *as* the God-Self. As you look down, see yourself surrounded by a cylinder, like a large beam of light that you have projected as the God-Self. Send so much love to yourself (down there) that you feel as if your heart would burst. Visualise that love coming down and over your physical body, strengthening the tube or cylinder of pure electronic Light-substance. Then come back down and feel yourself from the perspective of the human self, surrounded by this tube of light. You may want to affirm it again with words such as these:

'I AM' a child of Light. I love the Light. 'I AM' protected, illumined and sealed by the Light. I move in the Light and forever live in the Light.

Become aware, from this moment on, of your use of the words 'I AM'. Let it serve you as a reminder of the God-Self, the God 'I AM'.

You might want to say something like this:

'I AM' the circle of protection around me which is invincible and repels instantly everything discordant from my being and world. 'I AM' the perfection of my world, now and forever.

You always end with a statement of acceptance and with a benediction, an expression of acknowledgement, gratitude and blessing. This may go something like this:

As the consciousness 'I AM', all time and space is one. As these words are spoken, it is done! I know it. I see it. I believe it. I accept it. And I thank you!

The experience here is one of humility and yet power. In making the Call for your protective cylinder of light, as for all things, you exert your authority over physical substance and your responsibility for creating your world. But you also acknowledge your god-self and the power of Light which is Spirit. In the past we erred through employing either too much power (personally qualified) or too much humility. The first made us ruthless, the second rendered us ineffectual in the world.

The final phase of making a Call is the seal, the acknowledgement that confirms the physical reality:
SO BE IT. IT IS DONE. AMEN.

The Master Flame

Once you have fenced off your territory, so to speak, by invoking the tube of protective light from the Godhead, you need to work on the territory itself: in other words, yourself, your aura, your mental, emotional and physical self. You will need to confront and change, re-qualify and transmute trends, habits, impulses and compulsions, beliefs and even physical substance, disease and malformations, malfunctions and projections. As we have already suggested, you do this through invoking the energy of the seventh or violet ray.

The activity of this ray serves to transmute all energy and substance and is *primary to all alchemical work*. It is the 'mysterious' frequency of transubstantiation and grace. It is also what characterises this age, where old thoughtforms are being dissolved and where so much of mankind and the substance of the planet is being transmuted. In this sense the violet flame could be seen to exemplify purification and redemption, advocating transmutation and sublimation (which is actually the raising of an energy to a higher frequency).

Inner Alchemy occurs when the violet flame is drawn into a condition through the use of the three powers, with the intention of altering it. The violet flame addresses the intelligence within that substance, which then accelerates so that it may leap into another vibratory rate to produce a qualitatively different substance altogether. This activity necessitates a human being in embodiment, a creator of forms, a consciousness with direct access to physical substance, who by his very commitment to the evolution of the planet is in a position of authority over substance.

The violet flame is invoked and directed to each of the three lower bodies. Its presence will serve to bring up all the impurity or mis-creation for review and re-qualification; which means that we have to face it, look at it, deal with it physically, mentally and emotionally, while also regarding it from the perspective of the higher self and the transmutation process. We use our will and determination to re-channel the energy. And, in the case of physical disease or disturbance, we need to confront the causations behind the afflictions.

When faced and understood, these mis-creations are ready for release. The process here is called *etherealisation*. Etherealisation is the release of the building blocks or electrons (physical or non-physical) back into the formless; in other words, the process of dematerialisation. At this point a magnetic centre is created which provides a space for Light (the Holy Spirit) to descend and recreate substance in its likeness, which is perfection. This part of the process is called *magnetisation*. The violet flame is responsible both for etherealisation and for magnetisation at every level of substance, from the substances of Light to those of matter. You can perhaps understand now why it has been called the flame of forgiveness and mercy. Seen from the perspective of the personal self it is experienced as grace from God.

Besides the violet flame vortex suggested in the chapter on feeling, the violet transmuting flame may be used in the process of transmutation in the following way:

1. Visualise it enfolding your body. 'Feel' it, sense it outside your body and skin and inside your body, in your solar plexus, your genitals, etc. Also see it around you, extending to cover your aura within the protective tube of light.
2. Direct it into wherever you need it, physically, mentally, emotionally, and see it acting there, breaking up thought-forms and dissolving substance. (Watch what actions it takes, appearing at times to sweep, blaze, boil, spin, lick . . .)
3. Claim the transmuted energy. You may send it out as part of yourself with love and forgiveness, with blessing and goodwill, or acknowledge it within your own healing.

4. Test or check out its effects, acknowledging that the trigger-ing thoughts, ailments or emotions are no longer there.
5. Take action on the physical plane to seat and seal the operation.

It is not enough to pray vaguely. It is not enough to imagine. It is not enough to convince yourself that you have forgiven yourself or someone who has wronged you. It is imperative that all work be seated in physicality. You will need to embody the transaction through physical activity. You will need to behave with forgiveness and actually see or write to or telephone the person involved. You will need to check your habitual thoughts of lack and limitation to ensure that the condition will not be recreated in body, mind or feeling as well.

Your affirmation, or decree, for the use of the violet flame may sound something like this:

Beloved presence of God which 'I AM'! Blaze through and around me the violet transmuting flame, *now*. Purify and trans-mute in me and my world all which is not of the Light: all impurity, hard feelings, wrong concepts, including destructive etheric records – cause, effect, record and memory – known or unknown. Keep this action sustained and all-powerfully active. Re-qualify and replace all by purified substance, power of accomplishment and the divine plan fulfilled.

The way in which you prepare yourself for multidimensional work is to get into the habit of practising the visualisation of your tube of light and the violet flame. This protection separates you from the web of humanly constructed desires and thoughtforms, in order that you may transmute your own creations and proceed with your evolution, your life's purpose. Creating the habit will build the momentum of the thoughtforms solidifying and strength-ening it.

It is a good idea to practise protective shielding upon arising in the morning and upon going to sleep. In the beginning you will want to reaffirm it during the day, particularly if you have sensed any fear, doubt or irritation, as these lower frequencies will pierce through and destroy the finer vibrations of light that form your shield. Now you can see why it is so important to train yourself in holding positive patterns of behaviour.

When you visualise your protective shield at night before going to sleep, know that your physical body is held within the transmuting fire. Your consciousness, on the other hand, goes up through the tube into the higher vibratory realms. Without this pathway, you might get affected by the surrounding psychic and lower astral forces that interpenetrate our reality.

You may want to talk to your God-Self often; acknowledge it, establish a dialogue with it and direct your thoughts as well as your inner vision vertically. Listen for responses which will at first be vibrational, but which in time will come in the form of images and perhaps even words. If you did nothing else than practise these two processes, the alchemical secrets will unfold within you automatically.

Because of our limited perspective at this three-dimensional stage, we need to talk to it as we used to talk to the outer god. It's a device which works. Ask it for help. Ask it to take you there where it lives. Ask it to teach you, to show you, to perfect you. Ask it to show you what you need to do.

Surrender yourself in service, particularly when you go to sleep at night, that you may offer greater help in your out-of-body states. Soon you will connect with interdimensional reality. You will also begin to sensitise your own spiritual powers and begin to see what you look like (and what others look like) from the vantage point of the higher self. You will gain access to higher knowledge and insight directly, without intermediaries.

There will be times where you will be shown answers to questions or dilemmas in your life. You gain understanding about certain aspects of yourself, which cause you to behave in certain ways which may be different. Your personality will be revealed. The history of your individual life stream will begin to unveil. The akashic records will reveal your memory in visual and tangible forms for you, and will open dimensional doorways as well.

This practice of addressing your God-Self can also be used to address the God-Self of others you want to communicate with, simply by visualising it in others.

First, however, you will need to have aroused the sincere and fervent desire to know. In this way you create the space for answers and insights and direct higher communication to be given. The space is created vibrationally. Each time that you create the circuit and penetrate those higher frequencies, you are affecting your physical cellular structure as well. You are recalibrating yourself in patterns of Light-substance. You are becoming Light yourself.

Other Rays, Other Flames

When you were at the highest level of the God-Self you noticed that there were concentric rings of different coloration, indicating that you have direct access to each of the rays. The energies of the other rays may be used in Inner Alchemy to effect changes upon yourself and your environment. These may be used in conjunction with the violet flame, which, as I said earlier, is primary. You may surround, direct and enfold yourself and others with light and colour.

Perhaps the next most important colour used for the emotional body in particular is pale gold. Gold soothes, heals and stimulates healthy and peaceful activity of the solar plexus, which is the energetic seat of the lower chakras. The visualisation of a golden liquid light is especially helpful, as is the visualisation of a golden sun disc placed right in the centre of the solar plexus, or a golden shield or armour envisioned around the physical body. This armouring of light may be constructed in blue or violet as well.

Another favourite for the emotional body is pink, entering gently and swiftly where another colour might be too harsh or abrasive. A friend of mine likes to surround grumpy salesladies in New York department stores with pink light. In a matter of seconds, they are soft as kittens.

You might like to take another look at the chart on the rays and their uses. Feel free to explore the effects of colour on yourself.

In using colour, as in making the calls, you can invoke purity, healing, illumination of the intellect, abundance. . . . You will witness the colours emanating from the higher dimensions without your need to select and direct them yourself, or you may participate in the joy of projecting healing colours yourself, if you so wish. All you need to do is to affirm, 'I AM THAT I AM'. Wherever you direct your mind, that is what you become.

It is important to understand that you must not become fearful in either the use or the non-use of these protective or projective practices. To be so would prove counter-productive to what we are trying to convey. You must not feel bogged down by practices to such an extent that you feel burdened by using them, or fearful if you do not use them. These insights are gifts from Spirit and evoke the power of Light. They are to be used joyfully and not begrudgingly. They are to be used in deep understanding and not out of fear.

Love is the best protection. But, by the same token, you must not be so complacent and naïve as to believe that being indiscriminately vulnerable and open to everyone and everything is love. Love is also right action and discerning vigilance. Love involves consciousness and alertness. And that amounts to discipline and obedience to the Law, regardless of your chosen path.

The power of feeling serves to generate the fuel or energy required for all activity, particularly that of creation. In order for the fulfilment of your calls to take place, and for that which you are calling for to be released to you, you need to believe and act in partnership with your God-Self and you need to exercise discernment in your use of the spoken word. This is a twenty-four-hour job carried on in your working, sleeping, playing self, acting through your body, through your feelings and your thoughts, in your laughter, in your sadness, in your dying and your birth.

The Nature of Colour

Let's understand the mechanics behind colour, how this relates to sound and most importantly how we can use colour to affect our vibratory activity at the level of physicality.

Metaphysically, God = Life. Scientifically, Light = Life. To all of us light manifests as *colour* and as *sound*. 'In the beginning was the Word' could be taken to mean that in the beginning was also colour.

The Source, which I call the Great Central Sun, expresses itself dimensionally as the physical sun in each of the systems of galaxies. This physical sun radiates Light-Life by projecting from itself a certain substance or life force, which embodied into matter becomes life as we know it. The sun continues to feed this life with more life through its light, or sacred fire – which contains the primary matter of the rays and various flames responsible for all Life everywhere.

Light in the physical sense as sunlight reaches the individual through the pineal gland and the optic nerve. These affect the functioning of the brain and all vital processes, including the autonomic nervous system and the pituitary gland, which in turn regulates all bodily systems through the secretion of hormones. The effect of light and colour on our physical life is undeniably primary.

Colour in the environment affects behaviour. Breathing in the colour green by standing in nature is the best nourishment we can give ourselves. Green is the predominant colour of nature and is also the middle colour of the spectrum, as well as being the colour of the ray affecting the heart chakra. It is the colour of balance and harmony.

By exposing the physical system to the pure vibration of either colour or its counterpart in sound, we are able to balance the neuroendocrine system of the body. As we grow in consciousness we become more aware of colouring through our environment, our clothing, our thoughts and our music. There are many studies done on colour and the human body. I recommend Dr John Ott's work and the writings of Dolph Ornstein.

Colour Breathing

The most effective way of using colour that I have found is not only to breathe it but to direct it through the subtle energetic circuits of the body.

This is a method I obtained several years ago from a handbook on psychic development published in California (*Opening Up* by Petey Steves). I have since then developed different colour combinations. I still find it is one of the fastest ways of reaching altered states of reality, when the individual is able to visualise colour. If there is any difficulty in eliciting the colours, I suggest you buy sheets of solid colours from the local art supply store. Pin the indicated colour on the wall and look at it as long as you need to in order to transfer the impression to the imagination with the eyes closed.

This technique works, not only because of the vibration of the colours used, but because it utilises the energy currents within the body, affecting the various bodies, functions, powers and abilities inherent in them. It is also capable of affecting interdimensional faculties by activating the out-of-body chakras as well.

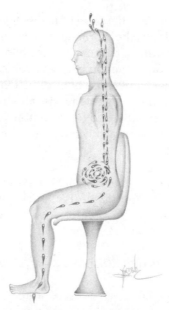

Fig. 2.6 Colour Breathing

Follow the same principles of colour as outlined for the rays, including strength for the ruby colour, peace and compassion for blue, joy for yellow, vitality for orange and vision for violet. Crystal, silver and gold and combinations of these also exist and affect subtle energy states with accelerated frequencies.

On this note it is interesting to observe that in a physical context GOLD (the traditional colour for alchemy) is a combination of orange and blue (the Alpha and the Omega). In the methodology of the Kabbalistic Tree of Life (the Hebrew esoteric alchemical tradition) this denotes happiness and beauty. Invoking gold brings instant energetic acceleration.

Invoking gold also brings into our personal consciousness the eternal flame of Life-Light. It ignites the mind and purifies the blood. It is the flame of rejuvenation. Invoking violet (the other pure colour used in alchemy), as already stated, brings properties of transmutation to our physical system, primarily to the blood, thereby affecting the light cells of all the bodies.

Begin by using the colour green. Visualise a deeper, forest-green shade for the Earth and a paler apple-green for the cosmic source. Draw streams of forest green from the centre of the Earth and pull

169

these streams in through the soles of the feet up to the pelvic cradle. Simultaneously draw the apple-green stream from the cosmic source through the mediation of your individualised God-Self and pull that down through the top back of the head, through the body to the pelvic cradle. Draw from both directions on the inbreath.

Holding the breath ever so briefly, visualise the two shades blending within the pelvic cradle and on the outbreath project the mixture through the body upwards and out of the front upper part of the head. Do this as long as feels comfortable. Soon you will be in an altered state.

At another time you might want to experiment with different colour combinations. You might like to try copper from the centre of the Earth and turquoise from the cosmic source; or purple and lavender, light green and sky blue.

Protective Visualisations and Affirmations

The tube of light and the visualisation of the violet flame are protective techniques that should be practised first thing in the morning and last thing at night.

These other visualisations may be practised anytime. It is always best to set a definite time and duration.

1. Visualise a clear crystal-like skullcap and armour over the body.
2. Invoke the power of the blue ray in creating a sword of blue flame. Hold that sword in your hand and swing it forcefully in criss-cross patterns with the intention of cutting yourself free of any lines of force sent to you or from you that may be keeping you bound and limited.
3. Invoke a cross of white fire and visualise it in front of you. You may intensify the protection by extending that visualisation to include a cross at the back, both sides, above and below you for a total of six. (Crosses of blue flame provide still stronger protection.)
4. Visualise yourself inside a nine-pointed star within the centre of a cross of white fire.
5. Picture a shield of golden substance over your solar plexus, or a revolving disc of light at the back.

6. Encircle your midriff area with a band of blue flame. (Also good around the throat.)
7. See yourself within an effervescent pearl of flaming light.
8. Invoke a star of purity to descend into the brain structure, then see its rays go out from your head like a sun; do the same for the chest area. You might want to seal this with an oval of light (outside the tube of light).
9. Picture a silver-blue light sphere within the throat.
10. See yourself within a pillar of light: violet, white, blue.... Then project that light outwards in all directions, beginning from your immediate environment and stretching out over your city, your country and the Earth.
11. Invoke the golden flame and see it descend into your skull like a great golden liquid spiral, coursing down the centre of the body and into the centre of the earth. Pause to let it flow into every nerve in your body and into every cell. Especially bless your feet and make the decision to allow the golden current to flow through you everywhere you go.
12. Make the call for the dissolution of all your negative etheric records, in your body, your mind, your emotions, in your environment, relationships and activities.
13. Surround your home, your car, your workspace with a pass-not ring of blue flame (or the crosses of blue flame).

Affirmations: (to serve as inspiration in the creation of your own.)

1. 'I AM' a white flame being from the Central Sun living within this body of matter, and expressing itself as perfection through every cell. 'I AM' the presence of my God-Self manifesting perfect health, youth and beauty, perfect intelligence, poise and peace.
2. 'I AM' the intelligence that knows everything that it needs to know. I see through everything which is not of the Light!
3. Beloved God-Self, which 'I AM', and all Great Beings of Light and Love! Secure me against everything that is not of the Light, especially:
all accidents, jealousy, injustice, gossip, discord, impurity, hatred (and anything else that you may need).
4. 'I AM' the presence of my God-Self, in perfect control over:

171

my mind, my feelings, my body; my affairs, my finances, my relationships.

5. 'I AM' within the Light of the Sacred Fire of the Godhead, which is eternal security.

6. Beloved God-Self which 'I AM'! Help me as I leave my body in sleep tonight. Fill my body and mind with rest and peace, with clarity and understanding, with all that I will require to do my day's work well, harmoniously and successfully.

7. See that I bring back into my waking consciousness the memory of what 'I AM' so that I may use it in my everyday activity.

(Follow the procedure outlined earlier for sealing your affirmation.)

Emergency, or charging visualisations:

1. After establishing the alchemical circuit, visualise blue rays in the form of blue lightning striking every form, feeling or thought that is negative or destructive (from you or towards you). Surround yourself in a mirrored shield and call upon the god-force, through your higher self, to be your guide.

2. See yourself receiving more and more Light from the God-Self.

3. Visualise someone you may be having difficulty with. Ask for permission to dialogue with their higher self. Address it from the perspective (and feeling) of your own higher self to their higher self. Ask it to help you establish the harmony you seek, or the message that you wish to convey. Trust that it is done.

It is always more powerful when you use the spoken word with your visualisations. In your own privacy create your own affirmations.

The Nature of Negative Impingement

Fear

We already know that fear and doubt are the primary gateways for negativity. These attitudes feed upon the consensus of belief that we are separate from the godhead. Let us now examine the dynamics behind fear.

Fear is intrinsic to animal life. It always refers to the body and to survival. Examine it and you will see that it relates to anxiety about being hurt physically, of feeling pain, about not persisting, about not having enough money to survive, about dying.

When you know that you are not your physical body, the mechanism upon which fear operates weakens. But the memory of fear is still imprinted within the cells of your body, as cellular or animal instinct. It is the way the body warns us of danger. When you are crossing the street and there is a car coming, the body will instinctively sense it and mobilise you. When there is a threat looming in the atmosphere, or a sense of impeding death or doom, you will sense it in your emotional body as well. You register oppressive or violent vibrations through premonition. Your mental body also serves to alert you by intuitive deductions. These forms of fear are part of the mechanisms of the lower bodies in their expression within earth life. They are part of the animal heritage and wisdom.

Manipulation happens when someone premeditatedly activates these mechanisms with the purpose of gaining control over people and situations. If you ask yourself *who* benefits from induced fear you will see that priests, politicians, the establishment, the authorities have used it for millennia. Fear creates bondage. When a person is afraid that their partner may leave them, they relinquish their power, their authority as a God-Being, their autonomy and their independence. They believe they need the other in order to survive.

When we are afraid of not being able to meet next month's rent we have accepted the belief that we are neither lucky nor resourceful. In some way we believe that we are not worthy. Lack of physical resources is heavily laced with guilt and fear.

In the same way people are afraid of aeroplanes, loud noises, communism, capitalism... you name it! We fear that pain or annihilation (death) will result if we stand on our own resources.

It is something of an art to learn how to decode the signals and sort out the real fears (which are realistic warnings), from the induced (propaganda) fears. Mastery will lie in ceasing to identify from the direct stimulus of fear (even when it is real) in order to free the higher faculties which will clear the way for us.

A good way of honing away at the accumulated beliefs in our aura is to affirm: 'I AM light', 'I AM divine protection', 'I AM truth, clarity, Peace', etc. By repeating a statement such as 'The Light of God never fails!' or the statement of Master Jesus, 'I AM the Resurrection and the Life', we reprogramme our mental and emotional circuitry and gain intelligent distance from our animal nature in order to be able consciously to direct it.

It is surprising how many people believe themselves to be a body, a name, a profession, a sex or a personality. Identity is a creation. One that can be carted aside and remade. One that is dispensable, illusory, unreal. This realisation will mark a major step in freeing ourselves from fear; or more specifically from the *fear* of fear.

As Frank Herbert wrote, 'Fear is the mind-killer . . .'. Fear *is* the killer. It opens the door to negativity, to manipulation and outer control. Experiential contact with the God-Self is the antidote.

Doubt is a form of fear.

Hypnotic Control and Suggestion

Life's code of ethics implies reverence and respect. This means that we should never intrude upon another life-stream's free will. The problem today is that people do not quite know what that is. They prefer to rely on outside authority and rules. Nobody can be hypnotised who doesn't want to be. The fact that *millions want to be told what to do* does not give anyone the right to dominate and control them. And yet it is done day in and day out all over the world, collectively and privately, from leaders of state to husbands, wives and children.

The voice of the collective unconscious controlled by outer authority's vested interests results in hypnotic beliefs and ideas. Hypnotic control is a result of mass mentality. If we hear something often enough, it becomes a fact. When people don't know who or what they are, when they are begging to be told what to do, when they want to be loved and accepted at any cost, because they don't love or accept themselves, what can we expect!

When, however, enough people are willing to risk standing alone, when enough people are happy, blissful, ecstatic in their aloneness, without despair or need or automatic, haunting fear, then hypnotic control will be impossible. You remove yourself from the mass. Once you enter the vertical dimensions of consciousness, it will be impossible for anyone to hypnotise you.

The hypnotic effect of a collectivity of voices saying 'This is ugly', 'That is beautiful', 'You're getting old', serves to influence us in subliminal as well as overt ways. We begin to believe what we hear. You may not be in the least hungry, but by the time you finish that movie on television, which includes the food advertisements in the intervals, you'll be ravenous. Subliminal messages are constantly bombarding our physical, mental and emotional bodies, stimulating our mouths, our sexual organs and our power instincts.

Hypnotic control works through the power of suggestion. 'Why don't you try this . . . or that . . .?' Suggestion is the layman's hypnotic control. It is given most of the time in total innocence, but unconsciously and out of habit, without regard to the effect that it can produce in individuals, in other words without sensitivity and care. People are continually giving their opinions, and other people are continually accepting them as their own. Very little more than lip service is placed on originality, individuality and authenticity, because this is revolutionary. Godliness is the greatest revolution possible.

Whenever someone advises you or suggests that you do something, stop for a moment. Remember your Self. You may listen out of politeness, or out of a response that is genuinely affectionate, but in the long run remember where your power lies. Remember the God within. Freedom is the highest value: freedom for the Self. Even love is second to that.

175

The best solution would be to learn to say, 'No, thank you, I'm not interested,' in a firm but gentle way. Unfortunately, even the mildest of do-gooders will be offended when you don't want to listen to *their* advice.

The individual must break free from societal imprints and forces and from the habit of intruding upon individuals in the name of 'good advice'. We must learn to respect our divinity and one another's.

You might want to hold a dialogue with your God-Self as follows:

Beloved God-Self which 'I AM'! Cut me free from all hypnotic control and suggestion. Clear my mind and feelings that I may see and feel and manifest you in my world.

Hypnosis and suggestion work upon the personality, especially over an individual who has not yet turned to higher values. Inner Alchemy offers a way of protection from forces that bind, coerce and limit us. Without the tube of light and the use of the violet flame we are just like anybody else, moving in a sea of influence and reaction. The greatest service we can render anyone is to envelop ourselves and one another in the violet flame. Not only does it protect and clear the way for you, it irradiates to all around you.

Psychism

Psychism operates under the principle of fear. Its influence is much stronger than is commonly believed. There are many psychic self-defence schools available today, which are exposing the dynamics behind psychic control.

Psychic power is closely allied to astral entities and astral reality, which is in turn intimately tied to lower chakra collective impulses and desires. In other words it is man-made. The vibrations are considerably lower than those of spirit, but they are very intense. They work on you through your own bodily desires, through emotional bondage and mental impingement, which operates even at a distance.

Psychic power does exist and it is a real danger. An individual who is identified with his personality is lethal. His personal desires are continuously seeking to control his environment. His motivation is far from humanitarian. He will unconsciously twist words and meanings to serve his own purpose. He will seduce. He will manipulate. He will even capitalise on people's increasing need to connect with a superior force. He, or she, becomes the guru. Such a person is often hard to resist, because he says the truth. But his actions, his very being is tainted with the density of personal desire. He may even possess a great degree of magnetism and healing ability.

The black magicians of old were usurpers of the powers of Light. There are lesser black magicians today, who use the power of hypnotic suggestion and fear to manipulate people into thinking that they are free.

Let's follow an explanation of the astral phenomenon, which may serve to encourage and fortify you to use your own faculties of discernment and activation.

Understanding the Astral Phenomenon

Everything pertaining to the emotions could be termed astral. Astral activity happens all the time, especially at night, when our conscious minds are off guard and the repressed emotional drives take over. Astral manifestations are responsible for wish-fulfilling dreams, including wet dreams and nightmares. The mind always seeks resolution and completion. Whatever is left undone or unsaid and which exerts a pull on the feelings becomes a driving subliminal force.

The astral dimension is not really a dimension, as we shall see in the section on interdimensionality. The astral is a part of third-dimensional reality. It consists not only of our own unfelt, unexpressed desires and fears, it consists of all the unexpressed, unfelt fears and desires of humanity that preceded us. There are millions of astral thoughtforms which roam over the surface of the Earth seeking expression. Every time we feel something similar we hook into the astral form (or it hooks into us).

In this manner, the so-called archetypal images were created and gods and goddesses, demons and spirits invoked, created and sustained by witchcraft and similar practices that prey on superstition and other dynamics of emotion.

The astral plane, as it is commonly called, is vibrationally lower

177

than our physical third-plane reality. It is denser, thicker, heavier. It has attracted substance from the first two elemental dimensions, which make the astral matter sticky and denser than an ordinary thoughtform, creating forms that last as long as they are fed by human emotion. We give these forms their power.

The oldest formula for the dissolution of these influences from our lives is the same method that is used in exorcism. Claim the power of the Godhead within you.

Understand first your own emotionality and seek to resolve it. This doesn't always mean acting it out. It means understanding, and disengaging from, the dynamics that unconsciously distort reality. Set these things aside, particularly in preparing for sleep. (See suggested Night-time Preparation Practices on page 175.)

Stand in your power, directly aligned with the God-presence above you, within the Alchemical Circuit. The more you create a habit of continuously perceiving the world as an extension of spirit, the stronger becomes your connection with the sourcing power, to the extent that it also carries through into your sleep. You will know that it has been deeply imbued when you find yourself using that power in your dreaming.

Whether in the midst of emotional turmoil awake or asleep, hallucinating or perceiving lower astral phenomena, you will need to use power words within the alchemical structure to command and impose the power of Light:

In the name of God, the Almighty, I command you to STOP/BE GONE (or whatever is required)
In the name of the ascended Jesus Christ . . .
Through the authority of the God-Self which 'I AM' . . .
With the power of Light . . .
In the name of Truth . . .

Use your authority to command everything which is not of the Light to BE GONE. If it persists, direct yourself to it and say with conviction and strength: YOU HAVE NO POWER! Repeat this as often as needed. And then, exerting the dominion of the purest and highest frequencies within you, affirm:

'I AM' THE ONLY POWER, THE ONLY SUBSTANCE, THE ONLY INTELLIGENCE ACTING IN MY WORLD!

Sleep Awareness Programme
(To be done before going to sleep)

Understand the nature of sleep and prepare accordingly. Under optimal conditions, sleep is a time for attunement, purification and illumination, as well as for service. Prepare physically and mentally for it as if you were going to be entering a temple to visit God Himself.

Sleep in and surrounded by fresh, clean bedding and scents. Clear your bedroom (and entire apartment) of psychic clutter by using a purification technique such as the violet flame, the crosses of blue flame, rays, etc. Invite your quarters to be filled by light. Re-dedicate yourself and your surroundings to the service of the Light. Erect and sustain a wall of light (visualised by you) around your apartment and more particularly, when you are ready to enter sleep, around your bed. (This can all be done silently, if need be, when you are with someone.)

Let your last thoughts of the day (as well as the first in the morning) be of light and your identification with yourself as Light. (Use any of the affirmations given or create your own.)

Below is a recommended procedure:

1. Review the events of the day. Train yourself to switch on the mental images of the day's events and yourself in them. Notice this unjudgementally but honestly. If there are any actions of yours that were unconscious and/or slightly hurtful to others, or if you were hurt by another, take note of how it might have happened differently.

2. Forgive yourself for unconscious behaviour and decide how you may right it through direct action later. Release others who may have wronged you by not harbouring a grudge. (See them surrounded by light and yourself healed in your lower bodies, as well as understanding the event deeply, i.e. how you attracted it to begin with.) RELEASE THE WHOLE THING, including *all* the events of the day. If there is any nagging process from preceding days or weeks, take it back to its inception and RELEASE IT. (This releasing process will allow you to enter sleep awareness with more sensitivity to the finer vibrations of your being, without the 'noise' from your physical life.)

3. Release, forgive and bless (picturing them in the highest light of their own higher self) those persons with whom you have lessons to complete. Speak to their higher self and ask for clarity and healing, and the cutting of attachments. Also call for the dissolution of any destructive etheric records between you. Picture perfection in them and extend it to your locality, your city, your country and the whole planet. (This picturing, animated by your feeling, is your 'absent healing'/service to humanity and the planet.) Now you are ready to enter into other subtler realities.

4. Create your protective shields, including the tube of light. (This tube will act as your interdimensional passageway as you leave your body and will prevent you from activating or hooking into the psychic or lower astral dimensions. It will take you into the higher frequencies directly.

5. State your intent, if you have any, i.e. if there is anything you seek in the way of guidance and illumination, healing or verification, define it, picture it, ask (verbally and *specifically*) for its revelation. Ask to remember what you encounter and see and determine to do so. (In time you will.) Ask to be taken to where you may be of greatest service.

Now everything that you invoke or picture before you go to sleep is impressed on thought-substance through thoughtforms and acts much more deeply and expediently while you sleep.

6. Fill your heart with gratitude for this knowledge of the Law of Light and let go into sleep in the certainty that your calls will be answered by your very own God-Self, with the help and protection of all beings of Light everywhere.

If you decide to activate the light-cells of your dream body consciously, or to witness the process which takes place, you need to train yourself to hold awareness through the different stages leading to sleep. Remember that the main ingredients are: awareness, determination and fearlessness. This last is achieved only in the understanding and acceptance of the power which comes from your direct circuit with the Source. When you know that you and your God are one, how can you fear? Understand that the nature of fear comes from body consciousness and is always connected to cellular memory and survival: it does not and cannot touch your essence. All training programmes will aim at facilitating the transference from identification with matter to identification with Light.

You may like to keep a dream journal of your activities, no matter how disjointed they may appear at first.

Always begin your day in praise of the Light within you.

Basic Alchemical Meditation Procedures *

The following instruction is used for inducing the accelerated frequency of vibration needed for all alchemical work, whether it concerns your own inner alchemy or your influence upon the world at large. It is introduced at this stage so that you may explore the possibilities for yourself.

Before you begin with any practice, acknowledge your identity with the Source. See yourself as a being of Light within matter. Emotionally acknowledge your place in the universe, your gratitude to Life, its beauty, its magnificence. Acknowledge the support that Life through its many forms – particularly your own – is giving you.

Below are suggestions on ways in which you can begin your practices, always including your physical body and all your senses and the assistance of a universe of light forms. You could say a prayer at this point. Most importantly, your *attitude* should be one of prayer.

The invocation that marks the beginning of every alchemical practice is done after you have built the momentum of your own physical energies. As your ability to generate energy increases, you will require less preparation time.

Physical Release
If you feel especially tense, or sense that your body needs freedom of movement, dance for a while or stretch your body in whichever way suits you best. Not only do you let go, you generate vital energy which can be transferred to subtler levels in your meditation.

When you feel energy coursing through you, that is the time to sit still and transfer it to the more subtle levels.

Etheric Activation

Now you energise what Jean Houston calls the *kinesthetic body*, by imagining that you are moving, swaying, dancing, raising an arm. You can create your own variations. The important thing is to notice the difference in sensation between physical movement and etheric movement.

For example: if you are sitting at this point, imagine standing in front of yourself. Imagine turning around. Imagine looking at the room or the floor from that perspective. Return to your physical body and try it again. Note the changes. You might begin to notice a buzzing in the ears, a heightened sense of sight or sensingness.

Imagine shrinking to the floor. Imagine growing taller. Imagine spinning.

Always end by transferring and integrating with the physical body energy.

Sonic Activation

You can also use sound. Try humming. Take note of the effect of humming upon your physical body. Hear the sound inside your body and feel the organs resonate. Let your whole galaxy of cells vibrate to the humming. You are activating all your bodies at the same time by using sonic frequency. Experiment with other tones and take note of the effects.

Colour Streaming

You may use colour. Use pastel shades. Breathe them into your body through your feet upwards. Breathe them into the chakras. Explore. A favourite of mine is to visualise a stream of golden light cascading through me. I've noticed that if I direct it from the feet upwards it accelerates my vibratory frequency. If I direct it from above the head down to my toes it has a healing, calming, soothing effect.

Use colour, particularly the cool tones to calm and soothe and the warm tones to enliven and regenerate. You may localise the colour in the form of spheres of light. Imagine holding a globe of bright electric blue! Or a sun of shimmering golden fire! Feel it, see it, sense it, smell it, hear it.

Combine the colour with sound or breath or with movement, if you like. You may choose to imagine yourself whirling, swaying, standing below a waterfall of translucent rainbow coloration!

Affirmations

These have the power of stilling the mind while engaging in dialogue with it. It is a way of consciously tricking the chattering mind by giving it something to do. It also hammers away at the unconscious, implanting thoughts and phrases that well up when least you expect, just as the advertising jingles do!

Whatever you do and say, make it as *real* as you can. Exercise your creativity. Know that you are designing something in thought and that you are animating it with your feeling. You are *creating*!

At this point you know that you have done as much as you can to generate your energies at the level of the first four bodies. You are ready to go into partnership with your higher self, with the Light, with the god-force.

The Invocation

Physically raise your arms. Open your heart and your feeling to the majesty of creation. Let your mind, body, feelings reach... reach up ... up ... up to that fountainhead of all Life!

Now join to that your words. Begin with the acknowledgement of your individualised God-Self in homage and thankfulness. Call on the Great Beings of Light from the Great Central Sun, on the healing forces, or the angels or beings of Light from this solar system.

Affirm Light. Be Light. Be in your physical body *and* be in your higher self at the level of the God-Self. Feel the connection energetically and as you feel it, know that you are creating the alchemical circuit through which all is possible.

As you call upwards, feel the energetic response descending. Be here; be there.

The Call, or the Request

Standing on the authority of your God-Self and through the authority that you hold at the level of physicality by virtue of being in embodiment, make your specified request or affirmation. This can be for the healing of yourself or another. It can be directed towards the well-being of any individual, country or the entire planet. It can also be as specific as you need. Do not be fearful of asking for yourself. Envision yourself in perfect harmonious surroundings, filled with boundless supply of all good things. And envision others in the same way.

Always call for the fulfilment of the Divine Plan, particularly if asking for another. You never know what motive or cause is involved in that condition or situation. All you can do is request for the Light to reach that person and help in the best way possible. If things don't turn out the way that you think they ought to, then you might be imposing your personal will. Affirm and trust the Light and don't concern yourself with whether it is right or wrong. Hold the picture anyway.

See that project manifest, see that situation cleared and healed, and stand by it. Affirm it with full force. And if possible let it be out loud. See it manifest already.

During this phase you may visualise a ray of light emanating from your God-Self and manifesting this for you. Know that in your affirming and holding the picture, you are drawing from that source. See yourself as an instrument of that source. Be its hands in action.

If you need to intensify the blueprint of what you want to see manifest, you may want to write down, draw, find pictures of that which supports your call. Again use all your sense and surround yourself with beauty at every level.

Benediction

Acknowledging the manifestation of your request, give thanks that it is done. Follow with the seal, as suggested in the previous chapters.

Know that it is done and don't dwell on it any more. If you wish to continue working on a condition or situation, establish a rhythmic practice of repeating the procedure regularly, each time afresh, each time with all your senses, each time with the full power of your acknowledgement in the Light.

SO BE IT. IT IS DONE. AMEN.

A Sample Meditation Using Colour

(Used to ignite the higher chakras, to heal and to awaken the inner senses, this meditation was originally developed by Duke University, Durham, North Carolina, to activate psychic perception.)

After appropriate preparation, lie down. Breathe long regular breaths for as long as you need to loosen your hold over the physical body and to relax.

Acknowledge your Self

Feel your body melting onto the surface of where you are lying. Feel the weight of it. Feel the ground supporting you. Imagine that you are getting ready to go to sleep and in that way are finished with the day's activities. Let go of your hold over the mind too.

Feel the energy coursing through your body from the inside . . . from the outside. . . .

Drawing from the power of Light by virtue of your identity as an individualised God-Self, imagine a focus of light in the centre of your chest, within the heart chakra.

Make this light a bright apple-green and watch, feel, sense it grow and glow to the size of a small sun (about three inches in diameter).

Feel the pulsation of this bright apple-green sun within your chest, sending out ripples of apple-green irradiation all around you.

Now sense this sun dissolving into vapour and slowly rising through the inside of your body, through the throat, head, collecting just over your head . . . about a foot beyond . . . and forming an apple-green cloud of irradiation.

Hold that cloud for a few moments and then sense the cloud dispersing down, over, under and around you, all the way down to the feet, enveloping you in a shroud of apple-green vaporous irradiation.

Now allow your physical body to absorb that apple-green light. Feel it sinking into your cells, all the way to the marrow of the bones, until it dissolves totally inside you.

Now, following the same procedure as for the apple-green light,

185

draw, from the God-presence which you are, a source of bright electric blue and see a bright electric blue light emerging within the centre of your throat. Let it grow and glow into the size of a small sun.

Feel the orbs emanating from this bright electric blue – like the blue of a beautiful stained-glass window – as it goes out in all directions. Listen to its sound.

Now sense this electric blue sphere of glowing light dissolving into a mist of blue and slowly, gently rising through your head to collect into the form of a cloud of vivid blue coloration just above you.

Hold the cloud there for a few moments and then see it spread over, under, around and down your body all the way to your toes, enveloping you in a mantle of bright, electric blue coloration.

Feel it, see it, sense it, as it is drawn into your physical body and dissolves within the cells, the blood, the marrow of your bones.

Finally, sense a sphere of bright, almost blinding white, a white as you have never seen before, without a trace of yellow to it, a white as white as virgin snow.

See this whiteness in the form of a brilliant light within your head, at the area of the third eye, and fill your entire head with it. Feel that there is a sun of brilliant purest white within your head.

Feel its orbs flowing out into all directions. Sense its pulsations; hear its sound.

Now gently witness the dissolving process as this pure white sun melts and its vapour rises to form a cloud over your head.

Hold the picture of this cloud over your head for a moment, and then sense the cloud spreading out over, under, around and down your body blanketing you, enveloping you, holding you within a cloud of the purest white radiance.

Gently feel your body absorbing this white radiance, as each cell drinks of it, is nourished by it, healed, raised, purified, until the whiteness dissolves completely into your body, all the way to the marrow of your bones.

Feel what you are now.

In that stillness, know 'I AM'.

Allow yourself to remain in this state as long as possible. Upon your return, endeavour to record what you experience or encounter, visually, sensorially, energetically.

The Return

You might want to visually delineate your physical form upon returning, just after you decide to come back or have been called back by a partner. Define the space that your body occupies and then identify with the sense of it, its weight, its currents of energy, the sense of temperature, the conditions of the room, the textures, smells and so forth.

One of the best ways that I have found to return to normality is to breathe into the belly, to come back to the awareness of the root chakra, the legs, to move and squeeze the hands and feet. It often takes time to readjust. Give yourself that time.

A nice procedure to follow at this point would be to dance. Play a particularly joyful melody and feel the magnificence of Life . . . of being able to be here . . . and there . . . and everywhere!

III The Spiritual Faculties and Interdimensionality

Introduction to Interdimensionality

The first aspect of work, as we have seen, has to do with defining the Self in time and space. It consists of personality work, concerning itself with the form and with who you are. It will relate to the horizontal aspect of time. It is sequential and operates under the law of cause and effect, or karma.

At this phase of inquiry, the self explores questions of identity, particularly in relation to others. All issues of relationship, body functions – including healing, causations of diseases, time travel and past life exploration – and the utilisation of talents inherited through genetic or karmic imprints, will pertain to this stage. It is important to understand that this is the emotional or psychological aspect of development which provides the mastery or transcendence needed through human faculties to reach higher vibrational frequencies of being. At this phase we learn the use of emotion and thought as applied to matter at the densest level. It is here that we learn the powers of creating and sustaining growing intensities of expression through the development of a unified consciousness of self.

The second aspect of development or Self-exploration, which is sometimes coincidental to the first, has to do with multi-dimensionality. At this phase of inquiry the individual is not concerned with the little self, or personality. He begins to develop

189

spiritual faculties and to explore higher and higher aspects of mind and spirit in what might be considered vertical dimensions. At this phase he concerns himself with pure faculties and with increasingly broad dimensions.

The third aspect of the work on the Self, which is simultaneous to the second, relates to the process of expanding consciousness, from the first through twelfth dimensions and beyond into spirit. It relates to the development of soul, or spirituality. Soul could be seen as an energy-substance formed by the activity of Spirit upon matter. It may be experienced as embodied light or intelligence which transcends its form-aspect to become pure sourcing energy. It is the dimension of Spirit which is spiral. It is the energy of creation, and our perception of it will reflect the degree of identification we have with the Creator and our role as co-creators.

The horizontal dimension is linear. The vertical is spherical and concentric. The spiral pervades all of creation. If you can visualise and sense the simultaneity of all three energetic activities, you will have a glimpse of yourself as you exist at all levels simultaneously.

The trick is knowing what is what. The perception of first and second level realities is often confusing. How can I know whether I am perceiving a past or future human life, whether I am partaking of an alternative reality or perceiving another planetary existence, whether I am viewing my own or others' astral projections or whether I am in out-of-body state? There has been no structured approach to the understanding of the interdimensionality and multireality of existence. What we do have has been veiled in religious and metaphysical terminology, too abstract, too removed from ordinary comprehension.

Everyone has access to all three aspects of reality in dream and fantasy states, in chemically altered states, in relationships and in certain states of exalted creativity.

Let's understand first that these states are intrinsic to our experience of living. The reason that they are not considered usual has to do with the myopia of three-dimensional perception. Everything that we perceive and communicate is perceived or projected through the language of this particular consciousness. Because we live in a three-dimensional existence expressing detail and sequence, we have hands and feet, digestive organs, transportation, a particular kind of housing and even logical thinking. These are all reflections of this dimension and are needed here only. In the dimensions beyond, we have no need of these functions. At the highest levels there may not even be a distinction between inner and outer reality, only space and pulsations of increasing frequency.

One of the most common forms of gaining access to what I call the spiritual faculties is through meditation. Through stilling the outer mind, the energy moves to higher realities. Depending on the unconscious, or supra-conscious, desire or motivation of the individual, past lives will unfold, interdimensional realms manifest themselves or formless, spiritual states open up.

I remember an experience I had during an operation, which made me recall similar ones I had undergone during meditative states. During the onset of the anaesthesia, I witnessed the gradual dissolution of my body. It was as if someone was turning the light dimmer and dimmer until there was an all-pervading greyness, like a primordial blanket enveloping all within the room. My own self, my doctor friend who had been allowed into the operating room and who was holding my hand, the doctor himself and all the attendants, the objects in the room . . . all dissolved into this greyness, which seemed to pulsate and give off a humming sound.

Within this pulsating sea of grey, little dancing particles of light moved about, each undifferentiated from the others. I was glimpsing substance, the basic stuff of all creation: of you and me and objects and reality. Everything was made of the one stuff. I could see and feel that we are all indeed one, moving in a sea of energy. When I came back to waking consciousness, I experienced the reverse process. From the one we became the many. From then on I knew that God is none other than everything, which of course includes ourselves.

At another earlier time, during the removal of a wisdom tooth under sodium pentathol, I had one of my first experiences of interdimensional activity. I had no recollection of leaving my body but suddenly I was propelled down brilliant lighted corridors. The walls and objects within the rooms adjacent to these corridors were of a bright substance. The colours were clean, vivid and beautifully clear. The people I observed were translucent. The feeling was one of peace and beauty. It was brief and fleeting. I travelled there in later meditations.

I have had moments of spiralling sensation where there has been no relation to linearity, where I have sensed myself and another as a pure presence, without form. And I have also experienced the heavy sensations of the astral plane of emotional pulls and attractions, moving heavily in a dense, though subtle, body, through physically familiar surroundings.

I have had these and other similar experiences during moments of heightened energy, while dancing and making love, at times of peak activity, focus or concentration. And so have many others. The extraordinary exists within the ordinary, if we only dare but look. But we normally put these experiences aside. We don't take them seriously. The clamour of our everyday activities takes precedence.

Have you had dreams in which you were looking at someone and communicating through thought? Where suddenly you knew what they were thinking, or actually hearing their voices in your mind? In your intuitions, your premonitions, your hunches and your inspirations are the faculties of the higher self. Artists, musicians, philosophers and scientists all have strong connections to higher dimensions of mind. They are plugged into these dimensions and are gaining access to this material constantly without recognising it as anything unusual.

It stands to reason, then, that if we were to know vibrationally and qualitatively what the different dimensions are and how to differentiate between them, we would be able to go there and consciously draw from these planes the information and abilities we require. It is my hope that we will all attain to these abilities, which are our birthright.

The basic principle is accepting that we are located in three-dimensional existence with faculties, language and densities appropriate to this. Understanding this, we may begin to transcend the obstacles that block our heightened perceptions, particularly the emotional feelings of anxiety, unworthiness, lack and limitation.

We are, as a planetary body of consciousness, transcending the attachment to a personal existence. But the movement is *through* not around. The personal experience gives us the energy, the momentum to engender greater and more perfect creations. We need to remember that we are so much more than the little self. In this acknowledgement is the nourishment, the stimulation and the energy that begin to align us with higher truth. Each of us is not just an individual located in a three-dimensional world. Each of us is a family of Self, co-existing simultaneously in twelve planes or faculties and coursing through three aspects of reality: in time, in space and in spirit. As each of us becomes more familiar with the parts of ourselves, we align with and regain that energy, that faculty, growing vaster and vaster, more and more luminously and powerfully.

Meditation on Multi-levelled Reality

The Beam of Light

This beam is the line of force which your Self as Spirit has used to project itself into the third dimension. It is the central axis around which the substance of your bodies has been woven.

Elemental forces build atoms around lines of force (whether they are the atoms of your bodies or the atoms of anything in creation). Substance is spun, first in a horizontal vortical spin and then in a vertical vortical spin. The web of these spins creates the atoms and substance around us.

In a very real way we are like atoms in a body greater than any universe we can conceive of. The beam of light (anchored in the heart) is the central lifeline and main connection to yourself as an interdimensional entity comprised of many aspects, bodies and consciousnesses.

Invocation

Close your eyes. Sit comfortably. Occupy your body fully and set it to rest in deep relaxation. Follow the same procedure as for previous meditation practices.

We call upon the brotherhood of Light Beings everywhere for assistance, guidance and illumination and to our own higher self and angel friends to open the way and lead us.

We seek to know you all (the various aspects of our Self), that we may work in partnership with you, in harmonious cooperation, for the enlightenment of all. We seek to embody the Light and to know the Creator at the highest levels of truth and love and deepest integrity.

Visualise yourself in relation to your individualised God-Self, using the vertical map. See that divine spark anchored in your physical heart. See the beam of light that connects your physical

193

self. Establish yourself within your tube of protective electronic force.

Ignite the flame in your heart. With deepest love and a feeling of immense gratitude for this light, allow yourself to soar up higher through the beam of light, reaching with all the love of your heart into those higher realms.

Meditation

Allow your head to be suffused with a golden glow.

Allow this golden light within the centre of your head to ignite now, and allow it to fill your entire brain.

Feel this golden light intensifying in brilliance through your entire head.

Make it as bright as you can. Keep intensifying it.

Now locate the beam of light from your individualised God-Self that is anchored in your physical heart and follow it up to the centre of your head.

Follow the golden beam of light right up through the top of your head and going higher.

Project your awareness over your head to a point of light or focus about three feet over your head.

Take notice of the vibration experienced in your physical body as you do this, and also of any images, sounds or sensations you may have.

Move up a little higher now, to another focus of light about six feet over your physical form.

Take notice of the changes within your physical body and in your perception.

Allow yourself to rise even higher now, through the beam of light of your consciousness anchored in your heart.

Go about ten feet high now . . .

Allow your consciousness to expand with a sense of light and brilliance, with a sense of love and space and peace.

The Call:

Beloved God-Self which 'I AM': I seek to know you.
Who am I?

Look around you. Where are you? Who are you?

Allow yourself to go higher still now, igniting that flame of love in your heart that takes you further and further.

Project yourself further into that source of all life, going higher and higher.

Allow yourself to reach right out to about thirty feet over your head, which in consciousness is much further out, out through the farthest reaches of this planet.

Beloved God-Self which 'I AM': reveal yourself to me.

Reach, reach, reach as high as you can and know 'I AM!'

Notice the atmosphere around you, wherever you may be.

Notice the bodies, structures or forms of life and coloration.

Take notice of your own existence at these levels.

Now, at the highest level of being available to you this moment, picture the focus of light, that individualised presence of God, your God-Self . . .

Embody, that, that luminous presence which 'I AM' . . . the 'I AM' in each of us. And feel and know yourself.

As you look down at all the selves that you also are, pause at the level of the seventh plane where your higher Self resides.

From there, project down to the third-dimensional self now. See your physical body and send your love to it. Embrace it with your heart's flame.

Now bring down with you the clarity and intelligence from the seventh plane, drawing with you all the parts of yourself above and below that into the physical body. Bring those consciousnesses down into the physical body and sense the feeling of fullness.

Open your eyes for just a moment and take notice of what and how you perceive through the body now. Allow all these parts of yourself to see through your eyes now. Just for a moment, and then close your eyes again.

We are going back up again now. All the way up, to the farthest outermost rim of your being.

Pause there for the moment, within the electronic fields of your Life source.

Now begin your descent again, only now leave the different bodies of energy at the corresponding levels behind you.

Separate from each of them, as you slowly come back, leaving

195

each of the sheaths behind, bringing back only your three-dimensional self.

Open your eyes again and look around briefly. Notice your perception and the sense of yourself. Close your eyes again.

Now we are going to invite our higher self to link with us through our beam of light, so that we can be in partnership with it.

Project yourself to the seventh plane. Feel yourself there and simultaneously feel yourself here in the third dimension. Visually anchor that feeling through the beam of light anchored in your physical heart.

'I AM' HERE AND 'I AM' THERE. 'I AM' THE CONSCIOUS PRESENCE EVERYWHERE.

Re-establish the energetic circuit between planes.

Project yourself back down to the three-dimensional physical self, having the vantage point of the seventh plane as well.

Be here, be there, simultaneously.

And very, very gently come back . . . here.

Interdimensionality

Interdimensionality is a frequency of the probable future, as it appears in the present. It is concentric time reached vertically. It is the arena of space – inner and outer space.

Living interdimensionally means being able to tap into simultaneous frequencies that exist at a faster rate of vibration than our three-dimensional reality. To understand these realities, we need to simulate the levels of our evolutionary journey into embodiment, as consciousness was projected from the formless into progressively dense forms. That passage from the state of Absolute Being through these levels of existence created vehicles at each of these points. These vehicles continue to operate independently of our awareness of them.

As intelligence, or consciousness, a spark out of the Source, we acquired these coatings which represent a progressive reduction in voltage at these transforming stations as well as providing vehicles of expressions for each modality of life. These modalities contribute to our life at the third dimension. In other words we use them without knowing what we are using. Each dimension then, can be roughly translated as a faculty, power or ability of ourselves as intelligence, from the most vast cosmic awareness to the most minute level of detail.

During the initial journey, each dimension continues to focus the incoming spirit, adding creative capacity through a system of specialisations, until it arrives at the fourth dimension, which is a mirror image of the third. At this point it is ready for the experience of the most complex specialisation yet: the acquisition of the physical substance of the planet in a highly detailed way, which, although seeming frustratingly myopic at times, serves to focus and to teach mastery in small dosages.

The third dimension provides the neutral coating of the physical substance of the planet itself, allowing for an intermingling with consciousness from all levels of mastery, which are also in physical embodiment At all other dimensions only like vibrations co-exist. In this way, this dimension serves as a learning and testing ground, a place where we can interact with others who may be more or less evolved than we are. That interaction creates karma, good or bad. We continue to inhabit this plane, repeatedly, until we can function in it in masterly fashion and responsibly. This includes redeeming all misqualified energies and forms that we create through relationships and deeds.

The part of ourselves that exists here at the physical level is that part of our mechanism that is best equipped to handle detail, or life at this level. It would be inappropriate to express purely cosmic powers in the marketplace, or to project physical dynamics onto cosmic space. Each level of ourselves is a faculty of Mind as expressed through substance.

By understanding the descent journey, we gain insight into the ways and means of how to become more of who and what we really are *already*. We learn how to gain access to interdimensional abilities.

We need to understand that if we communicate with non-physical beings, guides, masters and teachers in reality and not in fantasy, we can do so because we focus our consciousness at the same level at which they do. We are in fact communicating through our own selves at that level. We no longer need to empower outside forces. We can claim the information and perception that comes through our own higher selves. What sometimes appear as guides and teachers are often the perception of our own luminous figure existing in other dimensions.

The consciousness dwelling within the twelfth dimension may be translated as that part of us which is seed power – our individualised God-Self. This is the source of life and vitality, of all intelligence and light. Whenever we pray, or invoke, we turn to this source as if it were an outside figure, as if turning to God Himself. It seems so far removed from our characteristics that to us it *is* God.The formlessness and light recorded here in the silence and spaciousness of mystical and transcendental experience forms part of our ordinary life at that dimension. Religious experience will reveal any one of the levels beyond the seventh, where beings and reality appear much larger, more luminous, and vibrate at electrifying voltages of ecstasy and bliss. This frequency is reached through our seventh body and decoded through the physical body whenever possible.

The seventh dimension is our higher self. This is the level responsible for brilliant, intuitive faculties and superior unified intelligence. This frequency is reached through our sixth body while in physical embodiment.

The fifth body expresses the frequency at the fourth to sixth dimensions; and the fourth, or etheric, body, besides serving as a blueprint for the physical vehicle, acts as a messenger body for the consciousness of the first three vehicles. This body, as well as the fifth (the Higher Mental Body), also serves the higher mind.

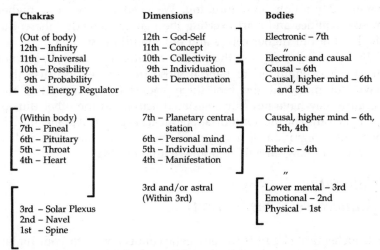

Chakras	Dimensions	Bodies
(Out of body)	12th – God-Self	Electronic – 7th
12th – Infinity	11th – Concept	"
11th – Universal	10th – Collectivity	Electronic and causal
10th – Possibility	9th – Individuation	Causal – 6th
9th – Probability	8th – Demonstration	Causal, higher mind – 6th
8th – Energy Regulator		and 5th
(Within body)	7th – Planetary central	Causal, higher mind – 6th,
7th – Pineal	station	5th, 4th
6th – Pituitary	6th – Personal mind	
5th – Throat	5th – Individual mind	Etheric – 4th
4th – Heart	4th – Manifestation	
		"
	3rd and/or astral	Lower mental – 3rd
	(Within 3rd)	Emotional – 2nd
3rd – Solar Plexus		Physical – 1st
2nd – Navel		
1st – Spine		

Fig. 3.1 Bodies and Dimensions: Interdimensionality Access Chart

The chakras located on the etheric body, which have corresponding forms of energetic activity on the physical body through the glandular system, *when functioning through the conscious personality,* cross over bodily and dimensionally, as follows:

Chakra	Body
7th – Pineal	Higher Mental Body – 5th
6th – Pituitary	Lower Mental – 3rd
5th – Throat	Causal – 6th
4th – Heart	Electronic – 7th
3rd – Solar plexus	Emotional – 2nd
2nd –Sacrum	Etheric – 4th
1st – Spine	Physical – 1st

Fig. 3.2 Relationship between Chakras and Bodies

I can't stress enough the importance of accepting and owning this information, of beginning to *feel* that God is within you, that His power, His thought, His desires and His feeling can be found (and *only* found) through your very own thoughts, feelings, desires as conveyed through your intuition. We need to claim our higher mental abilities and start exerting the mastery already inherent at the level of our higher selves and our interdimensionality.

Everyone has access to these parts of himself or herself, but not everyone is equipped to handle those frequencies, because they have not mastered the first three bodies (or personality), and because they have not fully mastered activity at the other dimensions as well. The most important requisite is physical plane integration: the integration of body, mind and feeling. As stated earlier: we are not going anywhere until we attain to that.

'Calibrations' (Audiocassette meditation)

The alchemical circuit is the energetic connection with your higher self and with your cosmic Self. It is your connection with the source, not only of your life and world, but of all that Is. By understanding it, you will gain spiritual mastery, a mastery which is reflected in the very quality of your life, in your body, in your environment, in your relationships. This primary energetic circuit links your delicate receptors (your inner and outer senses) to the earth and also to the heavens of which you are a part. You link yourself to the source point of all power, all energy, all light – your higher or God-Self.

As humans we partake of the godhead or pure intelligence which we call Light, and of the matter of the Earth. Our physical, mental

200

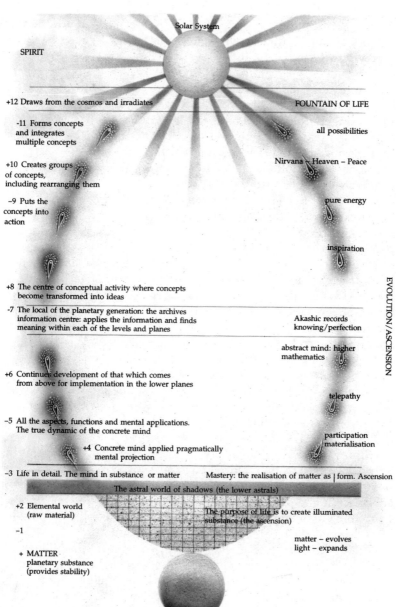

SPIRIT

+12 Draws from the cosmos and irradiates

FOUNTAIN OF LIFE

-11 Forms concepts
and integrates
multiple concepts

all possibilities

+10 Creates groups
of concepts,
including rearranging them

Nirvana - Heaven – Peace

-9 Puts the
concepts into
action

pure energy

inspiration

INCARNATION/INVOLUTION

EVOLUTION/ASCENSION

+8 The centre of conceptual activity where concepts
become transformed into ideas

-7 The local of the planetary generation: the archives
information centre: applies the information and finds
meaning within each of the levels and planes

Akashic records
knowing/perfection

abstract mind: higher
mathematics

+6 Continues development of that which comes
from above for implementation in the lower planes

telepathy

-5 All the aspects, functions and mental applications.
The true dynamic of the concrete mind

participation
materialisation

+4 Concrete mind applied pragmatically
mental projection

-3 Life in detail. The mind in substance or matter

Mastery: the realisation of matter as | form. Ascension

The astral world of shadows (the lower astrals)

+2 Elemental world
(raw material)

The purpose of life is to create illuminated
substance (the ascension)

-1

+ MATTER
planetary substance
(provides stability)

matter – evolves
light – expands

Fig 3.3 Interdimensional Map

201

and emotional parts are made of the substance of the Earth. In the fullness of our earthiness we connect with God in a way that is deeply transformative.

Allow yourself to be fully in your body. Feel each and every part of it from the inside. Sense it from within. Become aware first of its parts and then of the whole body as one unit. Feel its weight and also its fluidity, feel its fire and its space. Be sure that you are right in the middle of your body and not to one side or the other. And right inside your feet and not above your body.

Loosen your clothing. Be present to your body, its sensations, and to the sense of space around you.

Now direct yourself to the heavens and feel your connection with it. Feel your spirit reaching for infinity. Feel the longing and the joy that comes from that. You are both earth and heaven. You are the passage . . . and the circuit is within you.

Sensing the presence of the earth under you, sense the presence of yourself in partnership with it. Close your eyes and feel your body perfectly aligned, relaxed and open. Become aware of your breathing. Feel the gentleness of that breath inside your body, that life within you. Conceive of the miracle of breath: we breathe in not only oxygen but Light, Life-force. There is a subtle combustion each time you breathe: the cells of your body are renewed.

Let go of your hold over the physical body now. Let it lie and rest deeply. And let go of the hold over the mind, as if there was nothing to do, nowhere to go . . . In this way we will transfer the focus from the material to the very subtle but no less intense aspects of Life within and around you.

Within each and every cell or atom of your body is a point of light. This light is the seed of physical substance. The substance of your body is built around this light pattern. And this primordial substance is the same for the planet Earth as it is for your body. Everything in matter exists first in light. And light holds the pattern of perfection.

Within your body of matter, as we see it now, are billions of points of light which comprise your body of light, your original blueprint, and that body, that substance, is absolutely perfect.

Now, this mind has the power to enhance whatever it focuses on. Use this power to expand the points of light in the centre of each of your cells, and, as we do this together, know that as the light expands, it burns whatever is not perfection around it and thus heals and transmutes; it raises the level of vibration of your own vehicle, your body, and all that is housed within it, your mind and your feelings.

With the power of your mind, visualise these points of light. Sense and feel them. Use the power of your own feeling, that positive aspect of your emotions, to ignite life and the joy of life into each and every atom of your body. Visualise and feel billions of little particles of light glowing, intensifying all over, as if you are electrically charged (which you are)! Choose to identify yourself with the Light within you and with its perfection. Allow its reflection to recreate your body, your mind and your emotions in purity and love.

Part Two

Sense the points of light in your feet now and make them brighter. Sense your feet alive with the tingling energy of these points of light intensifying in brilliance.

Spread the sensation to your ankles, calves and knees, sensing the points of light expanding, filling the inside of your legs with more and more light particles.

Using the power of your attention – your visualisation and your feeling – bring your awareness to the inside of your thighs and up into your pelvic area, feeling the subtle currents flowing, glowing; as if you now had legs made of bright, bright light, and sensing this light igniting the points of light beyond it, within the organs of your body, within your belly.

Feel that light consume the density, setting the matter of your body aglow with Light substance.

Moving up, up through the stomach region . . . up your back and torso . . . and your chest . . . and even into the lungs and heart . . . and up to your shoulders now . . . feeling, breathing . . . being . . . Light!

Feel it coming down the shoulders, down the arms and setting your hands aglow. Arms of light!

Feel yourself aglow now, your own body responding to your direction . . . Feel the movement up through the neck and into the base of the skull; sensing the light bursting into crystal sounds at the base of the skull. The sound of Light: crystal gold, which is the colour of these points of light . . . and feeling like crystal gold. . . . Expanding now. . . .

Sense and feel and see the points of light within your brain, illumining it. See the grey matter of your brain become golden now. Feel that golden glow as your own brain seems to intensify in frequency, raising in vibration, that it may receive finer and finer impressions.

Expanding the points of light to set your skin aglow . . . the skull, the eyes, the nose . . . so that your entire body now, from head to foot, is one glowing body of light! Ablaze with light. And as that light is blazing, feel the burning, the consuming, of everything which is less than the perfection of your inner Self.

As the heavier, denser elements of your body seem to fall, like ash, to the ground, all disease, all fear, all limitation, all signs of age, excess flesh and tension seem to drop away, as you, once again, claim your body of light and all its powers, the dream body!

Feel yourself within this body of light within matter and sense how your level of vibration has intensified. You are within a body that is capable of tuning in to cosmic channels, a beautiful, wonderful complex instrument!

Now earth this body of light into the body of the planet. Sense lines of force going right through earth, rock, water, mineral, through the gems and gases and fires of the earth, reaching into the crystal core at the centre of the Earth, made of radiant golden light, just like your body now. Feel the homecoming and rejoice.

Send your love to this intelligent sphere, this being, this planet, for housing you and giving you of itself. And feel the solidity, the sense of form loaned to us by this great mother. It is in this solidity that we may stand, firmly, in our divinity, in our spirituality and our cosmic Self. Anchor yourself within the deep roots of the planet and allow your branches to reach for the highest!

Now you connect with that other dimension of your being, the dimension of pure intelligence, of cosmic space, in your dream body, your body of light.

That you may grow
and multiply
the glory of Light in matter.

The Twelve Dimensions of Consciousness

If you question the existence of multiple dimensions of being, share this experience with me for a moment.

I took a walk through Central Park last weekend. It was a beautiful spring day and everyone in the city seemed to be out. As my friend and I walked, it appeared as if we were walking through different universes. In one area, people were folk-dancing. In another area they were sunbathing, mostly alone, books in hand. Other strollers elsewhere were family types, children and dogs playing . . .

On the meadow people were playing frisbee, picnicking, playing soccer or football, while an aerobics demonstration was going on outside the Shakespeare Theatre. Then there were the squirrels' friends, the pigeon- and seagull-feeders . . . When we sat on the promenade, well shaded and reminiscent of an old world splendour, we sensed the depths of loneliness in some of the older folk, side by side with the nannies and babies in prams, the toddlers . . .

The cyclists were in a different world altogether, as were the horseback riders. The museum crowd by the Metropolitan section of the park was apparently insensitive even to the park itself, whereas the joggers by the dam were self-engrossed in yet another world of their own.

The wealthy and conventional Eastside crowd intermingled with the affluent Westside yuppies, while the artists belonged to the lake and the clouds and the infinite green of the foliage. The gays and the beautiful people had their own 'turf', sprawled over quite a large area towards the Westside, replete with costume and accessories . . . and here and there new lovers dreamed with each

205

other, oblivious of the presence of others . . . Each of these groups was living within a different dimension of being.

In New York City there is the best and the worst of all possible universes: Spanish Harlem, Black Harlem, the Bowery, the lower East Side, the Village, Chinatown, Park Avenue, Madison Avenue, Wall Street, Chelsea, SoHo, Brooklyn Heights and the Bronx, Riverside and Riverdale and on and on and on . . .

I have never been raped or mugged, and yet I live in a city where rapes and mugging are commonplace. You could meet the Mayor or dine with Donald Trump, shop at Bergdorff's or Orchard Street or attend a boxing match at Madison Square Garden. These are activities which are happening with groups of people living within certain dimensions of the city.

A dimension is an inner location for like states of consciousness that function in a specialised way. What determines the dimension that people live in is neither money nor education, neither cultural heritage nor upbringing. It is consciousness. Why certain things happen to some people and not to others is the result of a state of being, (which is a direct result of 'karma' or how one conceives of life). At the highest levels of being, you choose the conditions of your life.

Dimensionality is an inner phenomenon and relates to inner reality and perception. Each dimension, like a world that it is, consists of a form of life and activity. These dimensions interpenetrate and affect our ordinary three-dimensional lives, depending on the extent of our access (conscious or supraconscious) to them.

The people in the park were in different psychological frames of mind, but the very quality of their mental functioning was also distinctly different. We were not able to observe the inner dynamics of the mind of the visitors in Central Park. We could only infer through their physical activity, where they might be dimensionally. The consciousness of the lovers, for example, could be anywhere from the lowest chakras to the sublime poetic heights of higher dimensional activity, where one perceives emanations of light and force, which is transcendental in nature. The people who were reading books, the loners, the Metropolitan Museum crowd, even the joggers and the picnickers, could be operating anywhere from three-dimensional logic to higher quantum mechanics, while the squirrel-feeders might be immersed in a world of creation deep within the recesses of elemental life.

We reach higher mind when we transcend the emotional pulls of personality and the senses and are able to observe and commune with Life at the level of causation. But higher mind itself is separated into two levels. The first level is abstract but still personal, pertaining to the fourth, fifth, sixth and seventh dimensions. The second level of higher mind operates from the seventh to the twelfth dimensions, beyond personal identity. This is the spiritual realm of essence and spirit.

The reality of these dimensions consists of life forms and activities indigenous to them. As we touch these dimensions we not only draw from them but have our own experience within them. It is in this manner that we live within many dimensions at once. We are at best conscious of the faculties as they express themselves within our immediate world and only remotely conscious of the light forms, higher intelligence and scientific, musical and technological advancement of higher life forms, where we too have our being.

A person may anchor his consciousness in a world of higher mathematics, aesthetics, spiritual principles, intellectual exercise or technological expertise, musical genius or healing and clairvoyant faculties, depending on which frequency his vehicles are vibrating. Through the path of Inner Alchemy we can connect to all of these dimensions by raising our vibrations to the levels at which they exist.

The planes or dimensions of consciousness themselves correspond to bodies of consciousness that are similar to the seven bodies. These planes are located not only around our physical body and interpenetrating it, but also in concentric rings around the core of the body of the planet. One is seen as outer space, the other is experienced as inner space; these are experientially synonymous to each other. Understanding this requires a leap in our thinking.

Interdimensional Mind

Imagine now that you are throwing a pebble into a still lake. Notice the concentric rings around the spot where the pebble fell. The outermost ring is the largest; it has the greatest circumference (translate: energy or experience) and reaches the shore first. The progressively smaller rings follow the largest in wavelets; they have a greater distance to travel to reach the shore. Unlike the lower mind that operates in straight sequential logic, our higher mind functions in the same way as these wavelets, as does sound, radar and similar elements. The reality of interdimensional mind is concentric.

As our thinking develops beyond the personality and eventually beyond the personal itself, we are able to reach higher dimensional realms. In order to do this we need to generate more and greater frequencies of energy, accompanied by a finer degree of focus and attunement.

For us these dimensions might appear futuristic, as their development – highly mechanical and scientifically advanced from our perspective – is still untouched and highly suspect. Nicola Tesla tuned into his own activity at these higher levels and brought into our dimension useful inventions, many of which are still mysterious and considered dangerous to unevolved humanity. Wilhelm Reich was another genius of this nature, whose pioneering work in the field of human bioenergy is often misapplied and widely misunderstood.

But you do not need to be considered a genius to tap into these dimensions. Dare to tune in to your own energies. Explore raising the level of vibrations consciously. Give yourself permission to perceive and to remember, particularly in your night-time activity beyond body consciousness, where you contact these dimensions naturally and easily. Keep a journal of your perceptions. Focus your attention on the slightest changes of imagery in your mind. Finely tune your receptivity to include finer and finer levels of sensations. Register them without judgement or interference, no matter how strange or trite they may seem. Validate your perceptions. Call upon your family of Self – yourself as you exist in each of these dimensions.

Remember that at first your perception will be coloured by third-plane references. Draw from your alliance with your higher self and masters, teachers and guides available from the realms of Light, and gently, gently take yourself by the hand and patiently build your confidence. Don't compare notes with another. Dare to be alone, to feel alone. In that aloneness, remember, is your wholeness and your mastery. In that state you will receive direct responses to your questions and your needs. Believe in them as you believe in yourself. Remember who and what you *really* are.

You may use the visualisation and guided imagery method or

you may activate your chakras. You may intensify the points of light in the centre of the atoms of your physical body, or you may rise through the tube of light into higher dimensions of being.

Some people experience interdimensionality as an aspect of interiority, while others experience it as a dimension above and outside of this one. The ways are as multiple as the religions of the world, when we consider that each religion has been an attempt to reach and utilise systematically faculties and powers inherent to interdimensional life.

Whatever method you choose will reflect your nature. For the individual with a predominantly feeling nature the simplest form of connection to the Source and interdimensional guidance is prayer, directed upward in trust, in reverence and in deep gratitude for the Light. For the man of intellect and intelligence it may be through science and logic and systematic approaches that project mind through increasingly broad and more intense parameters. For the person of action and physical bent, the path of physical service and even dance is a form of prayer and a way of accelerating the frequencies of Life.

The key is always vibrational.

Interdimensional Dynamics

The higher planes are made of pure-grade Light substance, which at the highest level is pure Intelligence or Light as individualised spirit force, expressing itself as simultaneity and vast incomprehensible abstraction. At the lowest levels we have condensed substance in the form of matter at the third dimension, expressing itself as detail and sequence. The first and the second dimensions are inert primal substance, the realm of elemental life forces in gestation.

In the access chart we see that these dimensions are reached through our seven bodies as well as through the activation of the higher chakras. The planes are progressively more spiritual, larger, vaster (and our consciousness as a body commensurably taller) the higher or more accelerated their frequency.

All inhabitants are Light Beings, embodying greater and greater concepts. Within the planes dwell the consciousness of spirits in embodiment and also of entities serving there who may have been in embodiment. All are drawn there by the law of attraction.

209

Let's find out now what these dimensions are:

1. How does Mind express itself in each? In other words, what are the activities engendered in each?
2. What does it look (or feel) like?
3. What do you or can you draw from these dimensions?

The Third Dimension

This is the plane in which we are presently located, stationed here for the duration of our physical vehicles and returning to it for as long as it takes to achieve mastery over the matter of the three planes (or three lower bodies).

This is the only level in which we have the complexities and disturbances of humanly created emotionality, which makes this the karmic plane. It is truly the testing ground of spirit, where we build the abilities and muscle power utilised throughout all of creation.

Mind expresses itself as detail and sequence.

The environment is dense and made of myriad individual parts which are assembled physically one by one – into larger units for utility.

We live in this plane whenever we think in fragments or sequentially; when we identify with matter and mortality; when we feel alone and when we are emotionally disturbed. We learn management and control of energy and substance.

The Fourth Dimension

This is a mirror plane to ours, our parallel existence, but without the encumbrance of physical density. Here Mind generates practical usages for implementation in our plane. Whereas in the third dimension we proceed step by step, at the level of the fourth dimension we function by unit.

Objects appear in parts and mind assembles them. Mind precipitates (through the medium of thought substance), whatever it needs instantly.

The environment resembles ours except for structures of light. Here we are what we think. We draw from this plane every time we imagine how something might look or work; if we put this together with that. Here reside, in other words, the principles of manifestation and precipitation used in visionary thinking and planning.

The Fifth Dimension

Many scientists have direct access to this dimension. The developments of the sixth dimension are applied here.

Mind expresses itself telepathically as whole or complete. Objects are conceived in toto.

The environment is ultramodern, with open spaces of light.

We are here whenever we function telepathically or envision whole or completed activity, when we flash on what is needed and when we feel those strokes of genius. We experience mental realisation as well as answers to mental problems.

The Sixth Dimension

At this level, the mental activity from the higher planes is being reprocessed in the light of personalised (individual) application, before implementation can take shape in the fifth dimension. The reprocessing entails a continual generation of ideas, involving all aspects of Mind.

Mind expresses itself as the faculty of mobility and dynamic, continual growth.

The environment is electronically and mechanically futuristic.

We touch upon the sixth when we are in a creative vein of thinking, trying out different alternatives and making vast leaps in our thinking. It is an electric energy, sometimes moving so fast that we cannot grasp or understand it. Here we learn dynamic

211

mind control and penetrate living states of quantum physics and higher mathematics.

The Seventh Dimension

For purposes of our individual evolution on the path of Inner Alchemy it is especially important to understand the nature of activities of this dimension.

This is the arena of what I call the higher self, where the Christ-like higher mental body resides and from which it draws. It is where the *akashic* records exist and where all imprints of past activity are found for each individual spirit group and event upon the planet.

Here the activity is not only highly spiritual and conceptual, it is also individual and personal. This plane bridges higher and lower mind, higher and personal selves, inner and outer activity. It is a centre for research, information and philosophical speculation and a central station for intergalactic activity. We might say that is the galactic capital of the planet, where foreign planets hold office, and transportation as well as communication channels exist to link the various interplanetary stations.

At this level we behold the images of the perfection that we strive for in the lower planes. They exist here as fact. Below this plane is personalised life and applied mind. Above this plane is the highly spiritualised life and high abstract mind. All, including the vibration from the twelfth dimensional Self, must funnel through the seventh plane to reach us.

Consciousness on this plane experiences knowledge and perfection, uncovering realms of causation relevant to individual life streams.

Mind expresses itself as teaching, particularly as myth and fable.

The environment is one of large-scale living, including vast centres, airships and archives.

We are in the seventh whenever we explore the meaning of individualised life and the purpose of creation, i.e. philosophy and higher psychology.

The Eighth Dimension

This is the plane of demonstration, following the high abstractions of the planes above it. It translates individual concepts. Its scope is still highly abstract, however. The concepts from this plane leap over into the sixth dimension, where they are appropriately applied for our use.

Here Mind expresses itself as an effort to individuate. One could liken it to a sculptor's basic form before the perfection of a finished product (i.e. the seventh plane), which then gets interpreted subjectively by individuals.

The environment is electrical and pregnant with technical applications.

We are at the eighth when we know we've 'got' it, but we can't quite put one finger on it: the 'Aha' just before the blueprint. Contact with this plane brings about the intuitive perception of technology.

The Ninth Dimension

To us this is the realm of Probability, the level of ultra abstract science and research.

Mind animates ideas into motion and creates global systems.

The environment is one of sophisticated compilations, reflecting communications, electronics and mechanical systems.

If there is a way to do something, contact with this dimension will reveal it. When we are at this level we gain a broad understanding of systems and their universality.

The Tenth to Twelfth Dimensions

These must be explained as a unit. Their activity is largely conceptual and surpasses our understanding, no matter how evolved our intellect might be. We cannot understand these dimensions unless we are willing to disintegrate the very process of our thinking.

These dimensions have been relegated to spiritual and mystical

213

experience and what Zen has called No-Mind. We can and do, however, visit these planes and penetrate the faculties of pure intelligence indwelling there.

At the level of the twelfth, higher mind functions in the broadest parameters of philosophy and concept. It embodies spirit force in an individual way. This Spirit Being is our own God-Self, whose function it is to generate Life (which is an actual substance of Spirit as Life-force). It is a driving, radiating force of vitality. For example, if we remember our concentric rings on the lake, this largest sphere is the most evolved in terms of experience and the closest to the shore in terms of pure spirit. It serves to generate the force that moves towards the centre in order to draw the others towards it.

The spirit beings here then serve as the guardians of the threshold, as well as the individualised God-Selves of embodied spirits. Identity at this level is sonic and vibrational, echoing the individual frequency set by the Great Central Sun upon creation.

As we consider the eleventh plane we leap from pure light and sound into concept. From the effulgence of infinity demonstrated (if we can use such a term) at the twelfth plane, the eleventh represents brotherhood and unity.

To me the activity at the eleventh dimension is as if pure sound became musical notes, primordial light split into colours and intelligence gave birth to individual concepts. Contact with this plane is experienced as universality. Perhaps the greatest example we can give at this point is to say that this plane is responsible for the New Age ideas that are inspiring so many of us at this time.

Finally, the tenth dimension expresses the concepts of the eleventh through the majestic silence and peacefulness of order. This heavenly plane is responsible for the creation of nature as a living force. It is, for us, the realm of possibilities.

Summary

I must remind you that information from these dimensions is *already* coming through. We are reaching the fourth dimension whenever we talk about manifestation, affirmation and positive thinking. The influx of these ideas reveals fourth plane activity, including the ability to project instantly what we want.

To see things as a whole, forsaking the tedious elementary process of 1+1, is an intuitive leap into the sixth-dimensional level of higher mathematics. When you wish to penetrate problem solving, go to the level of mentation at the fifth dimension. Here we partake of the whole mind functioning, including high calculations and deductions. Here telepathic abilities exist as a natural function of whole mind.

Electronics and mechanics at a level higher are available at the sixth dimension. When you wish to know about yourself, when you seek a teacher or a teaching, you go to the seventh plane.

When you desire spiritual awakening and vitality, you may seek the help from the higher dimensions beyond the seventh where illumination and silence as vibration provide the answer at the level of soul and where nourishment is obtained in harmony, peace, spaciousness and light.

At the tenth nirvanic plane we find what the West has called heaven. This was the plane sought by ancient adepts who would raise their consciousness to that level of supreme silence and return refreshed, illumined by pure concept and the knowing that surpasses understanding. Through this gate they would also enter into the eleventh and twelfth dimensions and into the Void Clear Light.

The twelfth dimension is the realm of pure poetry and godhood. The realm is progressively distorted through form and definition. This is why Lao Tzu began his book of teaching with the statement that the Tao that can be said is not the real Tao. Higher teaching cannot be talked about; experience is untranslatable. It is pulsation; it is Light. It is pure energy.

The real alchemical teaching occurs through energy transmission.

And yet . . . we do need to integrate and embody these concepts of truth at every level. The teaching that comes through words points the way into experience. It will be inspirational, not didactic. It will lift and raise and beautify. It will allay our fears and gently coax us into non-attachment to three-dimensionality. It will reassure us and validate us. It will embrace and sustain us through each stage of growth. It will assure us that Life is eternal and that death is an illusion.

The earth is moving into greater consciousness and heightened awareness. We are moving into greater awareness of ourselves as not only children of Light but children of space, inner and outer space.

Understand that all dimensions co-exist within the present and

215

within the framework of three-dimensional life. We must assume that responsibility for our thoughts, our feelings, our actions, awareness and receptivity, as well as for how we deal with life through relationships and how we manipulate and create every moment.

As we grow in consciousness we grow in Light, and this means not only tolerating greater intensities of it, but also projecting and emanating it. The more energy we have integrated, the more people, things, ideas and resources will manifest themselves, attracted by the Light. There is more of us available, so to speak. There is more power, too, the power of Light. And like attracts like. It is that simple.

What we want to do is to keep our energy frequency high. Anything that lowers our frequency will diminish our power and our perception, our ability to attract Light and to radiate, manifest or access Light and things of Light in every way.

Spiral Meditation

This meditation involves the use of music and visualisation. It takes you through the experience of interdimensional space into cosmic and spiritual reality. You will need a partner or an audiotape and a timer as well.

Select a piece of music that can carry you through concentric space. It should be an even piece, fairly repetitive and with a slow, deep electronic resonance to it. One of the pieces I use is called 'Planetary Unfolding' by Michael Stearns. There are others which might suit you better.

Follow the initial preparatory stages that generate the energy you require to mobilise your higher bodies.

When you are ready, lie down spread-eagle on a mat on the floor. Turn the volume of the music loud enough for it to surround you.

You are going to be moving your energy through the power of your thought, in a spiral fashion. Counter-clockwise opens and clockwise closes or returns you to the third dimension.

Visualise a thread of silver light, the consistency of finely spun metal, pliable but not liquid.

Locate your vital energy at the level of the solar plexus. (This is the centre that provides the basic energy for all functions initiated at the level of physicality.) Now, from the solar plexus, visualise a thread of silver light spiralling counter-clockwise to the heart chakra and continuing the spiral to the second chakra ... onto the minor chakras on the shoulders ... down to the chakras on the palms of the hands ... up to the throat chakra and down again to the centre behind the knees ... up to the centre behind the face and base of the skull and back down to the feet.

Carry on up to the third eye ... back down to below the feet ... up again to the top of the head ... continue down below the feet ... over the head ... and around and around and around ...

And around ... and around ...

And around ... and around ...

Allow the spirals to become wider and wider, larger and larger ... beyond the city ... beyond the country ... beyond the planet ...

Around and around ...

Allow yourself to go as far as your can ... beyond the reaches of the mind ... beyond your ordinary states of consciousness.

Return after the period of time that you have allocated, or when the person you have entrusted with bringing you back calls you.

Bring that energy back with you, returning step by step via the spiral in a clockwise direction, coming from the outermost periphery into your aura ... From the top of the head looping down to below the feet ... the third eye to the feet ... to the base of the skull and the middle of the face ... to the knees ... the throat ... the palms of the hands ... the shoulders ... the sacrum and the heart ... and back within the recesses of the solar plexus.

Be still. Feel the universe within you.

Be extra emphatic about grounding yourself before returning fully to waking consciousness. After this exercise, and all exercises that take you to interdimensional space, you would do well to outline the space that your physical body occupies – both width and breadth – three times. Sense the space within your body and feel its weight. Be sure your energy is within that space and distributed evenly throughout your body.

E O Lihum

This is another of the Essenic* Light practices. This particular one is especially helpful in connecting you to your higher Self. As the

---

* The Essenes were mainly desert-dwelling ascetics with great knowledge of nature and natural law, light and energy.

teaching was channelled to Olive Pixley, a Christian living in Britain, who claimed that the practice of Light was used by Jesus himself, it initially suggested using the figure of Jesus the Christ as the model of the higher self.

If you wish you too may place His image in the place of your higher self. If you relate to another master, use another image. I find it is most effective to invoke my higher self at the level of seventh dimensionality directly.

Whatever outside master we invoke will only mirror the truth, the beauty and the love that our God-Selves are pouring through the medium of our own higher selves.

The exercise is done sitting. Silence and still yourself.

The sound is 'E' (as in 'seen'), 'Oh', 'Li-hum' (pronounced 'Lee-hoom'). Practise it a few times and feel the fluidity of the sound. The 'Lihum' is especially mellow and wisp-like.

Practise saying it internally now, combining it with the breath. On the inbreath say 'E-O . . .' and on the outbreath 'Li-hum'.

Visualise now a crystal-coloured stream of light, the colour of clear water and with like consistency, only in light.

See and feel this crystal-coloured light stream entering into your left temple. See and feel it coursing right through the inside of your head and mind, cleaning, clearing, cooling it.

Now picture your higher self in front and above you.

You are going to connect your mind with the higher mind of this higher self. You are going to do this by threading your mind with its mind, using this crystal-coloured light stream. As the crystal light streams into your left temple and comes out your right temple, it curves in front and enters the left temple of your higher self, leaves the right temple and spirals upwards into the God-Self.

You are ready to begin the exercise.

Breathe in, visualising the crystal-coloured light entering your left temple to the inner sound 'E . . .'. To the inner sound 'O . . .' (still on the inbreath) the light circles over to the higher self and loops through it. Then on the outbreath, to the inner sound 'Li . . . hum' the crystal thread spirals up into infinity.

Repeat as long as desired. Remain in that silence and that intimacy with your Self for as long as possible.

Interdimensional Activities

Third and Seventh Plane Relationship: Life

This is perhaps the greatest relationship of all, second only to that primary relationship with the Creator. I am, of course, speaking of the relationship to one's own higher self.

In religious history, particularly that of Sufi and Christian belief, this entity is seen as the epitome of love and beauty. The Sufis even call it the 'Angel'. And for Christians, of course, the figurehead of the higher self is Jesus of Nazareth, who was one with his seventh plane consciousness, Jesus the Christ.

When the fullness of the Christ-like higher mental body is sensed, or beheld, there is a feeling of total merger and belonging, as if one were blending with the greatest beloved. A flood of love and peace overwhelms the individual, however momentary it might be. One feels illumined, transfixed, ecstatic. It is in fact the greatest union of all, the one sought out by the seekers of the ages and the meaning behind the term 'yoga', which means union. This union between the higher self and the physical self, when permanently sustained, completes compulsory the cycle of earthly existence.

As we have seen, the seventh plane is the philosophical centre of the planet, the centre for erudition and evolution. Whenever we inquire into the nature of life and its purpose we are tapping into seventh plane motivation and activity. At this level we are stationed as an identity, as a flexible intelligence, mobile and available at not only interdimensional levels but as guide and support during work to develop the personality.

When the individual is still motivated by attraction, repulsion and desire, the higher self remains largely in its own plane; reincarnation of karmic impulse is mostly accidental. When physical

219

embodiment for a developed or fairly conscious spirit is sought, the seventh plane self will seek out the records and together with archetypical intelligences, which rule the quality of lower plane substance, will determine the nature, purpose and function of the life to come.

At this point, the etheric body moulds itself according to the vibratory frequency of its impulse and its needs. Physical substance from the genes of the parents adheres to this etheric blueprint. The composites of rays and astrological influences, the relationship to other beings, the influences of the time, etc., will determine the moment and kind of embodiment required to complete experience and to contribute to the consciousness of the planet as a whole. Now the awaiting third plane body of consciousness if individualised will again have a vehicle through which to perfect itself and learn mastery.

The first and second planes provide the raw materials (substance) for three-dimensional activity, while serving too as an elemental training ground for higher life.

In considering the third plane we must resist the tendency to view all hierarchy in competitive or judgemental terms. The third plane is a plane where we work out and inspire activity at the level of detail which influences *all* planes. At this plane intelligence integrates abilities and gains mastery through obstructions, delays, interference, distraction and a barrage of primal energies and forces coexisting simultaneously. It is the master laboratory for all the dimensions.

Once we master activity at this plane through the application of alchemical practices of conscious alignment and partnership with one's higher forces, we have raised our frequency high enough to meet and blend with the seventh plane consciousness, which has been guiding, influencing and attracting us as we draw closer to it through invocation and similarity of vibration.

Mastery over substance itself is a process of implosion. This has been happening gradually as our vibrations rise through the refinement of our lower bodies. The Light core at the centre of the physical atom ignites, expands and absorbs matter, recalibrating the vibratory activity and transmuting it gradually into soul substance.

As a consequence, the moment of physical death, the higher self, which has been moving between planes, linking us from the highest vibrational activity through to the lowest, may now merge or integrate with the physical self permanently. A new vehicle is created, more powerful and flexible than the etheric; one capable of expressing mastery both over matter and in light. This is the process of the ascension, or the rapture. At this point we become ascended masters ourselves, or assume the identity of the Angel, as this entity is known to some. At this point we possess what has been called the immortal body of light.

Third and Seventh Plane Relationship: Death

When an individual dies a natural death without having obtained full mastery, matter disintegrates into etheric components and spirit energy returns to the seventh plane. The higher mental body at the seventh dimension reviews the most recent experiences and integrates these with the experiences of the whole.

If during the physical embodiment the consciousness was not attuned to interdimensionality and/or spirit, the mental-emotional counterpart of essence will remain at a lower level, often surrounding three-dimensional life, until it disintegrates naturally, adheres itself to an embodying life stream or goes to learn at one of the dimensional planes surrounding the planet. These 'phantoms' are the spirits that mediums and psychics contact. Their level of development is usually not high, though sometimes inoffensive and good-hearted.

As we learn to tune in to subtle levels of reality while in the third dimension, it is important to distinguish between these phantom spirits and the perception of the higher Self, teachers, guides and masters. The only way of discerning is through the perception of the degree of emotionality and vibratory frequency. One cannot rely on verbal communication, as this is often misleading. To reach and communicate with the highest, you must be able to distinguish between emotional frequency and spiritual vibration. To do this you need to be vibrating at the higher frequency yourself.

We do not go to the twelfth plane until we are completed by the lower planes. The twelfth plane outpost continues to be our source of power, energy, light and inspiration. It also channels mighty and powerful rays into the Earth from cosmic sources, emanates Earth irradiation to the system and reflects to us celestial heights. This is, as stated earlier, the electronic body of the 'I AM' individualised Self. Beyond the planetary outpost there is a higher Godhead, which at this point we will collectively call the Great Central Sun source.

The Eternal Name or Sonic Imprint

The electronic frequency of the twelfth plane is sonic – individual and unique for each spirit. No one else has that vibration. This vibration is your individual name or frequency.

This 'name' was the sound of your life force as it was echoed at the moment of your creation, when your essence projected itself from the Source. It is the quality of your Life-stream: your pure identity.

As your ray of light moved through the different planes, it resonated in a particular way, which caused slight distortion of the original sound and created a diversity of 'names' in each of the planes or aspects of yourself. As you re-establish communication with the various dimensional frequencies, you blend your family of Self, including these names, faculties and identities, testing or trying out each name and the imprint or abilities that each one unlocks for you. Ultimately you choose the highest sonic frequency that pertains to you. This frequency will give off the ultrasonic frequency of the God-Self.

Each person may, with disciplined practice or through initiation, rediscover this 'name' or sound and through it gain access to not only the higher self, but to the Godhead within.

The best way of attuning ourselves to the dimensional planes that we have been talking about is through dimensional doorways. These are allocated right within our physical apparatus in areas which seem to coincide with the chakras. These areas are indicated below. The data given to us has come through a friend of mine, Bryce Bond.

As there are interdimensional doorways within our individual physical selves that connect us to ourselves in other dimensions, there are also interdimensional doorways on the body of the planet itself that connect with other galaxies and systems. The Bermuda Triangle is one such doorway. There are many others, places which allow access to states of being beyond our time, space and earth dimensionality, places where it is said that you may rework the

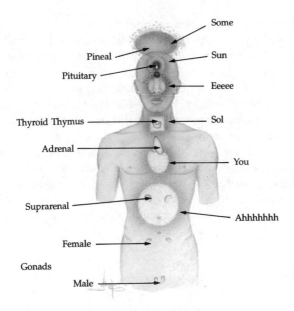

Pineal
Pituitary
Some
Sun
Eeeee
Thyroid Thymus
Sol
Adrenal
You
Suprarenal
Ahhhhhhh
Female
Gonads
Male

Fig. 3.4 Sonic Breathing
(Spiritual Centres)

past or construct the future, places where you may experiment and explore with simultaneous personalities and realities.

Interdimensional Travel

Mind is, if you recall, the essence and ability of consciousness, which uses different forms to express itself. In the first section of this book I listed three main levels of mind: the lower, or ordinary mind, the higher mind and the Christ-like mind. All of these use different bodies of consciousness.

Whereas we have access to interdimensional levels through telepathic imprint, or communication, travel happens through the etheric vehicle. This body then links up to the various consciousnesses dwelling in the different planes. As our own tolerance increases we come to inhabit our own higher bodies for longer and longer periods.

At the level of higher consciousness we go beyond the problem-solving functions to reach the levels of interdimensionality. But for

223

this to happen the individual cannot be under any tension that draws him down into the denser astral levels of fear and desire. He must have resolved his everyday life affairs to the extent that he can put them aside without them intruding, colouring or weighing upon him. At this point the dream, or journey, will be inspirational, prophetic, healing and deeply transformative. Even without the conscious memory of it filtering down into the lower mind, the effects are always uplifting.

Through interdimensional visitation we have access to our entire personal history and future realities. On the more immediately relevant issues, we have access to inspiration and higher mental abilities, including the advanced concepts, outlined earlier, of science, music and art. We are actually designed to work in perfect synchronicity with all planes.

Other planets

There is life in every single planet of our particular solar system, but not at the third-dimensional level. This is why scientists are unable to find life on Venus, Mars or any other planet. Unless higher mind is functioning, one may not reach the understanding of life in its multidimensionality. This higher mind works only when we have raised our energetic frequency through cellular recalibration. This acceleration naturally happens when old and highly inappropriate mind sets have been discarded through spiritual understanding and a genuine quest for perfection and light.

Through Inner Alchemy we may learn how to link up within ourselves to ourselves. Then we have access to the entire history, not only of this planet, but of the solar system.

All that we can see with our physical eye regarding our planet is that 8,000-mile diameter core. With an opened perception we may behold the concentric dimensions of existence surrounding earth, adding up to 2,266,430 miles in diameter. This same faculty would enable us to see non-physical beings and other dimensional life.

Interdimensional Bodies of Consciousness

As I mentioned earlier, all bodies and planes exist in polarity: positive and negative. Since all is energy, everything that carries energy (which would be everything in creation), is a battery made up of positive and negative poles or conductors. The same applies to the bodies of consciousness dwelling within each of the twelve planes, which correspond loosely to the seven bodies or layers of our aura while in physical embodiment (as outlined in the first sections).

Existence moves between the polarities of spirit and matter. Spirit is pure receptivity or negative polarity. Matter is substance that is available to spirit for transmutation and the creation of spiritualised substance: it is positive in polarity.

Spirit (–) takes on matter at the twelfth dimension, which makes that level positive (+) in polarity. From that point on to the third, the dimensions alternate in polarity. The third dimension as well as the seventh are negative in polarity, lending themselves to tremendous flexibility and growth. All negatively charged dimensions are levels of integration, absorption and application, whereas the positively charged dimensions are areas of crystallisations.

These polarities reflect themselves in the function or very bodies of consciousness. At the positive levels these fields are crystalline. At the negative levels they are spherical. Understand, however, that these shapes are only an indication of function. (See drawings, pages 222, 223.)

The use of ultra-sonic breathing practices (outlined in the previous chapter) vibrates these bodies of consciousness and gives more rapid and direct access to these dimensions. They open the

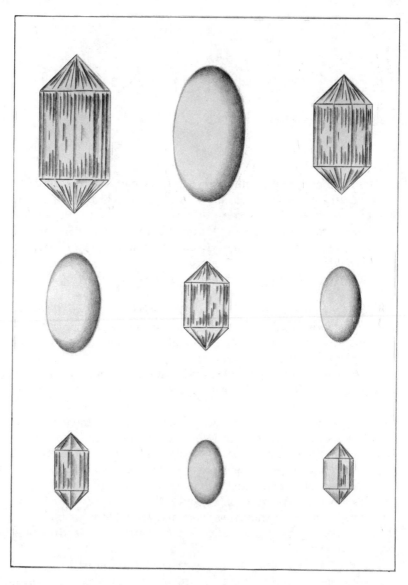

Fig. 3.5 The Forms of Consciousness

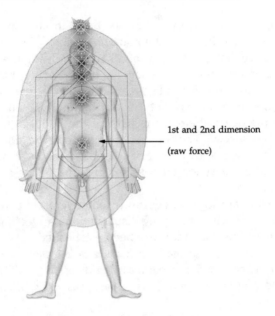

1st and 2nd dimension

(raw force)

Fig. 3.6 The Body and Interdimensional Forms

interdimensional doorways located within these bodies of consciousness.

You will notice that the location of these ultra-sonic areas coincides with the upper chakras, revealing that the chakras double up as interdimensional doorways. For someone who had not gained access to these doorways, these areas as chakras operate as energy distribution centres affecting personality development and the functions of the various bodies. When someone's consciousness and perception have reached a point of discernment, the chakras can serve as interdimensional passageways.

Methods of Entering Into Interdimensionality

The alchemical formula outlined in the first sections of this book is, in fact, a formula for interdimensionality. It is from this level, by the power of Spirit invested in the individualised presence of the God-Self, that all power, all intelligence, all energy and substance proceed. No change, particularly no transmutational activity, can

227

happen without the vibratory influx from that dimension, as the seed of all life upon the planet.

Once that frequency is attained by utilising the alchemical circuit, the process of gaining whatever one seeks is personally determined. Although the formula is essentially one, the ways, or styles, of connecting are as varied as individuality itself. There is the path of the heart, there is the path of the intellect, there is the path of active service. The simple person will reach through humble prayer and direct heartfelt communion. For many a more complex form of directed action such as the creation of the alchemical circuit is required.

Here are some suggestions to accelerate the vibratory frequency of your body, employing visualisation and feeling once the habit of the alchemical circuit has been established.

Be sure to use the visualisation of the violet flame (and any other protective techniques outlined earlier in the book) on a regular basis, and confront the reality as it manifests itself within you and in your world.

Suggested Techniques

1. Following the formula in my audiocassette 'Calibrations', intensify the points of Light in the centre of each atom in your physical body.

Sustain the feeling and visualisation as long as possible without straining the physical body. You will know this when the body temperature rises too sharply. You may take rest periods in between the visualisation. The suggestion is to build up the time gradually. You are actually transmuting the physical cells in your body, and your emotional and mental bodies will need time to adjust.

2. Follow the instructions for out-of-the-body travel in my audiocassette 'Dreamlife' (text included in the chapter 'Dreamlife' in the last section of this book), using the visualisation of the rings of light through the body. This process activates the out-of-the-body chakras at both extremities and takes you into spherical space.

3. Another way of entering into interdimensional space is through the conscious use of the five out-of-the-body chakras outlined in the chapter on chakras. As explained, these chakras work in pairs,

extending the polarity of physical substance into the etheric and working directly upon etheric energy, intensifying and activating it. When we activate the pairs of out-of-the-body chakras we are energising the concentric (or spherical) consciousness dwelling within higher dimensional reality. By expanding in both directions you come to occupy the larger bodies of consciousness, which, remember, are not linear.

You may visualise the pairs one at a time, being sure to sense the vibrational alterations each time before proceeding to the next level. Take note of each reality change.

4. Visualise entering into each dimension through the layers of your aura (your bodies) or through the interdimensional bodies of consciousness overlapping your physical vehicle and extending out into your aura. It is for this reason that the charts and diagrams have been provided.

You may also use the traditional vertical ascent through the visualisation of the chakras themselves.

5. Use the ultrasonic method of vibrating the interdimensional doorways located within your body and over the head, entering into intensifying vibrational space through sound. This method is perhaps the strongest, as you are utilising breath, sound, visualisations and feeling simultaneously.

6. Use the colour breathing method, flushing different combinations of colour through your entire physical vehicle to ignite and accelerate the chakras, points of light and bodies within and around you.

7. Project yourself through the protective tube of light that you invoke daily. Direct your request to your higher self.

8. Visualise golden light filling your brain and allow yourself to be lifted into other dimensions. This and any other methods that I may outline from here on will require faith. They are primarily spiritual. Addressing yourself thus, if faith forms part of your temperament, is perhaps the easiest and safest way.

Ignite the flame in your heart and know.

The chakras, bodies, interdimensional bodies of consciousness, etc, all move, evolve and expand synchronistically. I wish I could give you one simple method and say that it was going to work for everyone. There are individual styles. Be creative. In your individuality lies the key to your mastery and your ticket to God.

Most of all, remember that entrance into these spaces happens

229

naturally as your consciousness evolves and your energy tolerance increases. This outline is meant to provide understanding of something that is *already happening*. Inner Alchemy is as old as creation itself. As a matter of fact it *is* creation. Understanding it makes you a conscious co-creator with the Godhead.

Interdimensionality and Spirituality

Spirit is something that pervades all. It is basic Life, Light, Intelligence. The higher you go vibrationally, the higher the level of integrated spirituality. Pure spirit itself is beyond all form. We must not confuse technological and mental advancement with spirituality.

Mind, particularly universal Mind, has tremendous power, but the greatest power of all goes beyond that of mind: it is that of the source, that of Spirit.

The further out you go from the core of the planet, which may be translated as the density of your own physical form, whether this is approached externally or internally, the more spiritual force you contact. Conversely, the further inward you come towards the body, the less spiritual are the forces in operation, as they relate to sequence and detail and less to causality.

The integrative action of spirit upon matter creates illumined substance which may be called soul. This is achieved through the individual within embodiment, when he integrates his physicality with his spirituality. This matter, evolving as soul, contains greater and greater space or light, greater amounts of spirit so to speak. This manifests as body structure, mental attitudes, emotional balance, insight, intuition, creativity, joy and emanations of love and well-being.

The life forms dwelling within the twelfth dimension contain the greatest, purest quality and quantity of soul or spiritualised substance. Beings from the higher dimensions, when we are able to perceive them, seem larger in size and more luminous in appearance.

There is a downward as well as an upward progression happening. This means that the twelfth plane houses the God-Selves of those who are on the descending journey as well as of those who have attained to mastery and have returned 'home'. Our position in the third plane gives us the necessary depth (anchoring) to create the momentum to reach into the highest. While partaking of the level ascribed to the gods, we can transmute substance at the deepest levels through our alliance with it.

The Higher Self, Guides, Masters and Extraterrestrials

Your main guide *is* your higher self. People often perceive their own higher self in states of heightened awareness, but because they are not in the habit of empowering themselves, prefer to think of it as an outside guide or master.

Guides and masters are *not* extraterrestrial in the common sense. Few people understand extraterrestrial impingement. There is a great deal of fear surrounding UFOs and extraterrestrials, particularly over intervention, abduction and intrusion by alien beings. Although perfectly natural and even healthy, a lot of it is created by the media and exacerbated by the unenlightened animal fear which rules the masses.

I can't emphasise enough how important it is to work through the emotionality that blinds us, projects and therefore *attracts* fear, danger, discord and disease. Both the fear of and the attraction to alien beings denotes a certain irresponsibility and lack of awareness of the tremendous powers of the inner self. Whether extraterrestrial influence is well intended or not, the psychology of most devotees is tinged with dangerous and unrealistic messianic expectation, which opens the way for telepathic control.

Coinciding with extraterrestrial impingement there are beings from other dimensions on this planet, particularly from the seventh, who reach out to us in the capacity of helpers, teachers and guides. Some have come the way of physical birth, others irradiate courage, support and inspiration through angelic means.

The higher self as an entity lives a separate existence is most cases. As the ideal, it communicates with us through dream and fantasy. We usually don't acknowledge it as part of ourselves, and yet it is the medium through which we receive Light, Love, nourishment and teaching. Even when we invoke outside forces or authorities, help comes through our own life-stream as our higher self.

A true master is someone who is not presently in physical

231

embodiment, as being whose consciousness is anchored in dimensions beyond the seventh. This name is often applied to humans, but let me clarify that *it is rarely possible to be completely clear while in physicality*. No matter how spiritual the person may be, by virtue of physicality he or she is still subject to illusion and distortion.

A master is sensed rather than seen (even though masters may manifest themselves visually as well), and his or her irradiation is overwhelmingly intense. An ascended master is one who has been in embodiment and who has passed through the levels of mastery over matter to the point of having transmuted the physical substance of his or her cells. Ascended masters can materialise and dematerialise at will. They may also maintain the use of a physical vehicle for purposes of instructing, guiding and influencing world conditions.

There are masters who have never been in physical embodiment, who live and work from the higher planes and project help through rays, energies or intermediaries.

Angels and Elementals

There is often a clearing of the throat, a shifting of position or a suspicious glance whenever I approach the subject of angels and elementals. And yet there is also a kind of secret enjoyment, or conspiracy. Angels and elementals are kids' stuff. But, as the Kahuunas, the mystical priestesses of Hawaii know, and as the Bible also tells us, it is children who shall inherit the earth. Children have the heart to know and see, and the child within us is the key to our transcendence.

When we have tapped into interdimensional levels of reality and come to experience life at the different dimensions of being, when we have intuited the love, the teaching, the guidance that comes from higher realms through our own higher selves, guides and masters, when we know that life exists in multiple and infinite forms, some invisible to our eye, can we doubt that . . . maybe . . . angels do exist after all?

Besides the human evolution, two other modalities express themselves through evolving form. There are the angels and the elementals. Each expresses an aspect of the Godhead. The angelic kingdom is a vibrationally higher evolution than ours, and the elemental kingdom is a simpler, less complex evolution than ours. Man is in the middle, partaking of both: the material part of him is created by the elementals (whose task it is to build form), and the spiritual-emotional part of him is angelic in power and magnitude.

Both angels and elementals coexist with man and both serve as helpers to man. We can see, sense or hear them in proportion to our degree of sensitivity and quality of vibrational field; in other words in proportion to our innocence and purity. This is why children can communicate with them. Both angels and elementals are loving lifeforms that exist in the fragile capacity of service to humanity and to the planet.

Angels are sensed and seen as lightforms, conveying qualities of purity, harmony and beauty like wisps of fresh, clean peppermint air. If you have ever seen a soap bubble floating under a solid blue sky, on a sunny day, you have an idea of the colouring and substance of angels. Their wings are actually light emanations. Elementals have varying forms according to the element that they handle.

Angels can be as huge as buildings or as small as humans. Their evolution is not in substance as ours is; it is in ability to handle and direct light. The angelic mission is to absorb and release pure life-force which they imbibe in their very light bodies.

The angelic ministry is as complex as the human ministry. They keep a balance over creation. They heal and clear etheric substance, and guard and protect humanity and the Earth. Each embodied human has a guardian angel whose sole activity is to guard that person his entire life. This angel has a sonic 'name', as individual as ours.

It is a bit more difficult to see and communicate with elementals. I have never seen one directly, although I have seen its shadows and its motions in passing. My friend Marc Brinkerhoff, who speaks with them and draws them in minutest detail, said that the name of the elemental in my living room that takes care of a section of my plants is 'Eschu'. From that point on I started speaking to it, even though I couldn't see it. It responded by rustling the leaves and chasing my cat, Mia. Elementals love to play, their nature is in fact playful.

Elementals are simple creatures but they too, like humans in their interdimensional evolution into godhood, and angels in their expansion to the level of archangel, evolve to the highest level in the elemental kingdom, that of the master builders of worlds, the

233

elohim*. The elohim, like the archangels, at the highest ranks are seven in number, reflecting the activity of the seven rays.

Elementals serve through their identity with nature. Nature is the spirit's way of giving us nourishment at the level of physical substance, which is impregnated by the force of sun or light. The elementals are allied with each of the elements: earth (gnomes), water (undines), air (sylphs), fire (salamanders). Fairies and devas have reached the same elemental evolution in their capacity of overseers and friends to man. They are in charge of segments of nature and its activity. Elementals are best seen by those who are close to nature and to the salt of the earth.

Uniting the Three Kingdoms

We as humans have authority in both elemental and angelic kingdoms because we have our being in both. Ancient alchemists knew this. The Atlanteans in particular utilised this allegiance to command elemental forms into manifestation. The nature of elementals is to mimic (build the form) and execute the blueprint set by man's power of thought. Being of a simpler nature, elementals to this day continue to obey and follow man's whims and fancies, trapped often in forms that are inimical to their loving nature.

Angels, not having a body of substance, cannot be subjected to the laws of matter or to the misuse of man's will. Active collaborators with man, they simply withdraw their presence from our visible worlds until such time as our purity can again attract them and sustain contact with them.

The elemental, angelic and human kingdoms form a trilogy of expression that relates to the alchemical formula. Thought evokes the elementals, who carry out the patterns set by the mind. Feeling evokes the spiritual essence of angels, who irradiate the purity of feelings at the highest level and provide the generating power for creation. The spoken word formulates man's power to command vibrationally through his unique vibrational position of authority.

* Elohim are the seven powers behind the throne. They are referred to with great reverence in the Kabbalistic traditions as powers greater than the archangels. Some traditions say they are God. Mme. Blavatsky speaks of them in the *Secret Doctrine*. There is a good definition of them in her Glossary (cited above).

The day is soon to come when we will openly commune and co-create with angels and elementals in a world where the three kingdoms reign in peace in the fulfilment of the divine plan. Inner Alchemy draws its inspirations from this thought.

Opening Communications

Communication with the inner worlds is a bit different from the high intensity pitch needed for interdimensional perception, although you may tune in to it quite naturally along the way.

The best way I have found to sense angelic presence is to activate the outer layers of the aura. By expanding my awareness in such a way, I am able to receive their blessing – a softness of love that never ceases to melt me, even to tears of joy and gratitude for their presence with me. To hear them, on the other hand, I find it best to sit very very still, once I've called to them for help, and listen via the heart and throat chakra.

Elementals seem to respond to joy and mindlessness and to a feeling of vitality. My friend Marc, for example, is a picture of elfin charm, mischief and gentleness.

Once you have established a line of communication with either angels or elementals, or with both, you will find yourself supported in a world of higher manifestation – the creation of worlds. While we are in physical embodiment, this higher creativity pertains to healing and to the construction of harmonious atmospheres. In this capacity I would urge you to visualise the Earth enveloped in the healing love of violet flame, or pink or blue. . . .

You may simultaneously call the angels to purify and heal, and the elementals to construct and perfect. At the same time you can hold the picture of a clearer, cleaner world, a world of illumined beings in a planet run by higher principles. You can make the visualisation as specific as you like, directing it to Washington and Moscow, the Middle East, Africa and Central or South America, to leaders of state and Light workers everywhere.

Elementals (or nature spirits) have an especially difficult task handling the pollution of our earth. We would do well to bless them, which means addressing them lovingly with the energy generated from our higher selves through our physical senses, and lighten their load. They can use our help at this time, and of course our cleared consciousness too.

Angels love to be acknowledged and respond almost immediately to your call to them for help and support. Since angels work through radiance, you may ask them for qualities that will strengthen and uplift you, such as peace, obedience to the Law, purity, freedom and victory. They will then release these energetic qualities to you.

Another important way in which they can serve you is when you invoke them to dissolve (and requalify with their 'feeling') whatever impurities you may have generated or that have been projected towards you, and to cut you free from those lines of force that keep you bound in three-dimensional conditions. Although we are capable of generating these qualities ourselves from the twelfth dimensional God-Self, we can use the simpler, caring support that is offered us from the angelic realm. Speak to the angels and find out for yourself!

The elementals also help in purifying the atmosphere. Whereas the angels might radiate peace, harmony, healing and joy, the elementals, particularly the sylphs and the salamanders, can clear out psychic thoughtforms or debris from your environment quite easily. Invoke their help, and in the case of great density call on the stronger forces of the elohim and the archangels. If you can't observe the results directly, be attentive to your feeling receptors, which will reveal the lightened atmosphere of your worlds.

In the same way, playing music or talking to your plants, which has proved to be successful in promoting growth, is addressing the elementals that build the plants and the fairy or deva that oversees the entire plant or tree. Gnomes and elves likewise have been observed for centuries by the northern folk in their capacity as guardians of groves and mountains, rivers and lakes.

Explore the possibilities of co-creation, not only with your God-Self, but also with others among God's children, including angels and elementals.

The Alchemist's Stone

Crystals represent for Inner Alchemy what gold did for the medieval alchemist. Crystals reflect the power of Light. In particular

Ray	Elohim
	(male/female)
1st	Hercules/Amazon
2nd	Cassiopeia/Minerva
3rd	Orion/Angelica
4th	Clair/Astrea
5th	Vista/Crystal
6th	Tranquillity/Pacifica
7th	Arcturus/Diana

These names correspond to a sonic vibration and create thoughtforms that link us to the particular energies outlined above.

The illustration below depicts the order in which the rays appear within the spiritual centre *located in the area of the third eye*. Historically, these rays were seen as emanations of light surrounding the head and conveyed the power of the divine ruler in the form of a diadem or crown.

Please note that although the rays represent primary colours, they act in combinations of colours, as reflected in the illustration below. Each of the flames in the forehead is the domain and activity of an elohim (the highest consciousness and office held in the elemental kingdom).

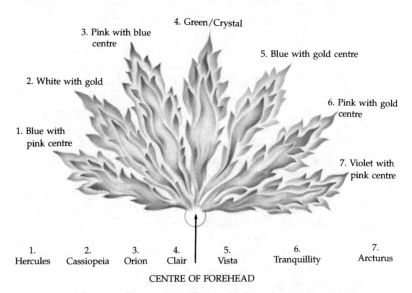

3. Pink with blue centre

4. Green/Crystal

2. White with gold

5. Blue with gold centre

1. Blue with pink centre

6. Pink with gold centre

7. Violet with pink centre

| 1. | 2. | 3. | 4. | 5. | 6. | 7. |
| Hercules | Cassiopeia | Orion | Clair | Vista | Tranquillity | Arcturus |

CENTRE OF FOREHEAD

VISUALISING THESE FLAMES ACTIVATES THE SEVEN RAYS AND INVITES THE ACTIVITIES OF THE ELOHIM WITHIN YOU. *IT IS A POWERFUL PROTECTIVE MEDITATION*

Fig. 3.7 The Seven-Leaved Flame

237

quartz is pure Light-substance generated through the power of Spirit. All crystals magnify or amplify the feeling energy and as such serve to act as a purified emotional body would. They do not do the work for you, no more than anything will. They simply reflect your energy and intensify it. The ultimate power lies within.

Crystals, like precious stones, are Light-substance that was projected here from cosmic sources, through the activity of the rays, with the purpose of irradiating purified energy and maintaining a balance on the planet, serve to neutralise negativity in many instances.

A personal crystal, particularly a wand or a double terminated one, can be charged by the individual in such a way that it serves to heal or to facilitate meditative and spiritual experience. You charge a crystal by projecting the desired qualities onto it visually, through touch, by directed breath or the use of power words. The hand transmits energies tapped at the higher levels to the crystal. When the crystal is used repeatedly, the energy accumulates within it and it becomes an alchemical tool.

I often visualise healing love into my crystal. I may visualise a sun, a bright sun like our physical sun, and project that image into the crystal, so that when I place it over the body or on the soil of a plant, it will give off the quality of the sun. As a tool of light, you can programme a crystal to do anything for the good.

A crystal evolves just as individuals do. In particular milky crystals are known to clear in a matter of months in proportion to the acceleration of the individual. By the same token, crystals affect vibrational frequencies in the physical body as well as in the mind and feelings. A few people may feel headaches or other ailments upon using a crystal, not because the crystal does anything but because their own discordant energies are amplified back to them.

Crystals have six sides. A large crystal will generate enormous energy and will maintain that energy. Smaller crystals will need to be cleared through any one of a number of methods. There is massive literature on the subject of crystals, which contains methods of clearing and cleaning them. As for all the other information on crystals, as with everything, your own higher self is your best guide and discerning power.

I prefer the simplicity of using only quartz and amethyst. Amethysts convey the properties of the violet ray and for this reason are already alchemical, functioning as purifiers, transformers and

238

transmuters of substance. Wearing an amethyst is protective. The amethyst will also repel negative energy. Some alchemists used amethyst and quartz together in their invocations: the amethyst was placed on the left (receptive) palm and the quartz on the right (active) palm.

Remember: in order to effect any change anywhere, you must embody that change yourself. The secret to alchemy lies in the alchemist himself.

Working with Crystals

At some point during alchemical work I may suggest the use of a personal crystal and I may use crystals on the individual. Crystals arranged in patterns around or upon the person's body help in the recalibration process. But, unlike some crystal practitioners, I do not advocate the need or use of crystals alone. Alchemy happens without physical crystals as well.

The chemical nature of quartz crystal is silicon dioxide, SiO_2, and any doctor will tell you that there are traces of silicon throughout the body. These are what are called blood crystals, which can be charged just like the physical crystals. Although the process of crystallisation is a negative medical condition when it applies to the condition within the blood, etheric crystallisation (at the level of thought) is highly beneficial to the alchemical quickening process. I sometimes see crystals within the body and use them to heal and balance. I also project crystalline light through my fingers and hands, extending the forcefield of my own blood crystals.

In Atlantean times crystals were used not only to generate and magnify energy but as interdimensional passageways. Crystals can be used as such today, too. Simply project yourself inside the crystal (or enlarge the crystal around you through the power of thought) and use the acceleration that the crystal (light) produces around your own aura field to access other dimensions. There are numerous other techniques of using crystals, and many books to familiarise the reader with the possibilities for experimentation.

When I discovered that the dimensional bodies of consciousness were crystalline and spheroid in nature, I made an interesting connection. The crystalline bodies of consciousness (i.e. the fourth, sixth, eighth, tenth and twelfth dimensions) corresponded at one time to actual physical crystals of the same angles. The only natural crystals that we have today have six sides. In Atlantean times, crystals with twelve, ten, eight, six and four sides were used, each to give access to the different dimensions and their properties.

Both Marcel Vogel and Frank Alper did experimental work with the use of different-sided crystals. Marcel Vogel was especially brilliant in his application of crystals to time photography and other inventions. Dr Frank Alper's books on Atlantis and the use of crystals are thought provoking.

Review

In the opening pages of this section I asked: how could I know that what I am perceiving is in any way real? How could I tell whether I am in a past, present or future reality? How could I tell whether I am astrally projecting or out of the body? Is there a difference? And, does any of this make any difference to my everyday life?

Knowing who you are personally and multidimensionally certainly does make a difference in your life. It is the primary purpose of this book so to acquaint you with the dimensions and levels of reality of yourself that you may begin to transcend limitation, that you may ultimately achieve freedom in the highest possible way, that you may come to create yourself, your world and greater and greater and more abundant life everywhere.

A serious student of Light, or one who is on the path towards initiation, does not concern himself or herself with whether he or she travels astrally or interdimensionally. What matters is that our inquiry go beyond the so-called ordinary and into the intuitive possibility of perceiving that we are more, infinitely more, and vaster than we thought we were.

Through Inner Alchemy you will begin a journey of self-exploration and mastery that is exciting and fulfilling. Not everyone needs physically to climb Mt Everest. But those who did felt that it was worthwhile, and those who read about their experience are enriched in a personal sharing that can make a difference in their lives.

If you are *emotionally* involved in your experience of the levels of reality you can be certain that your participation is *not* interdimensional. There is every possibility that you are projecting desire or fear. There is a world of difference between the astral and the

240

spiritual levels of consciousness. When the astral or desire body travels, the experience is emotional. The experience of astral projection is like walking through thick water or syrupy liquid. It is slow and tiring to the physical body. When the projection is through the lower mental body, as in thought projection, the experience is swifter, not as clear, and also subject to illusion and personal prejudice.

The consciousness of the astral or lower mental body distorts perception. The best out-of-body projection is the projection of consciousness through the tube of light in sleep or in meditation, directed by the higher will.

The only way of knowing where you are is to ask. Ask your higher self. It comes down to establishing that relationship with your higher self. It comes down to building the alchemical circuitry and using it. Practice does make perfect.

Spirit

There is little that can be said directly about the purely spiritual experience, since it is so far removed from our reality and possibility. Remember the feeling that you have in your longings for the highest love, the greatest beauty, the greatest good, the ultimate truth . . . In that longing resides the echo, the memory of Spirit.

In your love and in your joys are the whisperings of Spirit. In your prayer, in your dreams, in your gratitude and in your creativity are the workings of Spirit. Look around you everywhere, particularly when you are sad and down. Notice the beauty of the flower or of a sunny day, the magnificence of Life everywhere. Touch a kitten or a rabbit, remember the innocence of children. Look into the eyes of a child . . . There you will find Spirit, the force of the Creator.

The Creator is in the created and you . . . you, my dear friend, my brother, my sister, are both the Creator and the created. Spirit is everywhere around you, and Spirit is in the innermost recesses of your depths. In your ecstasy and in your sadness is the sound, the living sound of Spirit.

The greatest alchemist bowed before its power, its magnificence. 'Your will be done!', He said. And then 'I AM the Way', it said within Him and 'I AM with you always.'

Meditation: Drawing and Irradiating Love

Open your heart to the deepest innermost longing for the highest within you. Reach for the greatest love. Fan the fire of that love within your heart, the Sacred Fire Heart. See its flames ignite and soar, enveloping you in wings of light . . .

BELOVED GOD-SELF WHICH 'I AM'! I SEEK TO KNOW YOU!

Direct your feeling upwards and visualise the beam of light anchored in your heart. Follow it up through all the dimensions of being to the twelfth plane. Sense its vibration streaming down through that beam of light into your own physical heart and flooding you with its love, its light, its healing, nourishing, compassionate understanding. Be loved.

Feel yourself here . . . *and* there.

Now, drawing from the power of your own god-Self into your physical heart, send out rings of love to all directions of the Earth; to people you know and to people you don't know; to the animals and plants of the Earth; to the lands and seas and waters of the Earth; to the minerals, gases and substances of the Earth. . . .

Feel these rings expanding, like concentric orbs of light. Become a sun . . . irradiating light, emanating, pulsating light through your very own body!

Expand that power now to include the dimensions around the Earth. Fill the entire space with your love, your life-force. Feel it spiralling, spiralling outwards to infinity, reaching, reaching, reaching, exploring . . . and simultaneously emitting your love-light to all that is.

Continue the process for as long as you can. . . .

Gently reverse the process. Feel the love of infinity pouring back into you, concentric rings of light falling into an infinity within you . . .! (Continue . . .)

Be Blessed.

Come back, gently, reverently, gratefully.

Bow before the creator and the creation. And bow before the magnificence of your Self. *'OH BELOVED GOD PRESENCE WHICH I AM'!*

Illumination Is Your Nature

(Text from audiocassette 'God I AM')
I AM Light . . . I AM all Light . . . I AM the Light of God within you, bringing peace and joy and power regained. Illumination is your nature.

You are Light . . . The endless creative flow, the ebb and flow of life, continuous life. You are a projection of light into matter. Your home is light.

Feel yourself as light now; a beam of light projected onto Earth.

243

Your body is a function of that light. Each atom of your physical body contains a tiny sun of Cosmic Light. You are a scintillating galaxy of shining stars, right here within this flesh form. You are this light right now!

Now. Within this body of scintillating suns is a focus, just around the heart area; a Central Sun to your million suns. Look within it now. It is so brilliant that it is a white beyond any white that you have ever seen. All colours vibrate around its orb in magnetic rings of throbbing splendour, but within its centre, within this infinity of crystalline white is a flame, your flame, the source of your life, energy consciousness; the seed of your God-Self.

Allow yourself to be within the flame in the centre of your heart. You'll see that the flame has three main tongues. The centre portion is golden, rich flickering tones of warm golden hues. To the right is an exquisite blue flame; deep electric blue with swirls of the palest blues. To the left is a soft pink flame with specks of a deeper pink, magenta. Together these flames form one magnificent flame which is the centre of your power. Once this flame was so large that it enveloped your entire physical body and extended outside it as well.

Allow the tiny flame in your heart to grow again into its full size . . . to glow brighter and brighter and expand larger and larger. Larger and larger . . . You feel as if your heart ignited and expanded.

I AM Light . . . I AM all Light . . . I AM the Light of God within, bringing peace and joy and power regained. Illumination is my nature.

Keep the awareness of your physical body as a form of Light, encased within matter but allowing that light to shine through. You are a body of light within matter. Within your heart is a magnificent sun. Within that sun is a flame . . . now expanded to contain all of you. Feel the power regained by this light. Feel the joy and beauty that you now are, that you have always been; only you had forgotten.

Remember now. Allow yourself to remember.

Illumination is your birthright.

Let yourself move and sway as light. You can do this physically or through imagination. Experience the freedom of light in matter. The release! The joy!

You will notice that wherever you go there is a violet glow around you; and around others. This is the ultraviolet fire of transmutation.

The ultraviolet fire of transmutation around you is a manifestation of your Lightself and is the healing flame. Feel yourself as a centre of healing, transmuting love, reaching out in tongues of violet to purify and set the world alight. Be healed, and be a source of healing.

Illumination is your gift to life!

You are a sun of light within a greater sun. You are a child of the Light. Light is your nature. Illumination is your birthright and your gift to life. Let your thoughts wander now and picture the people and the places you'd like to bless with your love-light. Let it travel the world over, over space and time. There is no limit to where you can reach with your love-light.

I AM Light ... I AM all Light ... I AM the Light of God within, bringing peace and joy and power regained. Illumination IS my nature!

IV Alchemy In Our Lives

Esoteric Hygiene and Spiritual Protection

This chapter has to do with optimum ways of preparing and sustaining your organism for increasingly intense vibratory states on the path of Inner Alchemy.

Your Body

You have to start with how you live: the foods you eat, the exercises you do or don't do, your sexual behaviour and so forth. Your body is used to certain habits, so begin to observe what they are non-judgementally. You might want to keep a journal.

See how much sleep you get and what the pattern is, what do you eat and how often. Do you eat meat? Do you exercise and if so, what kinds of exercise? How regularly do you bathe? And wash your hair?

And what about your clothing? Do you wear tight or loose or both? What colours do you like to wear? What textures? And how often do you launder your clothing? This includes the linen that you sleep in and the towels.

Do you take vitamins? How many and how often? Supplements and diet foods? Do you go on binges? What kind of binges? Examine your excesses and your privations. How do you go about maintaining and governing your body?

How do you care for your face and your appearance? Do you use creams and lotions? What are your feelings and judgements about beauty care? How often, if ever, do you look into the mirror and see your whole body . . . your face . . . looking deeply into your eyes? How do you feel about what and *who* you see?

Your Home

Describe where you live. How clean do you keep it? How organised is it? When was the last time you cleaned out your cupboard? The refrigerator? The kitchen shelves? Do you have plants, and how do you care for them? Do you have an animal?

What colours predominate in your apartment or home? Which are your favourite areas and which are your least favourite? How does your apartment smell?

Do you like going home? Being at home? Do you like being/living alone? If you live with another, is there any space or place that is just yours? If so, how is this place different from the rest of the apartment or house?

What takes up the greatest space or importance in your home? Is it the kitchen, the bathroom, your bedroom? Or is it the study? Is it books and magazines, or maybe your papers? How neatly or organised do you keep them?

Your Friendships and Relationships

Examine them. How many? What is the pattern of your friendships and relationships? How much time do you spend with friends? How important are they in your life? How intimate are you with them? In what ways?

What is the ratio of male to female relationships? Which do you prefer as friends? Which kinds of relationships are the most difficult for you?

How do people see you? How does that compare to the way you see yourself? Are you living any lies or pretences?

What about relationships that are long distance? How strong is the relationship? Do you think of them and how realistically can you image them? Can you feel them? How do they influence your life?

Are there any enmities, any unfinished relationships where

people may harbour a grudge against you, or you against them? Who hates you? Dislikes you? And whom do you hate, or dislike? In general, what kind of people do you not like?

Procedure

No one can tell you what to do or how to go about cleaning up your life. Be as realistic as possible. Gently and consistently begin changing your habits. The purpose is to make each act as conscious as possible. Let your every action be an expression and a reflection of you. It's that simple.

Put your love, your sense of aesthetics into everything within, on and around you, and this very much includes yourself. Choose colours that express purity and beauty. Choose clean, beautiful surroundings. Choose uncomplicated, nourishing foods that respond to your need and without excess also to your craving. Don't censor but also don't indulge in excesses.

The way you look, the way you live, the way you eat and sleep all reflect your state of mind and reflect your level of consciousness. A messy or cluttered home reflects a messy, cluttered mind. Ragged underwear and socks with holes in them say a lot about the way your feel and treat yourself.

The argument that you can't afford it doesn't hold. Simplicity and cleanliness, orderliness and purity don't have a price-tag. It takes awareness and care – the two basic ingredients for consciousness. Everything you do is connected to everything else within you and within the universe of form. Spiritual mastery begins with clean linen and a healthy, although perhaps prudent, bank account.

Energy Deterrents

Here are a few of the things that I have found to interfere with my energy. Some of these are, for me, absolutely *lethal* to my consciousness-raising practices. These are marked with an asterisk (*).

*cigarettes
meat

alcohol
*drugs
aerobics, jogging
synthetics
loud music
diet foods and sweeteners
*violent or lustful movies
dark rooms and furniture
*unclean smells and appearance
*pornography
dark, impure colours (apparel)
*overeating
*sleeping with someone I do not commune with
*harbouring a grudge ...

Anything that goes against your sensitivity, your heart's feeling, your good, the good of the whole.... Most of you would agree with the last items, but many of you would object to the first five. You need to try things out for yourself. Observe what these and other things that we take for granted do for you. Go without them for a while, if you can, and then try them again and notice their effects on your energy or your state of consciousness.

I spent eight years without eating any meat, fish or dairy products. My sensitivity was so keen that it was embarrassing and downright unpleasant for me, especially when I moved back into New York City. So I decided to ground myself gradually. Fish helped, but when I tried chicken, I found I couldn't sleep well.

Unless the animal is killed in loving surrender and consent, as in the ancient days (and as the American Indian tradition still upholds), there is violation. This energy goes right into the cells of your body and registers discord.

You may not sense the chicken the same way that I did, but you might observe other reactions. Take note. And then decide for yourself. Ultimately I am sure that you will want to go for harmony and constructive vibrations.

You are constantly giving off energy and absorbing energy through your senses, your organism, subtle and gross. You are constantly taking in from your environment. There is a perpetual circulation of energies through you. You are responsible for what you put into yourself and for what you give out of yourself. You put in food in the way of sound, colour and nourishment. You give out colour and sound vibrations as well as the emanation from your own psychology.

Becoming aware of what you do is the first step towards protecting who or what you are. This includes the way in which you treat your body. We are constantly abusing our bodies through excesses of all sorts. Quite common are rigorous dieting and exercising regimes. There is a fine line between taking care of the body – which includes honouring and bending to its needs – and forcing the body to follow our will.

We seem obsessed with imposing our will. Sleeping with someone is an act of utmost intimacy. This is so even if there is no sex. When the motivations are unclear or when they go against your natural intuition and the needs of your Spirit, you will feel depleted or disrupted in some way. In order to ensure your own protection, you must know when to say NO and when to say YES. If you don't take care of yourself first, you will be unable to function in responsive and responsible ways.

Once you have cleared up your physical, mental and emotional reality and have made choices, you are ready to use conscious protection methods. Remember that 'like attracts like' and that if you are untidy, unclean or filled with violent, unharnessed impulses and vibrations, you will be easily influenced by others' needs or demands at the same level. Protection techniques will be of no avail. Psychic self-defence practices and spiritual methods of protection will produce results proportionate to your own energy level and to your own integrity.

People ask me for techniques that can help through everyday irritating and conflicting situations. They seem to want things to do. It is *what you are* that protects you. People who are beginning on the spiritual path and discovering the inner radiance of the heart believe that being loving and open to one another is enough protection. It isn't.

Real love calls for strength, for individuality and tremendous personal integrity. It is not blind surrender to a guru or a doctrine, or even to life. It calls for discernment. However we look at it, living is hard work. It requires consciousness and choices. It requires the power of love and not the love of power. It requires decisiveness and ability to act.

Once you begin the path of spiritual development, everything

251

will become heightened. You become aware of all that you have not done, your misuse of energy, and your mis-creations. Your own thoughtforms will return to you. Although the world will continue as always, when you begin to awaken, you will start noticing your own and others' projections. Your emotional body will undergo tremendous fluctuations of energy. Everything will seem to strike against you. You will become impatient, particularly with traits that you have worked hard with in the past and thought you had overcome.

You will lose the control that you had before, when your actions were automatic. As you become conscious, habits lose their hold over you. You will begin questioning how much of what is happening is a reflection of your emotional states. You will be working on your personality as you work on the spiritual levels.

As the ascended master, Saint Germain, has told us, 'Stand, face and conquer.' You know now that there is no escape.

Psychological Awakening

You will begin investigating your actions and your motivations. You will reflect, 'Maybe she is *not* this way, but my mother was.' And, 'He or she *reminds* me of my mother.' Or someone will remind you of the father you ran away from at an earlier age. That feeling will haunt you until you forgive and forget your father, until you accept and integrate that experience into your consciousness.

People are attracted to you for some reason. Your entire emotional history reflects you and the way in which you have responded. And according to each response (or lack of it) you create other responses. It is 'karma', the law of cause and effect, and there is no escape from this. Even in non-doing you are doing. By evading making a choice you are also making a choice.

The highest Eastern moral principle is the Buddhist notion of harmlessness, *Ahimsa*. Harmlessness means purity without extremes: the middle way. When you stand in the middle you can 'Stand, face and conquer'. Only then can you perceive without the barriers of your own desire.

Beware of your righteousness. You may be justified in certain of your reactions, but irritation can be a reflection of a certain intolerance or impatience in you. You may be absolutely right in your belief, but wrong in your righteousness about it. There are ways of saying things which need to be said in a way that doesn't create karma for you. If the other is offended, you have to deal with the effects. You would need to re-examine your motivations, and your delivery.

Hold others, especially discordant people, in the image of godliness. Get into the habit of visualising their 'I AM' selves above them, connected to their hearts. As you begin to see people like this they will respond appropriately. You will begin to live change from the inside. This is the real revolution.

Miracles are possible. People may be reached through the use of methods of light. If they don't respond immediately, that energy stays on the periphery of their being until they open to receive it. Maybe they don't respond to you directly, but they will respond later on, to someone else. It doesn't matter. Try not to see the world so personally.

Part of why the world is the way it is, is because of our personal investment in being right, and this includes spiritually right. But don't be heavy with yourself. Above all don't be heavy! Be gentle, loving and tolerant with yourself. Treat yourself as you would a child who has made a mistake. You're not going to beat up that child, are you? You're going to talk to it, teach it. And yet you beat yourself up.

If I were to see you irritated with someone who is perhaps arrogant or judgemental, and acting upon that irritation with more petulance and impatience, I would immediately assess that you are looking at the other in the same way that you look at yourself – critically. You don't love yourself enough. You need to develop more love and patience towards yourself, loving the you that makes mistakes, even loving the you that loves the Light so much that he becomes just a little bit fanatical sometimes.

Your attitudes about yourself, and through yourself about others, are absolutely basic to the kind of protection you may have.

Psychic vs Spiritual Protection

The basic difference between psychic and spiritual methods is the source of the energy or power used. Psychic pertains to the personal world; spiritual draws from the Godhead.

In using spiritual protection techniques you are continually aware of being an instrument of the Light. You acknowledge this Light as the Source of your life and activity. You acknowledge that everything that comes to you, comes via the higher self from the God-Self. You acknowledge your participation in an intelligent universe of Light beings working in harmony and in brotherhood.

This acknowledgement in itself is all that you need to be shielded by the Light. The visualisation and feeling that accompanies this acknowledgement creates the wall of light around you. We move in a ocean of influences and we are subject to them at all levels. Besides the constant use of the violet flame surrounding your form, your environment and your affairs, in the way of review, here are a few of the methods suggested:

For the physical body:

— Bathe frequently and wear clean clothing
(clothing holds the energy from the environment for hours).
— Take alternate hot and cold showers, which strengthen your resistance to disease and also your physico-etheric balance.

— Treat yourself to a massage often. I especially commend shiatsu and acupuncture, which address the whole organism, particularly the energetic system.

— Love your body from the inside and from the outside. Look at it with appreciation.

For the emotional body

— Use the visualisation of light, particularly the golden light that soothes the nerves and brings peace, around the solar plexus in the form of a disc or sphere.

— Surround the solar plexus with a wide belt of electric blue, shielding your entire midriff front and back.

— Visualise a suit of light covering the entire body (this is good for the physical as well as for the emotional).

— Hand mudras (or postures) that shut down the intake of

emotional energies from the outside include: —— Thumb, second
and third fingertips touching.
—— Clasp hands, interlacing fingers.
—— Cross arms across the solar plexus.

— Visualise a mirrored shield around yourself, returning all energies which are not of the Light, to sender.

— Picture crosses of blue flame (or white or gold) before you at
the level of the solar plexus and belly, or as large as your physical
body (or slightly larger still). This is a general protective visualisation, good for everything.

— See a stream of golden liquid light pouring from your God-
Self into you, particularly washing over your spine and flowing
through into your entire nervous system, especially covering the
brain. (Also good for the mind.)

— Picture yourself within a gold sun-sphere of protection – the
presence of your God-Self or any being that you may have
invoked. (This is a general protection, which becomes a tangible
reality once you commit yourself to working with the Light.)

— Imagine wielding a sword of blue flame and cutting yourself
(or another) free from any lines of force or influence that may be
impinging upon the freedom and sustenance of Light. (This is a
dramatically powerful act that brings results at every level,
especially if you accompany it with the affirmation, 'You have
no power!')

— Call upon the angelic host. The names of archangels Michael,
Raphael, Gabriel and Uriel hold special power. Invite them and
their legions of angels. You may also address the angels of any
quality you need: victory, freedom, purity, peace, healing, etc.

For the mental bodies:

— Hold the presence of Light within the physical brain, particularly golden light. See it transmuting the grey matter of your

255

brain into light golden substance, raising the level of vibration in your brain that you may receive the higher impressions.

— Visualise a cap of bright white or crystal light, shielding your skull, or wear a band (à la American Indian) of golden light around the head.

— Invite the luminous presence of beings of Light to overshadow you, to clear your mind, to help you think better, or remember.

— Visualise the flames of the seven rays upon your forehead, which relate directly to the activity of the elohim. (Illustration may be found within the chapter on angels and elementals).

These visualisations have been given by the Brotherhood of Light over the years and happen quite spontaneously without our having to do anything. But given our need to *do* and the fact that this doing evokes the spirit and vibration of Light, we may avail ourselves of them at any time. As your meditation intensifies and you are able to attune yourself directly to the source of these energies, more and more variations will be revealed to you. The world of colour and light of the higher octaves of vibrations are magnificently beautiful, nourishing and uplifting. There is no greater power than the power of Light. Remember that. And dare to live it.

Establish times and rhythms for your meditations. No matter how brief, be sure to begin and end your day with a practice of light. Before you leave your home or apartment, protect it and yourself and your vehicle. You might even want to visualise yourself shielded in an armour of light! Or you might want to picture the old tried-and-true visualisation of the magical 'ring-pass-not', used by magicians, sorcerers and alchemists of the ages, around yourself or the area that you wish to protect with a ring of light.

Remember the power of the spoken word. Pay attention to your speech and to your empowerments. For whatever you think and say will come to pass in some way, at some time . . .

And then, know that the Light that is growing in radiance within and through you shines forth upon everyone you meet. In this way as you purify, perfect and protect yourself you are purifying, perfecting and protecting others by serving the eternal Sacred Fire of Spirit.

Visualisation: Gold Spirals and Blue Circles

This and the next exercise from Olive Pixley's Essenic repertoire are best done in the evening before going to bed. The first one clears away the thoughtforms, feelings and impressions accumulated during the day and from the past, cuts through our unconscious resistance to a new quality of life and protects us by sealing us in a blue aura.

Stand relaxed. Be sure that your body is aligned – knees are loose (not locked), pelvis is tucked in a bit to permit the flow of energy up and down the spine, shoulders relaxed, chin is down allowing the energy from the spine to course up and down from the brain.

Feel yourself held within the beam of light that is anchored in your heart and which also comes right through into the earth.

Sense your feet firmly planted on the ground, the weight distributed evenly between the heel and the ball of the foot.

Gold Spirals

Now, visualise a long gold thread, like a flexible golden wire, with which you are going to thread yourself through the spine nine times. Each portion of your intersected body is cut with each succeeding spiral.

You will see on the illustration that the spirals start at the nape of the neck and are drawn over the head from back to front.

Do each cut on an inbreath. Draw it over the head and through the throat on the first breath . . .

On the outbreath take it through the throat, out via the back, up and over, piercing your body at the level of the breastbone on the second inbreath . . .

Continue in this way until the trunk of the body has been cut nine times down the spinal column.

Note:

This gold light is an actual substance which cuts through other substances without effort. It is not an easy exercise to do; often light will not cut straight down the centre. It may dart aside. The more this happens, or the more difficult it is to feel and see the light piercing through, the more important it is to do it.

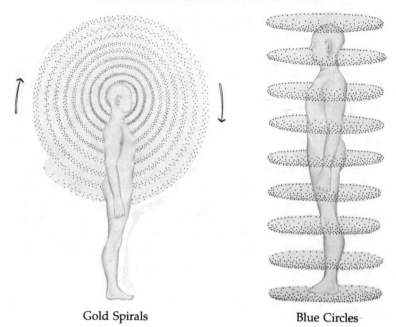

Gold Spirals   Blue Circles

Fig. 4.1 Gold Spirals and Blue Circles

Blue Circles

Visualise a circle of glorious blue, like the glow of a living sapphire, just above your head, wide enough to encircle it but not to touch you. Below and around your body are eight more circles, the last one, as illustrated in Fig. 4.1 right by the soles of your feet.

On an outbreath, pull the blue ring above your head down to the second ring. Hold the picture for a moment... and then allow the two rings to coalesce.

Then pull the rings down to the heart level... and see the three rings uniting into a unit as well.

Continue until you have encircled yourself nine times, descending each time with the uppermost rings. When the nine-in-one rings surround your feet, they vanish.

You can do this exercise three times.

When you get into bed, you can visualise yourself as a cross of light, from head to feet and across the shoulders.

Sah-Vay

This one is also done standing and includes the entire energy circuitry of your bodies.

Visualise a golden half-moon above the head on the right side, and another half-moon of deep blue between the feet and containing them.

To the inner sound 'Sah', on a deep exhaling breath draw the golden half-moon down to the ground. Simultaneously, the blue one is drawn up through the centre of the body, all the way up to the top of the head . . . where it is filled with light.

Now, on an inhaling breath on the inner sound 'Vay', the gold half-moon rises and the blue one descends.

Again on the outbreath (to the inner sound 'Sah') the half-moons return to their original positions. Visualise the light which poured into the blue half-moon being distributed down the body and into every cell.

Do this exercise three times as well.

Alchemy and Human Relationships

Emotion and Religion

The power behind the dynamic of the emotions is mammoth. It is the power released by the pressure exerted upon matter by the consciousness. In other words it is the force behind transmutation. It can move mountains. At its purest it can lead human emotions to express the power of faith, of prayer. Ancient sages knew the force inherent in human feelings and attempted to teach the masses about the concept of godliness in different ways.

The East posited God as the Guest – He who comes unexpectedly at any moment. The seeker, or devotee, lives within the shadow of this all-powerful greatness, which will manifest itself unannounced ever so subtly, whimsically at times. He must live a good, surrendered life of ever-sharpening awareness and sensitivity so as not to miss the moment of visitation.

Judaeo-Christian tradition saw God as the Father-Son, who relates emotionally to his children through punishment and reward, through action and through grace earned. Time is short and there is only one life. Prayer here is a dialogue becoming at times a form of barter, a give and take which in the absence of real love is still echoing 'an eye for an eye, a tooth for a tooth.'

The Sufis saw God as the Beloved. The aspiring seeker assumes the role of masculine solicitation. God is to be conquered and seduced. Prayer is a love song and emotion is raised to the heights of ecstasy and rapture.

Muslims understood God as the Friend and the virtues of good conduct and reverence were raised to the art of ritual within the fabric of everyday living.

The American Indian beheld the Great Masculine-Feminine Spirit, within which all function and power reside, all manifestation and all teaching. This is the path of the warrior, essentially underlying the mysticism of the Americas.

Religion, as we have come to know it, is primarily emotional interaction with the Godhead. It is rooted in belief and in subjective emotional experience. Emotion is the driving manifesting force. And emotion, as we know, is an aspect of the sexual drive.

Because the emphasis has been on desire-based emotion and not on genuine feeling or sensibility and the autonomous circuit with the inner source itself, man has come to believe that power lies outside of himself, that God is an outside force. The primary relationship being with the creator, all other relationships will reflect that. We empower another and desempower ourselves.

The Longing

As with the sexual urge, the longing within an emotional relationship has its roots in the primary drive to merge once again with the Godhead, in that primary oneness and wholeness which is but a faint, though basic, subliminal memory. This yearning gets translated into our relationships with one another. Of course, we set ourselves up for disappointment. The relationship with the Creator at its essence is not emotional – it is not reciprocal or conditional. Secondly, it is not outside of ourselves. And thirdly, it cannot be consummated, in its totality, at the level of third-dimensional physicality.

If we *really* understood this, we wouldn't get ourselves so entangled in human relationships. We wouldn't come to expect and demand, to manipulate and to engage in any one of the barrage of emotional reactions that ensue, including rejection, betrayal and grief.

The Alchemical Marriage

The union between two people, particularly of the opposite sex, provides a dynamic forcefield which parallels the very dynamics of creation itself. It is the union of positive and negative polarities at every energetic and dimensional level. This reflects the process that happens individually within each person at the cellular level; the meeting between Light and matter in the creation of consciousness.

The outer relationship reflects the inner relationship with one's Being or Source. I can meet and see others as they truly are in proportion to the degree to which I have met and see myself. If I have not seen myself, I will project what I refuse to see or accept within myself onto another, and this includes the negative as well as the positive. In its practice, human relationships serve to mirror back to ourselves what we project emotionally, mentally and physically.

I know of two psychotherapists who came together very strongly, united by the common vision of service – working together for the Light. Both are highly evolved spiritual beings with tremendous awareness of the responsibility that Life empowers us with, and both are also physically sensitive. Both have good reputations and hold seminars and workshops. Both are 'authorities' in their own right. Their coming together reflected that which they had achieved and presented to the outside world.

After an initial honeymoon period, this couple began to show signs of extreme discomfort. The other side of the mirror began to reveal itself; in other words, the perfection that neither of them had yet embodied; their faults. These two spiritual beings began bickering and screaming in ways that surprised each of them. And each blamed the other for the discord. It took a while before they could see, with the help of artful guidance (where each of them was helped to see the situation from the perspective of their higher selves), what was being enacted; their privations, their pretences, the gap between that which they wanted to be and that which they actually were at the personality level.

The male in particular found it difficult to accept his anger. He had developed a smooth, soft veneer of spiritual surrender, with the accompanying values of harmlessness and unconditionality, poverty and non-competitiveness. His success in the world, particularly in relationships, was being challenged repeatedly, he admitted, especially in this relationship with a powerful female who, from his perspective, seemed to emasculate him.

She, on the other hand, mirrored his unexpressed anger back to him, in her attempt to elicit the strength in him that she needed in order to feel safe. What she projected onto him was her fear. She had never been able to give herself fully to a man. She lacked trust in the human sense and had become secretly embittered by relationships which, in her estimation, were always exploitative and disappointing. The relationship, on the personality level, was a disappointment to both. The meeker he became, the angrier she became. And on and on and on . . .

It was an emotional impasse from which neither of them could extricate him or herself, except through spiritual means. From that perspective they could begin to weather the gap within themselves. These two individuals, as it turned out, came together to learn the lessons of love and the transcendence that typifies the psychological lessons at the level of the heart chakra.

Both were playing at being independent, givers and showmen (being therapists); together they were learning the rhythm of giving and receiving, through the refining process of fire into light. Their emotional entanglement was a necessary process. By generating intense emotional energy, and the accompanying fire which results from activating the lower chakras, they were forced into a confrontation that produced the transmutation of the fire into light – a light that was far greater than that produced by each of them individually. Their confrontations, both positive and negative, proved to be an (alchemical) arena for spiritual growth.

The true meaning of the alchemical marriage has been lost. We find it only within ourselves and in union and partnership with one another as independent, conscious, creative individuals. In that state of homeostasis, the marriage that results from the merger of equal wholenesses can produce miracles. The coupling at this level intensifies the resonance and vibratory frequency, not by addition but by multiplication.

The alchemical marriage unites fire and water – the creative force of the sacred fire of the Godhead with the power of the fluid energies of personal feeling. It occurs within. The outer is not only a reflection of that inner state, it is meant to help and trigger that inwardness. Through the medium of polarisation, the separation into positive and negative modalities, is created the yearning that takes us beyond the boundaries of rationality into the world of the heart, the world of pure feeling through which we intuit, in greater and greater quantities, the majesty of the Source. Human relationships at their core are intrinsically frustrating – they are the tease of the divine.

Sexual Energy

The greatest lesson we learn through relationships is the lesson of loving cooperation. We learn to be ourselves while allowing the other to be himself. We learn the art of give and take, of compromise, of co-creation. And we do this at a level of vibration of extreme and confusing intensity. The sexual energies inherent in all relationships, whether celibate or not, exert a tremendous pull to earth, to density, to third dimensionality and linearity. The sexual energy is the rhythm of the flesh seeking to procreate; it is the vibration of the animal within matter. It is louder than all the other resonances within us. It is the bass drum that obscures the still small crystal voice of the higher self, unless we learn to orchestrate properly.

This was the original purpose behind the ancient discipline of Tantra, which utilised the energies of sex as a path to the Creator. The ancient religions knew the undeniable power of the sexual drive and made provisions to include it within the codices of spirituality. The ancient sages knew that the power of transformation, and ultimately transmutation, is contained within the energy of sex.

The proper use of this energy is another matter. As with all energies, we are meant to learn mastery over it, not oblivion or suppression, not indulgence and self-justification. In a better world, where we are not continually controlled by hypnotic and cultural suggestions that drone into us and create compulsions to food and sex and alcohol, we will be better equipped to understand and contain the energies of sex. This better world begins with you, the moment you decide to stop the world.

One of my clients, a young woman in her early thirties, first came to me out of a confusion about her gender and a devouring guilt about what she construed as homosexuality. Her parents had been physically undemonstrative. Her mother seemed to be warm and the two had been 'close', which added to my client's confusion, but never physical. The child had grown up with fantasies of women's bodies which seemed to intensify to epic proportions in later years.

She was a sensitive, spiritual child and began meditating in her teens. She had no problem reaching interdimensional realms of light and effulgent beauty. Her problem was with the earthlife, and in particular with her sexuality. Most of my work with her consisted of bringing the energy down her body and into the lower chakras. This is different from the usual procedure with ordinary, somewhat materialistic, people, whose energy needs to be refined, accelerated and brought *up* through the chakras.

The gap between her personality and her spiritual identity was actually a chasm. Her relationship with her mother only intensified the atmosphere for learning the lesson that she came to learn: embodying the spiritual aspects in a physical body or form. In other words, bringing light into her sexuality. The raging passion within her was proportionate to her denial, mirrored through the lack of physical relationship with the mother.

The process was intensified by her fantasies of sexual practices in witchcraft and shamanism, typical of life-streams who indulge in excesses; excessive privation alternating with excessive indulgence. These feelings create a tremendous confusion in an advanced soul who has decided to work on the dissolution of these tendencies. The fanaticism and self-recrimination expresses itself in guilt and suicidal thoughts. I helped her to see that the energy *behind* the self-condemnation is the same impulse towards purity and integration that hallmarks her current purposes. It is a friend and not her enemy.

Slowly, slowly, with the understanding of her own energetic circuitry and the spiritual force of the highest dimensions that were so accessible to her, she was able to begin to dissolve the tension that the two polarities had created within her. She also began to understand and accept the nature of the bodily drive. If you know that the body is not 'you' but an intelligence that is elemental and under custodianship, you are freed from identification with it. You can tend it, love it, feed it and lovingly discipline it. Sex is a bodily drive, plain and simple. What we add to it is our creation, the excuse for our wants.

Romantic love, if you will dare to notice, is often the emotional embellishment of lust. It is sex acted out emotionally and raised to

265

aesthetic proportions that suit the style of the individual. As beautiful as this romantic love may be, it is all too often illusory.

There are three levels in the expression of love; lust is the basic physical core, romantic love is the emotional counterpart at a higher frequency of vibration, and spiritual love or compassion is the highest resonance available to a spirit who is embodying polarity within matter. Only at the third level do we transcend the pull of sex. Only at that level have we transformed the energies that bind, blind and manipulate.

At the level of lust we learn to stimulate and project energy, to use and satisfy the drive. At the level of love, with the added ingredient of emotion, we learn to give and receive, to care for and to honour ourselves and the other. Once this level is mastered, we begin to long for something more. We realise that physical and emotional union is not enough. Emotional love opens the doors of the heart by taking us through the tests of anxiety, doubt and fear of our own existence and identity. Emotional love teaches us how to couple the energies of feeling with the primary substance that generates the sexual drive.

Love, human love, is the gateway into godhood. The passionate intensity at the level of feeling, whether it be directed towards another individual, or towards the search for God Himself, sets up the momentum for more and higher creativity, by expanding our definition of ourselves. Love is inclusive. In love we are more than our individual selves. Love in itself is a quantum leap that takes us to the fringes of the ultimate leap – into interdimensionality. Through loving others we expand, or accelerate our own vibration to the point of merger with the higher self. At that point we are in cosmic or spiritual love. At that point we become what in the East is called a Buddha – a compassionate one. To become a Buddha is not beyond anyone's reach.

The Art of Relationships

Learning the art of relationships requires a certain knowledge or understanding of the energies involved in relationships. Most importantly it requires that we understand the difference between meeting and merging. In love the drive is to merge so totally with the other that we lose ourselves. And herein is the danger. Losing ourselves in the energies of love is different from giving away our power, our identity. Instead of being two pillars, as Khalil Ghibran prescribes, we become a shambles. We empower the other and lose ourselves simultaneously. Remembering this is the key to the art of relationship.

The lessons of love are the lessons of the proper administration of power – power over ourselves, power over others – ultimately leading to the acknowledgement of the highest power through us.

In our over-romanticised societies we rush to merge with one another, hoping to find in the illusion of the other what we lack within ourselves. In this manner two deaf people meet, two blindnesses converge, hoping to see, to hear through the other, disillusioned when they can't and then blaming the other that they did not deliver the goods as promised.

Energy Dynamics

The sexual link with another opens up an energy conduit between the persons through which are projected all of their personal history. When you sleep (particularly when you have sexual intercourse) with someone, you are sleeping with everyone they have ever been with, with all the people they have been with and with everything that they have done or not done. You are blending with all human creation through lives upon the planet. You are inadvertently taking upon yourselves their load. You are karmically bound. Casual sex and casual meetings are one of the fundamental causes of emotional pollution.

If we understand that we are an energy field filled with abilities, impressions and perceptions and that this energy field is extremely sensitive to other vibrations of a like nature, we can begin to care for it, protecting it and preserving the purity of its functions.

When we meet someone we feel attracted to, we will know the source of this attraction, without condemnation or illusion. We will be free to meet or merge with this individual and we will be aware that the choice is ours. We are not compelled or driven by blind forces that we neither understand or care to understand. We have taken responsibility for our actions and the effects of these actions. And hopefully we will have done this with love.

At the moment that we link sexually (physically, mentally or

267

emotionally) with someone, we open up the function of the chakras in a horizontal way. We begin to form energy circuits with them.

A further complexity arises when we consider the psychological characteristics of each of the chakras (see the chart on 'Chakras'). The lessons contained in learning to manage the different energy frequencies and qualities at each of the chakras is what is commonly referred to as 'karmic'.

At the base chakra, remember, the lesson was purity and the right use of personal will. At the second centre the lessons concern the use of emotion and the attainment of individuality, as well as learning the balance between social and personal reality. At the third chakra, the lesson is control and submission, cooperation. At the heart level the lesson is trust, unconditionality and the joining of consciousness and matter.

The lessons contained within the higher chakras are; at the level of the fifth, or throat chakra, creativity and divine will; at the third eye, concentration and consecration; and at the seventh, cosmic consciousness and transmutation.

Each of the chakras presents a lesson that can only be learned in relationship, as it pertains to the right development of personality in alignment with higher self. The stage is set when the energy that seeks to be integrated (at the level of the chakra involved) reaches out and finds the corresponding energies out there that will help it to express itself and force a resolution.

For example: if I need to learn humility, which is a lesson of the heart, I will be attracted to people and situations that will bring out the proud and the arrogant in me, or that stifle and repress the proud and the arrogant in me. Either way, the momentum of the energy intensifies to such a proportion that it explodes into consciousness, stares me in the face, so to speak, and I *have* to deal with it. If I don't learn the lesson this time, then I suffer again and again in increasing dosages until finally I do. It is my own energy that provides the situations: my own incompletedness.

I am seeing a client at the moment, a woman. She is involved in a relationship that is typical of the lessons provided by the solar plexus bond. Each of the parties is trying to dominate the other. There is a compulsive attraction and equal proportions of hate involved. They can't be together; they can't be apart. Their link is strengthened by a strong sexuality and a deprived (equally intense) emotionality.

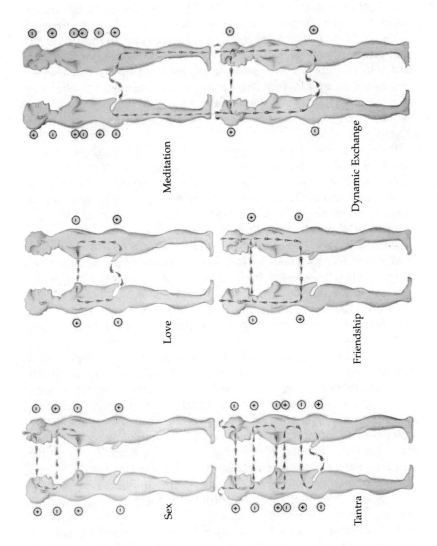

Fig. 4.2 Energetic Interactions between People of the Opposite Sex

Typically the male partner is ambivalent to commitment; the female is starving for it. She cannot stop thinking about him, what he might be doing, who he is with. I have explained to her that in order to bring clarity into the situation, we will have to work energetically as well as verbally. Understanding the issues is not going to help one iota, if the emotional energies are not stilled. In order to do this, we will need to develop methods of distracting the mind from the stimulus, bring some harmony at the level of the energies, and then look again. As I work with her mind I am working with her emotions. At this point we can hardly invoke the spiritual energies.

Whenever she reaches a point of stillness (through my use of spiritual healing methods and energy rebalancing practices), she experiences fear or rage. She is afraid of forgetting her fear, her anger and immediately brings up the thoughts that again trigger the emotional response in her body energy to perpetuate the situation. She would be called an obsessive.

Behind it all is the echo of her childhood voice, 'Mommy, don't leave me!' She had been a child actress, primped by an ambitious stage mom who was unable to love her at any depth. To this day she is acting out her need for mom's approval through her partners. This time she found an ideal mate, whose very presence intensifies her fear of abandonment and rejection, her feelings of worthlessness.

Conventional therapy would hash and rehash this psychological situation to a pulp and nothing would be resolved. The woman is emotionally tied to her partner and to her mother. Most importantly, she is coming face to face with a characteristic of revenge that has typified her personality, in other words, a misuse of the power centre – the solar plexus. The energy at this level is calling to be brought back in. She is learning to control herself rather than another. She is being thrown back to herself, to her own resources, to the power within. She is at the point of qualitative change. Either she takes the leap into spirituality through forgiveness, or she aggravates her misery longer.

This emotionally packed relationship could easily be between people of the same sex. As a matter of fact, homosexual relationships are typically more intense than heterosexual ones. The tension of like energies magnifies the activity of the emotional body, and particularly where sexual energies are involved, the craving for

270

touch, feeling and sensation can create a tremendous addiction, which, like all addictions, is difficult to break.

I am, of course, assuming that we all want to be free of addictions.

Circuits are formed between people of the same or opposite sex with varying intensities, depending on the kind of level of consciousness of the parties. In homosexual relationships, although the bodies may be of the same sex, there is almost always a psychological energy distortion which predisposes one to being more masculine and the other to being more feminine. These distortions, in my opinion, come from a personal history that transcends the current upbringing.

There are so many variations on the dynamics of attraction that it would be impossible to cover them all here. Suffice it to say that we may have mental homosexual relationships too, even if physically the parties are of opposite sexes. The lessons involved in homosexuality are usually related to learning integration at the level of physicality.

Particularly where high souls are concerned, attachment to sensation and emotion provide a safe way of life. They are avoiding the refinement of their energies. They fear the loss of sexual pleasure, sexual stimuli and the sexual game in general. This, of course, applies to the great majority of our culture. This fear prevents the individual from reaching higher and finer degrees of ecstasy. In a more refined world, sex will be seen in its right perspective, as a way of meeting, merging and giving love and pleasure to another. The obsession with excessive sex is a reflection of a regressive culture fixated on the stimulation of the denseness of physicality.

The same principle of addiction and attachment applies to relationships that are rooted in the emotional body, such as many parent-child relationships, and even spiritual relationships that carry on through lifetimes. There is great difficulty at the time of separation. Only the energy of the Godhead can carry us through the process of transcendence and transmutation.

Commitment

Monogamous relationships are on the rise, both because of the threat of AIDS, which has made people re-examine their sexual

271

behaviour, and because of the growing awareness of a spiritual dimension to loving, expressed through a need for closeness and intimacy beyond the psychological and the physical. This kind of relationship requires commitment and integrity. Relationships are life, whether we are engaged in a committed relationship or not. We actually make a commitment to love itself, to its purity, and to the awakening and deepening of that in one another. We do *not* commit ourselves to the individual psychology of the other in a pact of possessiveness and exploitation. True commitment is of the heart and it echoes the yearning of Spirit.

We are constantly interacting with and affecting one another. In the light of this, we are coming to recognise the need to bring sex out of the closet and up from the darkness and the gutter into the light of love and purity of heart. Love itself must be refined to include our every conscious expression, act, thought, word and deed.

Karma

Karma is the Sanskrit term for the circle of energy created by individuals whenever they interact. Every action brings about a reaction. Karma refers to the law of cause and effect as applied to the workings of the three lower bodies. Karma works through the energetic circuits at the level of the chakras. It works interpersonally and affects every creation at the level of personality.

This karmic circling stops the moment you step into another level of being and into the law of grace. At this point you live from the perspective of cause. You become master over the effects in your life by establishing an awareness at the level of causation. You are no longer at the mercy of the haphazard effects. You are now within the realm of Inner Alchemy, in the domain of the higher self and the God-Self. What this means is that your energy, instead of moving horizontally (as the chakra energy at the level of personality does), moves vertically. You relate in terms of the higher self, in you and in the other.

Normal interactions are predicated on attack and defence. Usually the best defence is an attack. Our defence structures vary according to our abilities. We can have a physical style of defence, a mental armouring style of defence, or we can use emotional manipulation as a defence. These are all within the scope of psychology.

As you step out of the wheel of cause and effect, these defensive and aggressive patterns prove ineffectual and unnecessary. You begin using spiritual protection methods. You begin to use your higher powers in alignment with higher law, and you attract that which you have come to embody: Light.

Stepping Out of Karma: Completion

How do we step out of the wheel of cause and effect, which in the East is called the Wheel of Samsara? Through forgiveness. One of the parties in a relationship has got to do it.

For example: two persons are involved in a karmic bond of tyranny that has lasted a long time. It may be that they have taken turns in tyrannising the other. One may do it to the other, who in turn takes his revenge by doing it back to the first, and so on and so forth. Or the pattern may be that one consistently does it to the other. Every time that the assaulted one tries to get on his feet, the aggressor in some way knocks him down.

Now, at some time, the assaulted or masochistic one wakes up to his or her situation and decides to get out of this song and dance. If he or she gets even, it will perpetuate the activity yet further. If he or she waits to reach, convince or negotiate in any way with the other, it may take even longer. The best and only recourse is to change oneself. He or she stops putting out the energy that creates the circle. He or she stops the charge. He or she turns the energy elsewhere and, in sum, forgives.

The other party, the aggressor, is left in the lurch. He or she has lost the dance partner. He or she will attempt to elicit old responses and failing that will go elsewhere and work out the pattern with someone else.

Completion of life lessons, particularly the completion of relationships in which one may have played out many roles and learned many lessons together, can happen only in love. Only love releases and sets free. Completion and release happen in deep love. If only people who divorce, parents who watch their children leave home, lovers who become separated from the loved one through death would release the other in the fullness of love, with gratitude for

273

the lessons learned, saying 'goodbye!' and 'thank you!', 'We are going our separate ways, richer for having known one another, different now . . .'.

Love

Love is eternal. Once you have really loved someone, you love them forever. It is still difficult for my ex-husband to believe that I love him, as deeply as I ever did. It is difficult, in our three-dimensional existence, to conceive of love without possessiveness.

I like the image of love being like an open hand, where the lover may come and go like a bird . . . free! In that freedom is true love and respect. In that freedom is dignity and the fullness of each moment lived intensely.

Love is not a set of rules, or an excuse to manipulate, attract or control. Love is not a sex performance, improvement technique or a justification for blame, judgement or indulgence. Love is not an ego-gratifying scenario to defend one's need or fear of aloneness, in order to create dependency and exploitation. Love is not an argument for possessiveness, exclusivity and separateness. Nor is it a psychological encounter, analytical process or biological laboratory. Finally, real love is not escapist.

Love is a consciousness-awakening process; a way of learning cooperation and respect for individuality. Love is a way of learning to express more love, a validating experience based on the equality of difference and higher purpose. Love aligns with higher law: blessing, sharing and expanding. Love reflects true commitment to life and to beings, through an awakened, illumined commitment to the self. Love sets a pragmatic psycho-spiritual stage.

Relationships are the arena of love, the bridge between lust and compassion. They stimulate, balance and nourish. Ask yourselves:

How well do I see another?
How deeply do I meet with another?
How much do I reveal of myself to another?

Whether your relationship is in nature of friendship and shows up as a meeting of complementary, parallel or opposite forces; whether your relationship is passionately sexual and emotional;

whether your relationship promotes growth, expansiveness, play and sharing; whether it includes the learning of karmic lessons such as forgiveness, empathy, selflessness, creativity and authenticity . . . our quest in relationships is for identity, power and that merger that leads to co-creation and the sharing of a vision.

There is no relationship without a common vision. In this common vision there is a dance of forces playing from the inside and from the outside, interacting and intermingling. In friendship, which is the highest or purest form of love, there is always equality. There is unconditional giving, not buying or trading of love; there is acceptance of the other, and not a demand that he or she be different.

For relationships to exist as a dynamic and conscious force there needs to be an acknowledgment of boundaries. We need to know when to be apart and when to be together. We need to refine our discernment to include the fine lines between the personal, subjective reality and the objective. We need to recognise and provide a sacred space for the individual and a sacred space for the relationship. The good of the couple must never take precedence over the good of the individual.

In a relationship we need to continuously reformulate the initial commitment. Each moment should be lived to its fullest, as if it were the last. Each meeting should be as the first, never taking the other for granted. We must learn to get close without absorbing the other. We must learn to surrender, with dignity, to love itself – not to the other. Each party in the relationship is a leader, whole and autonomous, coming together in honesty.

When there no longer is joy or freedom, we need to have the courage to go our separate ways. Freedom is a higher value than love. When we begin to notice that routine, or monotony, has set in, or that we are repeating emotional patterns of rejection and betrayal, the relationship is no longer serving us. Have the courage to risk all and step out of it. If there is love, the other party will be benefited enormously by your courage. He or she will feel the effects without any great arguments or further emotional entanglements that are demoralising and undignified.

There are several ways of effecting this change and any of them are appropriate. The important element is your attitude; the motivation behind your move and the way in which you do it. You may physically leave. You may withdraw your energy emotionally, or direct it elsewhere. Or you may use the alchemical formula to purify the energies within the situation and manifest the harmony that you seek.

One of my clients actually transformed his relationship by speaking to his partner's higher self over a period of months. Every morning, after his protective visualisations and affirmations, he dedicated three to five minutes to addressing his girlfriend's higher self. He asked for help in harmonising the relationship. At first the changes were slight, but as he kept it up, miracles seemed to happen. His relationship improved and he is now applying the same procedure on his relationship with his son. Whether the son is ready to open up to the influx of his higher self or not, is irrelevant. True change, real revolution, happens from the inner planes through the intermediary of the highest relationship of all, that to your own God-Self.

And then . . . when we begin to see through one another, in the transparency of intimacy, harmony, and the intensity of feeling raised through ecstasy into light, we come to know the secret behind relationships. We come to experience what the Sufi mystics did when they proclaimed, 'La illa ha, il alla hoo!' (Nothing exists but God.) At the very highest frequency we are indeed one.

For relationships are the little death. And death . . . the death of the little self is the ultimate alchemy. Relationships are a dress-rehearsal for Life eternal.

Alchemy and the Art of Relationships

As for all transformational practices outlined here, the practice of Inner Alchemy requires that you utilise the alchemical circuit, which by its very creation necessitates that you identify with both your personal and your transcendental self. Moving every moment of your conscious life with the awareness of this circuit is what creates mastery. Your relationships should be no different.

Recognise the higher self in the other as a vibrational presence. See and support that highest vision of the other and derive from it the inspiration and illumination that you require. Behold the magnificence of a God-Being like yourself. In order to do that you must first be that. In order really to be able to be together with someone, you need to know the experience of being alone – all-one, whole within yourself. As a deep experience, you need to know that all resides within you, that the universe, existence, is ready to give you what you ask for, if you but dare to ask. Within this realisation comes the dissolution of neediness. You can then come together with another out of abundance, not lack.

You may be thinking 'How do I get there?'. 'I seem to be so far away from that realisation, from that experience!'. It may take several relationships for you to come to that realisation, or it may take one. It may take your entire life or it may take one second. Each relationship, each intimacy with another throws light upon the blanket of experience of our lives, enriching, embellishing, strengthening the varieties of interpersonal experiences. As with the development of consciousness during lives, we need to experience all things. We are forged by the fire of emotional experiences.

Be where you are, so fully, so deeply . . . In the depth of experience is the transcendence. Be present to yourself: it's that simple, and that difficult.

In the meantime, endeavour to apply the truth that you intuit at the highest levels of perception to your everyday relationships. Understand the nature of the emotional triggers and automatic reflexes, and do your best to transmute them. Use the violet fire and the affirmations. Create the protective shields around yourself that ensure that you work upon your own creation. Hold the silence. And most of all be patient.

My students are constantly telling me how their mates and partners respond as their own responses refine and become more aware and keener. Everything that you do to yourself you do to the person who is closest to you. It rubs off energetically by your very proximity. Especially when you sleep next to someone, your very emanations are going to act upon them. You actually bless the world and everyone in it by refining yourself. Physical recalibration is a direct result of proximity to Light.

Most of all become aware of the quality of your relating and deepen it. In your lovemaking, let there be an awareness of yourself in the present moment, free of fantasy. Go tenderly, with open eyes, before your love and behold the grace of the Godhead. Stop your inner chatter and your mental projections. Regardless of how many techniques you follow, the quality of your experience is up to you and your decision to stop whatever prevents you from living fully in the moment. This is the bottom line.

Live as energies with one another and not as personalities. Sit silently and feel one another's presence. Be sure to meditate and sit silently with yourself as well. Honour yourself as you do the other. And when you unite sexually, let it be relaxed. Remember God. Remember your Self. And in the fullness of your ecstasy, remember to share. In that sharing your love is multiplied.

Alchemy in relationships is living the God in you with the God in the other, so that all of creation is enhanced.

Forgiveness

Forgiveness is an energetic release that sets parties free from the momentum of cause and effect. We enter into 'contracts' with one another, which may last lifetimes and may include not only the individual life-stream but the entire group or family with which the individuals are connected.

This 'contract' is like a bondage that exists, compelling individuals to react and affect one another in certain ways. Quite often this agreement, although created initially by lower impulses, was affirmed on the seventh dimension for the purpose of experiencing certain lessons. The relationships between parents and children, for example, are *always* karmic. There is no possible escape from the condition dictated by parents to the apparently helpless infant. Sometimes the incredibly arduous early experiences have been accidentally inflicted, but even in the cases where there has been no prior personal contact, parents set the conditions for experience that you need, in one way or another.

The same principle often applies to love relationships, particularly marriage. We feel compelled to create or experience oppressive conditions way beyond our understanding or control. Forgiveness is the application of the fire of pure love onto the subtle, psychically engendered chains that bind us karmically.

You don't need to believe in past lives or anything of the sort. You may complete a lesson that was started with a different partner or by somebody *else*. The lesson is humanity's. What matters is resolving it *now*. The following are three ways in which you can affect energies at the highest levels, effecting the release and ultimate dissolution of the lines of force that tie you as a member of the human race.

Release Through Affirmation

Visualise the person(s) to be released before you, sitting under the same alchemical hookup system as yourself. Emphasise not only their connection to their own higher self, but the connection between your higher self and theirs. Talk to their higher self through yours.

Through the power of my God-Self and with your permission, I address you as a being of Light. I ask for your help in freeing —— and me from the entanglements of the lower bodies. Transmute the energies between us into their highest form in the fulfilment of the Divine Plan for each of our life-streams in this embodiment.

Pause, and then:

I release you, —— [three times] and I release myself [three times]. With your greater clarity, courage, direction and protection, which is eternal, you, ——, are free! [three times] Receive my love, gratitude and praise!

And then:

I AM free! [three times]

(Feel it. See the lines of force dissolving, and the energies returning to each of you.)

With a Partner

Especially good for group or family release. This technique is drawn from a practice followed by the Kahuuna priestesses of Hawaii and involves the entire cellular history of the individuals. A basin of water is placed between the partners, which serves to wash away the karmic debris. At the appropriate moment of release, the person speaking sprinkles the water around himself and the person he or she is releasing.

This process can be done with the person with whom you are having difficulty, provided you both genuinely desire it. It may also be done *for* another – in other words, with a substitute. In some cases it may be done alone, switching places with the imagined party and speaking for him or her.

It is essential that both parties are acknowledged as speaking.

Part One
Invocation. You may choose your own, or you may use the Kahuuna version, 'Divine Creator: Father-Mother-Son as One!'

[Now addressing the person that you want to forgive and be forgiven by:] If I/we ——, my/our families, relatives and ancestors have ever offended you, ——, your families, relatives and ancestors, in thoughts, words, deeds and actions, from the beginning of our creation to the present, humbly, humbly I/we ask you all for forgiveness for all efforts, resentments, guilts, offences, blocks and attachments we have created and accumulated. [And then ask, looking directly into the eyes . . . :] *Will you forgive us?*

Part Two
[The partner answers:] *Yes, we forgive you.* Let this water release us all from spiritual, mental, physical, material and karmic bondage!

[And addressing the God-Self:] Pull out from our memory bank and computer, sever and cut [emphatically] all the unwanted, negative memories and blocks that tie, bind and attach us together. Cleanse, purify and transmute all these unwanted energies to pure Light. Fill the spaces these unwanted energies occupied with divine Light. Let divine order, light, love, peace, balance, wisdom, understanding and abundance be made manifest for us all and our affairs through the divine power of the divine Creator: Father-Mother-Son as One, in whom we rest, abide and have our Being, now and forever more. Amen.

It is important that eye contact be maintained and that the person receiving the release (if present) takes time to *feel* that release and to *accept* it.

The entire process is repeated for the other partner.

The Rhythm of Forgiveness

None of us will be *free* until there exists no person in the world – no relation and no one-time friend – against whom there is a fear of disharmony or irritation, a barrier, a reserve, whom we retreat from even in our minds.

Forgiveness is freedom from illusion of conditions. Forgiveness is forgetting, the washing out of conditions. We are unable to forget, because such memory lies in the mind. In the heart there is no memory.

Vibrations are held by the earth, which is sensitive to all impressions. Our bodies will hold on to impressions and memories until a greater force or identification takes over.

This next exercise is the last Essenic practice we are including in this book. It consists of a flash of light which carries away permanently all memory of the past, unless we choose to keep recreating it.

Remember, it is the last act in our lives to be absolutely free of any claim in regard to anybody. Don't look upon forgiving people with any sense of virtue. It is an urgent necessity.

The exercise:

The rhythm of forgiveness is a zigzag rhythm of eight. Begin with the invocation. Create the alchemical circuit. Strengthen the personal heart-connection to your higher self and make the call for forgiveness. An especially powerful colour to use in connection with forgiveness is deep pink Light-substance. Wash yourself in it. Absorb it . . .

You are now ready to return the gift back to the Creator. You are ready to offer up all the imperfections which prevent you from loving yourself (and others). The rhythm of forgiveness starts the moment you wish to release your hold over substance in the way of thoughts and feelings in your aura and return it to the Source.

The light is flashed *on the inbreath* from the left side of the back to:

1. A point on the right side under the right arm.
2. The top of the left shoulder.
3. The same point on the top of the right shoulder.
4. The left ear.
5. Through the head to the right ear.

Fig. 4.3 The Rhythm of Forgiveness

6. To a point on the side of the head, halfway between the left ear and the top of the head.
7. A similar point on the right side.
8. It flashes out of the top of the head *on an outbreath*.
   Do this as long as you need.

God 'I AM'
Rainbow Self
(audiocassette text)

Fill the container of your body now with the presence of yourself, igniting the centre of each atom within your body with a tiny sun of pale golden light.

Allow each cell to be filled with the joy of Life and see them expand and become brighter and brighter. Feel your entire body aglow with the presence of yourself, millions and millions of tiny suns within your body, a body of light within your physical body.

Now. Direct your attention for a moment to the body of the planet and go directly through into the centre of the Earth. There, in the centre, is a crystalline structure of pink and golden Light-substance, just like those little suns in your body. Your body is part of the body of the planet.

Connect with this heart centre of the planet. Feel yourself held there. Anchor your own form into it. Feel safe, held within the solidity of the mother and your own body.

Now. Direct your attention to the centre of the chest. Go within and locate the heart centre. It's like a globe of iridescent light within which is a three-fold flame of intense radiance and power. Here is where your divinity is anchored, your spirit, the Light which you are as intelligence, consciousness, life and vitality.

Leave your body within the safety of the mother and follow the beam of light that is anchored in your heart up into the greater source above you. Follow the light beam right up through your throat and head and continue upwards.

Become aware of the changes in vibration, or the inner sounds . . . sensations . . . as you move up this vertical map to your God-Self . . .

Until you reach at the same time a space of infinite peace and intensity, an immensely brilliant luminosity which you are.

283

Know that you are in a body of matter *and* you are also a source of Light. I AM HERE . . . I AM THERE . . .

I AM THAT I AM

Beyond millions of suns . . . 'I AM' . . . crystal light with rainbow hues, a great central sun within suns of glorious light, concentric spheres of colour expanding.

I AM an infinite brilliant WHITE as of a thousand suns. A blinding pearl of unlimited creative force . . . expanding.

I AM a shimmering GOLDEN sun-sphere suspended in space, infinite peace and knowingness . . . expanding.

I AM a glowing effervescent globe of scintillating PINK, healing, nourishing love . . . expanding.

I AM a jewel of RUBY love, sheltering depth, protective shield . . . expanding.

I AM a VIOLET flaming heart with orbs that reach into infinity . . . transmuting, purifying grace . . . expanding.

I AM the verdant embers of APPLE-GREEN suns . . . abundant life and wealth . . . expanding.

I AM the glorious cosmic BLUE of cosmic purity . . . the matrix of all creation, the backdrop for all my forms . . . expanding.

The sacred fire breath of God I AM, pulsating Life, pulsating Love.

God 'I AM'.
God 'I AM'.
God 'I AM'.

Death: The Ultimate Alchemy

Evolutionary Development

Let's trace our steps back to our beginnings. That which we are in its complexity is made up of varying layers of substance, of both light and matter. Our essence takes on the substance of the planet itself when it seeks the experience of learning management of energy and substance at all levels.

What dwells within substance is intelligence, or consciousness. Consciousness proceeds from individuated spirit and reflects levels of integration within different planes. The interaction of consciousness and substance, particularly within our dense physical substance (the core of the planet), creates soul, or spiritualised substance. This spiritualised substance when created is highly malleable and directly responsive to the direction of spirit – which is intelligence at the highest level.

Activity at the level of physical embodiment provides the best and only possibility for mastery and the greatest release of soul substance. In fact, the purpose of physical embodiment is ascension – perfecting matter at the level of the physical, emotional and mental bodies. At the moment of ascension we as a conscious presence within matter blend with our higher selves anchored at the seventh plane and complete a cycle of physical possibilities.

We have been integrating with ourselves (or better still developing our faculties) at interdimensional levels during our lives. The more we have of ourselves (i.e. the more we have developed our awareness at the different levels), the more energy, momentum and power we possess to reach the vibrational intensity of the higher self in order to cooperate with it. The apprenticeship served at the level of physical embodiment then leads to other apprenticeships at higher and vaster levels.

If we stop to think for a moment on the process of apprenticeship itself we will come to the realisation that in order to be at this (human) level of development there must have been previous stages of apprenticeship.

Most third-dimensional scientific thinking believes we descend from the animals. The truth is that we do, but in a wholly different way than has been explained. We, as individualised consciousness which animates matter, do *not* descend from the ape.

The process of evolution begins when Spirit projects a *part* of itself and penetrates into matter at the simplest amoebic stages. That part develops into greater and greater complexity, as we have been taught, until it is able to merge with itself as Source.

Elementals are consciousnesses within a realm, or kingdom, as I have already defined in a preceding section, which is parallel to the human. It is inferior only in the sense that it is simpler and collective. Elementals are the builders of form. An elemental is a consciousness that is learning to create form from the simplest to the most complex, just as we are learning to express mastery from the simplest to the most complex systems of creativity. Elementals grow and develop according to the degree of complex creations they can handle. They begin by building an atom, then molecules and then organisms. . . .

It is elementals that build our bodies and everything in form, including our synthetics. All is derived from substance made available to us through the activity of elementals. Obviously a tree is more complex than a plant or algae. A human body is more complex than an amoeba. All form is built by elemental activity under the direction of higher intelligence. Elementals follow the blueprints set by the mind. As the amoebas and the human organism, so is the animal form created by elementals.

These forms created by the elementals are inhabited by consciousnesses at parallel levels of development. The consciousness that dwells within animals has nothing to do with the consciousness that dwells in a human body. There is a group soul that oversees, so to speak, dogs and cats, cows and rhinoceroses. This group soul is elemental in nature and qualitatively different from the potentially individualised consciousness of a human being, who contains the possibility for leadership and the attributes of supreme intelligence, which are of the Source.

Now, as elementals function by imitation, they are especially prone to mimicking human qualities (to wit the elves and gnomes, fairies, salamanders and sylphs). Elementals individuate (i.e. can develop an individual soul) through sustained contact and proximity to human beings' consciousness. This is why we see our domestic animals expressing human qualities. They are 'almost' human, and many of us would argue that in fact they appear more human than some humans. But they are not yet within the realm of human evolution.

When an animal dies, the love it gives and receives from humans has developed a longing in it to express itself as a human. It is believed that this impulse may take it into the initial stages of human development. Some thinkers disagree, however, that there is a leap from the elemental into the human, and argue that the relationship with the animal only represents our own life force in expression which may enhance the specie as a whole but does not result in human individuation. Being human would be only one of the possibilities that the instinctual soul of our beloved human-animal is exposed to. As a complex and highly evolved elemental spirit, it may move into other complex and greater creations, bypassing the human levels altogether.

The human evolution is unique in that it builds individuality and awareness of Self. It is the alchemical path, designed for the purpose of learning mastery and co-creation with the Godhead. Each human is a godseed. Each human soul in embodiment is a potentially individualised consciousness of the Godhead, with all its powers and unlimited, although not yet integrated, possibility. The animal, as all elemental life, serves the human, or godseed evolution.

Beyond and parallel to the human there are other evolutions as well. When we as humans have mastered the human plane, or ascended, having performed the ultimate alchemy, we are also faced with a leap similar to that of our evolved elemental spirit into another modality of expression. We may choose to remain in the aura of the planet, move on into the other systems or enter into the angelic realms. The possibilities are vast, and more than I could outline here.

The Ordinary Death Experience

What happens during the activity preceding the ascension, where the individual is learning through the working of karma, or the laws of cause and effect, how to create and manage increasingly complex systems of energy? What happens to the individual life-stream?

Although the body substance disintegrates, its counterpart at the level of the lower mind (the identity formed around the body or personality) lasts a while. Then that too disintegrates or reforms into something else.

Understand that all substance that has not been integrated into light, such as in the creation of soul, or the immortal body of light at the ascension, dissolves. In this way the lower bodies, the physical, the emotional and the mental bodies disintegrate after a period of time. This cannot happen at the higher levels; the higher bodies are not, so to speak, perishable. They have become self-luminous by the liberating, redeeming faculty of applied human intelligence through the use of the Law of the One or of Light.

It is possible to experience death emotionally and mentally while still in embodiment. It is possible to experience the death of the ego, or of the identity, and recreate oneself consciously. This is part of the workshop practices within Inner Alchemy.

Psychology and Ego Death

Psychology as the working of the three lower bodies, or personality, is the key to understanding the evolution of the individual personality within the body of the human race. Psychology *is* the personality, or particular identity impulse of the individual life-stream to persist.

There is basically no difference between a living person and a disembodied spirit, as far as psychology is concerned. A common spirit still has the identity of a personal world and will relate through that personality as long as he holds onto it or is fed by surviving humans who feed that identity. When a spirit as a personality devoid of matter but not yet individualised in the spiritual sense has no knowledge of anything beyond earthlife, he will mentally project reality in earth ways that are recognisable to him. He sees his own projections, just as humans do in bodies. There are the spirits that we contact in seances and who haunt houses, and who continue to act as if alive, even if they may have recognised that they are no longer in bodies.

I have worked with what are called 'spiritualist rescue groups' in England. Their main function was to advise the newly (and sometimes not-so-newly) departed of the 'change'. Because these spirits knew nothing of the afterlife, their perspective was earthbound. They responded to us rather than to the helpers who were in bodies of light.

It was our function to work in cooperation with groups of helpers from 'the other side', and to direct these spirits to those who could guide and instruct them appropriately.

You might conceive of that stage of the afterlife as a kind of Grand Central Station. There are helpers ready to guide spirits, but they must be opened to seeing them and receive their guidance. It was our function to help them accept their 'death' and in this way allow their consciousness to separate from the subtle matter, and let each consciousness (that of Light and that of matter) receive its rest and rehabilitation. The consciousness of Light, or intelligence, would then be able to rise to higher realities.

This kind of activity happens at astral levels within three-dimensional reality, but without the anchoring of the physical body of substance. The new arrival gravitates to vibratory frequencies of the etheric counterparts of places, people and things according to his desire for them and his capacity to use thought projection. A good description of what happens at this stage is given in the movie *Made in Heaven*, where the protagonist learns to steer himself through visualisation and feeling. There are guides to teach him and according to his quickening for higher truth, he is led to schools and centres of learning where he awakens further.

When he is ready (i.e. can tolerate a greater energy input), he reviews his immediate past life, makes the necessary assessments and depending upon his level of mastery chooses to embody and work out whatever is needed to complete his apprenticeship on the earth plane and settle old accounts. If he is not vibrationally acclimated to the higher self, the decision to embody will appear to be made independently of him. He may also decide to work from the out-of-the-body state for a while, as a guide or teacher himself, or as a guide to people who are in bodies and who are undergoing similar lessons to those he is mastering.

At some point he, as the unit of matter (personality-in-process-of-individuation), must complete the physical experience. As explained earlier, the third dimensional plane provides the arena, or raw materials needed, for the development of skill. The physical body serves as the vehicle. The transmutation of this very vehicle in the process of ascension provides the magnification, the amplitude, intensity and momentum required to exist permanently at a qualitatively higher level of vibration. In this way, what is reincarnated is not wholly individual and neither is it spiritualised *yet*.

Another Way

The teachings contained within the Books of the Dead were perhaps the first spiritual teaching upon this planet, and very possibly the only teaching needed. This teaching was interpreted by many cultures and came down to us *The Tibetan Book of the Dead*, *The Egyptian Book of the Dead* and other scriptures including the Mayan, Hopi and Vedic traditions. Recently, in the psychedelic and meditation revolution of the 1960s and 1970s, when people started getting in touch with interdimensionality – formless reality and worlds of sonic and colour frequencies of light – modern interpretations of the *Book of the Dead* included Timothy Leary's version and E. G. Gold's *American Book of the Dead*.

I researched these books and created workshops around them, developing an experiential scenario for the understanding and refining of our power to create reality. At first I called these workshops, 'The Personal Bardo Experience', which was a variation of 'Bardo Thodol' or journey through the afterlife. The process lasted from four days to an intensive restructuring phase of ten days. The culminating experience was that of ego death through a consciously elicited method of consciousness projection beyond the known parameters of the lower mind.

At these workshops we sought to sharpen the faculties of thought, feeling and the spoken word and alchemically evoke forms of thought and feeling that suited our intention: to recreate ourselves in the image of the higher self. We discovered that great transformations of the personality are possible, which affect and influence the physical structure and the entire web of personal reality. It is possible to give birth to oneself, not only in spirit (as the Christian and Hindu scriptures indicate), but to physically and psychologically remould oneself.

At the very end of the workshop I recite a compilation from the various Books of the Dead, applied to Inner Alchemy and called 'The Book of Life'. This consists of a step-by-step journey through the 'Bardo'. I use the same visual map of symbolic lights and colours as in the underworld or shadows, otherwise known as the astral dimension. The Tibetan, or *Bardo Thodol*, represents energies and faculties of the higher self.

The Bardo Experience

At the first moment of departure from the physical vehicle, when the impulse is at its greatest, consciousness comes into contact with the twelfth dimensional self in all its glory and power. Unless awareness at that level of consciousness has been trained to sustain that intensity, it cannot remain there and comes down to the next level, the eleventh dimensional self, continuing to descend until it settles at a vibrational level where it feels comfortable. This first stage I call the 'first and second glimpse' of reality.

During the next stage, which is the bulk of the journey, the individual consciousness confronts the reality of mental and emotional projection and the creation of thoughtforms. At this point, the various lights, which for the East were represented by deities, begin to appear, attracting or repelling the individual consciousness according to its own development and ability to embrace these qualities within itself. This process occurs during different timespans, which were called 'days'.

The lights are primary colours which represent the vibration of space and of the elements that compose the three lower bodies, or personality. If the individual consciousness has mastered even partially the lessons at the levels of the three lower bodies, he or she will be able to blend with these lights and avoid the reactionary and negative aspects of the journey.

If, on the other hand the individual has not 'done his homework' in life, he will continue to project distractions, obstacles, fears and all kinds of horrors before him (proportionate to his own guilty conscience), causing him to lose control and yearn for the limitations of a physical body and the conditions which are familiar to him. At this point unconscious rebirth is possible.

The rest of the journey provides for the individual consciousness the opportunity for the highest possible rebirth, under optimum conditions for spiritual evolution and mastery.

When unable to blend with the frequencies of the twelfth, eleventh and tenth dimensional selves, the individual consciousness will separate itself into parts and project a higher self, a god, a deity or an authority outside of it. In this way an average consciousness is encouraged to evoke the highest teachers or aspects that he has known for support and emulation, to serve as a drawing force into the highest vibrational frequencies. He is continually reminded that 'I AM THAT I AM', which acts as a subliminal pool of remembrance.

The psychological process outlined here is available in my audiocassette, 'The Book of Life'. My book, *Death and Rebirth: The Ultimate Alchemy*, describes the entire process of filtering mechanisms in operation during the entire human experience, which are intensified in the death experience.

Alchemy and the Life-Death Process

There is an infinity beyond life. Whether we are in a material body or a spirit body, the process is the same. Life and death consist of the *same process*. If we are afraid of death, we are also afraid of life. To live fully, present to the Self in its multifaceted expressions, conscious to the Life all around, is to know eternity beyond the myth of death and dying.

The journey through the afterlife as taught throughout the ages exposes us to several trials. Each aspect of the journey calls for a certain skill. Each of these skills has been taught to humanity by Eastern and Western schools of thought from the Vedic to the shamanic. The elements of the journey are the same for everyone. The Tibetan map may vary from the Hopi or the Australian Aboriginal in appearance only. Each school of thought throughout history will endeavour to exercise the individual human being in the use of the skills he needs to have in order to attain to mastery.

Each spiritual path will require that we learn to exercise totality as well as discernment, surrender, appropriate resistance and an ability to sustain heightened levels of intensity and focus. We are asked to develop the ability to resist illusion and 'apparitions', those skeletons in the closet that form our baggage. We are shown how to embody power in its different expressions. We are encouraged to silence the chatter of the mind in order to perceive the real behind the illusory, and we are taught how to still the whirlpools of emotions through developing purpose and integrity. We are propelled into practices that put us in touch with the transience of form, its permutations and the entire world of energy as expressed through sound, colour and light. We are instructed in how to channel feeling into form. And lastly, we are coaxed into alignment with the godhead and into claiming our legacy – existence as our playground.

Whether your journey through the afterlife resembles a Tibetan tapestry or a Christian calvary, the experience is the same. To succeed in such a journey is to attain levels of mastery; to fail is to be thrust into a lower level of life to which our habits attract us. Either way we are confronted with life, with our creations, with ourselves.

Death provides us with the opportunity for the ultimate alchemy. But you don't need to wait for the moment of physical death to initiate this ultimate transformation.

Should you wish to prepare for the experience of ego death, you can follow the suggestions given in my book, *Death and Rebirth: The Ultimate Alchemy*. Understand that the journey is through the astral worlds of desire and wish-fulfilment. Meditate on practices that expand and contract your auric field. Keep a journal or a diary of your developments. Meditate on light and on colour, through breathing practices and prayer.

Dreamlife

Dreaming is another important aspect of our lives. Whether awake or asleep, dreams are the very stuff upon which creation spins.

Imaging

Every time you look, think, remember, plan or deliberately imagine, a visual image is created, filed away and impressed upon your memory. Massive psychological studies have been done to document the essential role that images bear upon memory, experience and thinking itself. The most relevant to us here are the studies done by Robert Masters and Jean Houston at the Foundation for Mind Research in New York State.

Masters and Houston found four levels of thinking in images. Each of these levels is experienced differently for each individual. Depending upon his or her temperament the images will be sensorial, visual, auditory or emotionally activated. The levels range from the immediate factual input of sensory data, through the mental process of assessment and integration within the memory bank, through the stylised mythical phase of the collective and into the luminous experience of the spiritual level. Every level of thinking consists of a corresponding visual imaging process.

Even blind people will have constructed corresponding forms that act as a reference point for thinking and functioning in life's activities. The image itself is not what is important. The process of using and constructing forms is. As breath is to the human body, so are images to intelligence.

Mind is a faculty of intelligence and it is also a warehouse of images: images from our current life and beliefs, from those of the time, from past and future possibility, from interdimensional activity, from cosmic sources . . . and from every conceivable area of activity in the universe.

Everything that we perceive is interpreted through our experience. We will see reality through the lens of our personal history. We construct and gain access to images corresponding to each level of Life. We dream dreams within dreams, with every breath, with every wink . . . consciously, subconsciously, supraconsciously.

Dream Levels During Ordinary Sleep

As we have seen, when we fall asleep our mind does not stop functioning. If we have not resolved an issue during the day, this issue will seek to be completed in the dream state. So the first level of dreaming will refer to our immediate three-dimensional reality: our bodies, our relationships, our affairs. . . . The conclusion reached at this level of dreaming will be expedient – positive and negative. At this level we dream of drinking out of a deep well if we happen to be thirsty, of making love if we happen to be sexually frustrated, of punching the boss if angry at work or calling the friend who returned the day before. Here we may find the answer to threatening situations and prophetically intuit the situations of people with whom we are involved with emotionally. This is the level of physical, mental and emotional immediacy, the most common level of dreaming.

Say we have somewhat resolved our activities of the day and there is no tension exerting a pull over us in that direction, the next level of dreaming will be wish-fulfilment: our desires, our hopes and aspirations. Coupled with these for some there will be the sabotage tactics of the deeper levels of the emotional body, the levels of the subconscious mind: the guilts, the fears, the catastrophic projections of violence or disaster, the haunting nightmares. . . .

If we happen to be clear about our everyday lives and know what our hopes and dreams are about, and perhaps have given them some creative outlet somewhere, the levels of dreaming from here on will pertain largely to interdimensional life. At this level abide too the solutions for problems posed by the higher mind, as in the cases of great scientists who have reported finding solutions to great mathematical or scientific problems through dreaming, or awoke to find the answer immediately after. This domain of dreaming pertains to the life of the higher mind (beyond personality thinking) and the spiritualised life of the highest planes.

At this last level of dreaming we find the symbols, from the collective to the highly abstract colour formations of the higher dimensions; here too the transfiguring encounters and the sometimes vivid experiences of humanity's past lives which seem to unfold as if in a movie; and the prophetic dreams (that do not pertain to the level of immediate personal life) . . . the meeting with wise figures, the archetypal figureheads of myth and fantasy.

These levels of dreaming relate to our experience within the worlds of images of the lower, higher and Christ mind, and can apply equally to the waking as to the sleeping states. This includes fantasising, daydreaming, meditating and intuiting flashes of precognition and inexplicable or unfamiliar recall.

Dream Bodies

Let's go back to our basic seven bodies, the ones contained within our aura and which have been outlined within the section on human energetic anatomy. Each of these bodies not only serves as a vehicle for experience in the higher aspects of expression and interdimensionality, but has also a kind of mind replete with memory and images.

At this point the term 'dreaming' applies to an activity that goes beyond the notion of fact or fantasy. It is the same meaning that ancient shamanic cultures give to this activity when they refer to the dream journey: the multidimensional journey through time and space.

When the consciousness is lodged or stationed at a certain vibratory rhythm that corresponds to a body other than the physical, and is trained in holding the awareness of this vehicle, the individual can tap into the mindset or memories of the body in question and enter into a dream journey.

The Dream Journey

Beyond the level of the physical body, which plays out the scenarios of everyday life, including physical discomforts, disease and repressions, lies the second or emotional body. This body is easily stimulated by vibrations and sensory impressions. It projects visions of loveliness which are extensions of the senses. Songs, mantras, scents and colours affect dream states in this body of poetic and romantic vision . . . of Krishna and his Gopis, of the Muslim heavens and the Christian hells . . .

The third, or mental, body, contains within itself the attitudes and impressions of the past in general. It operates sequentially and deductively. This dream body travels in space, beyond the fear of death. Its experiences are adventurous, Homeric even. Its scope is the past and present.

The etheric body dreams of the personal past or future. Yogic and Tantric methods of fasting and sensory privation of the past have stimulated the creative realms of this body by provoking its mobility and creating a distancing, a witnessing of the Self. This body dreams interdimensionally, and often brings impressions of other planets and other worlds.

The fifth is the higher mental body. This body crosses from the personal to the higher self and concerns itself with consciousness as a whole, including the knowledge of past existence and the myths of creation. It is a body of high individuality. At the level of the fifth body, we can dream simultaneously with another individual at the level of fifth body dreaming. To move beyond the level of dreaming of this body we would need to go beyond the concept of individuality itself.

The causal body crosses the threshold of personal consciousness and travels into the realm of cosmic myth such as that of Brahma and the Eastern concepts of 'maya' or illusion to experience Oneness. This body dreams the stuff from where religions originate, and weaves the web of great systems with the Creator. At this level we dream a dream without a dreamer.

The last or electronic body plunges us into the experience of nothingness and infinity, and into dreams of unending silence without boundaries or time. The language and images of spirit, if any, are so vast as to appear non-existent or incomprehensible to us.

Living and dreaming are one and the same thing. When we come

297

to accept this, we can begin to tap the unlimited potential that is within us, within our reach every moment, every breath, every step . . .

Dreamlife is the greater, vaster life of the master alchemist, who *dares*, as Cervantes might say, 'to dream the impossible dream'.

Instruction

If you intend to extend your consciousness to include the dream states, you would do best to prepare yourself accordingly, not only to enter into the dream state but to sharpen the very faculties that you will need to decode the perceptions in the dream journey.

Sharpen your awareness à la 'don Juan' to include all subliminal impressions, visual and energetic. Know your physiology as well as your psychology, so that you can understand and bypass the ordinary physical body dreaming. Create the arena for your explorations by clearly delineating your intent. Call on your higher self and on the beings of Light for help and guidance. Never fall into the arrogance of thinking that you can do any of this alone. Know that your 'call' never goes unanswered. Ask to be taught. Ask to be taken. Ask to remember. Endeavour to maintain the thread of awareness, the continuum of awareness right into the dream state.

Maintaining the continuum of awareness takes practice. At first it can be an insomniac's nightmare, as it heightens the vibratory frequency of the body, giving you more energy and making it more difficult to slip into ordinary unconsciousness. And then when you do fall into sleep, the impressions may not be all that clear at first. Keep trying. Don't give up.

What you bring back from your dream states may not be very clear at first. It may be simply an energy, a melody, a symbol . . . Whatever it is, validate it and yourself. Write it down. Train your focusing and visual faculties, as well as your capacity to sustain the images.

And as you are training yourself, notice the changes in your vibratory frequency. You might like to use a biofeedback device or one of those brainwave machines that monitor the change from beta to alpha to theta waves. When you are approaching the theta stage, just before your eyes close and you are ready to slip away, don't forget to give yourself permission to travel to these higher realms. You might want to use the text given here to help you remember your dreams, or create your own audiotape.

Remember that your mind is just like a computer. You can pro-gramme it. Focus your desire for the highest truth and allow the Light to guide you.

There is no real difference between sleep and so-called trance, especially for the training alchemist. In trance we penetrate heightened states of awareness through the intermediary of the higher self and our faculties at the different dimensional realities. In these states we commune with nature and we co-create with the godhead. We are in partnership with Light. The dream journey is a conscious trance state reached through one's own activation of the different dream bodies.

In this kind of journeying there is no room for darkness or for lower vibrations to enter, particularly as you have created the habit of surrounding yourself in your tube of electronic Light-substance. This tube is, as already mentioned, not only protective, it creates a very real passageway, an interdimensional passageway through which you rise, through a tunnel of light, right into the higher planes, bypassing the lower astral realms which are the ordinary abode of shamanism, witchcraft and black magic. Your tube of Light is your protection by day and your passageway by night. *Use it.*

Night Procedure
(Inner Alchemy Techniques for Protection of the Various Bodies)

Once you begin the practices of Light, your activity in altered consciousness states increases. This is due to your intensified inten-tionality. As this activity increases you are subjected to greater energies. Being that matter always exists in polarities, the more you embody light, the more darkness will also be attracted to it. This same light is what has attracted your past mis-creations to you for transmutation, requalification and reintegration, which constitutes the path of Inner Alchemy.

Your physical body is especially vulnerable when you sleep. Atmospheric energies impinge upon your physical and emotional bodies, resulting in stimulation, depletion, or other alterations.

These include astral influence from disembodied entities or emotional thought projection from people in bodies. Remembering that 'like attracts like', and that you are working through much of your old unconscious habits and desires, you can see why it is important to shield yourself and to invoke the help that is offered you by the intelligence from realms of Light.

The practice of constantly relating to all manifested three-dimensional reality in terms of alignment to the God-Self above you creates the most important connection. This visualisation strengthens the protective tube of electronic Light-substance around you, which is enough in most cases to protect you during the day. At night, this tube serves as the passageway into interdimensional levels of reality. While it may still be maintained around your physical form, stronger methods of protection are prescribed for the night.

I suggest that when you retire at night, you leave the physical body clothed in a pillar of flame – the violet flame, a spiral blue flame or the sevenfold flame from the forehead, expanded to cover the entire body and the aura. Direct yourself to the electronic presence of your God-Self and determine to go to the electronic belt around the physical sun. This electronic belt would mark the most exalted vibrations of light.

The violet flame produces the action of purification and transmutation of substance. Visualising a spiral blue flame creates a powerful vortex of first ray activity that cuts impure substance at the etheric level and is protective. The sevenfold flame in the area of the pituitary or third eye joins the activity of the seven primary rays of creation and represents the activity of the elohim, or the builders of form. Expanding this phenomenon creates a powerful force that serves as a shield. Finally, the threefold flame within the heart hallmarks the operational seat of the original sacred fire substance in relation to the elements. With this visualisation you invoke the partnership with the godforce (yourself) at the most direct and highest level.

The electronic belt around the physical sun denotes the vibratory frequencies of your twelfth dimensional God-Self. At that level you can connect with the godseeds of all that exists within this solar system, including the seat of physical forces and energies, such as the temples of healing and of the highest instruction. From that perspective, too, you are guided or inspired to the best work appropriate for you at the present moment. Your influence as an irradiatory presence upon the planet itself is heightened by conscious contact with that dimension.

The next step, before going to sleep, is to call upon your God-Self to clothe your physical and etheric bodies with an armour of light. This looks somewhat like a suit of armour and includes a crystal-like skull cap and a brilliant crystal cross. If you remember, the symbol of the cross, particularly in light, cuts across all lines of force and represents the most complete and immediate protection.

If you should awaken in the middle of the night, always endeavour to remember where you have been and, as suggested earlier, record whatever you bring back with you. Should you awaken in any way that is disturbing, such as in a nightmare, take courage at that point and try to go after the cause of the disturbance. Once you have located it, either intellectually or energetically, flood it with violet flame and, if you like, call upon the Beings of Light to annihilate that cause. Reaffirm your circle of protection and go back to sleep, knowing that is so.

If this is not enough, repeat out loud whatever affirmation is appropriate to cut through the hold of the energy over you. You might like to visualise yourself holding that sword of blue flame and physically cutting the lines of etheric energy around you, while declaring again and again: 'Through the power and authority of my God-Self, I command that you be consumed by the fires of Light and Love! . . . You have no power!' These affirmations, although pronounced energetically with great power, must *not* contain any fear or anger. Allow the decrees to come through the voice of the God-Self within you, and remember: 'The Light of God never fails . . .!'

Permission to Remember Dreams
(Text from the audiocassette)

In a few moments you will begin entering into another, less ordinary level of reality. You may begin to feel more awake or alert than usual, and yet your body will begin deeply resting. You will feel more present and yet you will sense your body resting deeply.

Just allow your body to relax now, to sink softly, comfortably into the mattress. You can let go of your hold over the body now.

You can let go of your hold over the mind too. No need to go anywhere. No need to do anything. No need to direct or control anything. Your body and your mind deserve a rest. Anything unresolved can be finished tomorrow, if you still want to. For now just allow yourself to relax. Allow yourself to trust now.

You can give yourself permission to begin to remember your dreams and your activities in other levels of reality now. As time goes by you will remember more and more of your dreams and activities at other levels of reality. As time goes by you will be able to follow the thread of consciousness through sleep and waking more and more easily. Soon you will begin remembering more and more of your participation in other states of reality and you will remember more and more of your dreams, so that you can record them and bring that information back with you, gaining clearer insight into your essence, your flowering, and also that of others. This is a process that will happen as quickly as you want it to happen, so take courage.

Remember your dreams ... Remember your Self. ...

Keep love in your heart. Surround yourself in light and allow this light to lead you where you need to go.

Rest now. Trust in your God-Self.

Trust.

Move towards truth and love.

Remember your Self.

Remember that you can tune in to your own God-presence, which is Light and consciousness, anytime.

Remember your Self!

In the morning, you will awaken refreshed and alert, remembering your dreams more and more accurately, remembering your nature and understanding the nature of reality more and more clearly. You will awaken rested and eager to welcome Life and the new day.

You are loved.

You are Love.

Remember your dreams. Remember your Self!

Fine-Tuning the Dream Body
(Text from the audiocassette)

Now, prepare for sleep and know that you will journey through other realities and other dimensions of being where you too have your being.

Lie down. Let go of your body weight completely and become aware of your body from the inside. Wherever you direct your awareness, know that you are directing light. Fill your body with light and know that all tension, all darkness, all density will be dissolved by the light.

Become aware now of any tensions in the mind, any worries, fears and expectations – any busy-ness – and allow the thoughts, memories and emotions to slide away . . . slide away from the mind. Feel your mind liquid now. See it as a clear flowing brook, cool, a flowing without obstacles.

Remind yourself now of your intent to become more and more aware, more and more conscious, more and more of a witness, a witness to your body, to your mind and to your spirit.

Notice your breathing. Allow it to become more and more relaxed as you let go of your hold over the body and your mind. Your body and your mind are not needed now where you are going.

Sense the energy field within and around your body now. Within you is an ocean of energy. Around you is an ocean of energy. Inside . . . Outside . . . Allow the inside and the outside to merge into the totality of yourself this moment. Pure energy . . . A vibrant energy field.

Note the pulsing, throbbing vibrations that make up your body and your energy field. Notice them and enjoy them. Allow them to be pleasurable. Let them lift you into peace, bliss.

Surround yourself in the colours of love, in the feeling of love. Sense a field of deep, deep blue . . . or violet . . . or pink . . .

Now imagine a golden ring wide enough for your body and your energy field to go through. See it right over your head and sense it coming towards you. Pull it towards you and allow it to slide right over your body: over, under, and around. . . . See and sense and feel this glittering, electric gold substance surrounding you now . . . Hear its sizzling sound . . . Feel it as it gently slides over and under and around your body, slowly lighting and quickening your entire energy field. You become finer ... finer ... more intensely finer!

As this golden ring slides gently, steadily down, down, down ... to your feet ... and beyond them ... three feet beyond, hold it there ... and release it. See it disappear into infinity below you, and sense another ring, like a wave, returning to you. See and feel it gently rising around, over and under you ... as if pulling you higher and higher ... gently ... steadily rising to your head and then three feet beyond it. Hold the feeling of this golden energy ring three feet over your head ... And then release it. Follow it as it dissolves into infinity above you.

Allow another ring to descend now, just like the first one ... right through and around you ... into infinity below; and another ring to ascend now, extending upwards ... gently, steadily rising through you and around you ... into infinity above.

Stretching downwards ... and upwards ... ; a continual flow of energy rings pulsating through and beyond you ... into infinity below, above and around.

Continue feeling these golden rings of Light-substance, like waves rising and falling, up and down your body ... and allow your body to dissolve within them ... endlessly streaming with all that is!

Feel your consciousness rising higher and higher, wider and wider, into and through the rings ... in and through the tunnel of light into pure spirit ... where dreams are real and reality is but a dream! Awaken to the endlessness that you are.

Conclusions

The courage to stand alone

Life has a wonderful way of taking care of us. Our part consists in maintaining harmony by establishing a balance between activity and inactivity, between mind and no-mind, between giving and allowing ourselves to receive. If we really believe and dare to put the practices of Inner Alchemy to the test, we will come to the realisation that nothing is impossible. Through the application of this law and partnership with the forces of Light, all is possible.

In this partnership is all that we require, within and without. We find the wholeness or the oneness with ourselves in vertical dimensions of being. When you feel that fullness, the presence of your Self; when you feel all-One; that is MASTERY. You are now ready to play . . . to apply it to life.

The balance between outward movement or interactivity in the world and withdrawal into inner realms, or the receiving of divine sustenance, is the rhythm of life. As you live this way, in harmony with your Self, life takes care of you. What this means is that your higher self is able to act through you, guide you, direct you and use you to attract directly that which you need. Automatically a space for relationships, for example, *right* relationships is created.

Entering the path of Inner Alchemy means living consciously without identifying with the materialistic point of view and incorporating multidimensional thinking. Questions like 'When are you getting married?', 'When are you going to have children?' or 'How am I going to be able to . . .?' disappear. We understand that our fear gives these thoughts life and form; and that trust coupled with right, creative thinking and action is what actually shapes our lives.

As the planet itself, and all consciousness upon it, moves through the initiations of the heart, we come to integrate upper and lower vibratory frequencies, Eastern and Western philosophies, planetary and cosmic influences. And as the heart expands within each one of us, we come not only to see and understand more, we come to love more. But here just a few words of warning. . . .

You will become affected by the conditions around you, particularly the suffering. Your attention will grow even keener. You will see and feel much, much more. The choice between the human and the godly will present a constant dilemma for you, in your every act and thought and feeling. You will see darkness or you will see light.

When you see suffering, you will feel and sense that part of yourself, your humanity, which is still identified with the old values of a dying world – whether it is the Eastern chains of karma, or Judaeo-Christian guilt ethics. And then you will live through that qualification. For example: when you see suffering and feel it, a part of your mind is qualifying that energy with heaviness. You are thinking, 'Poor . . . thing!' You are projecting that weight onto the person you are feeling for. Instead of lifting their burden you are adding to it.

Now, if, when you look at this person, who is for some reason that you cannot possibly comprehend in such an 'unfortunate' state, you see the Being of Light within . . . you will actually reinforce that light, that beauty which serves to lift the one you are beholding. You may choose to do something not out of guilt or fear – which is the usual motivation behind charity – but out of your own abundance and positivity.

The Real Ecology

The real ecology begins with yourself. As you train your perception and the mechanism of your mind and feeling to affirm Light, you qualify energy positively. Instead of adding to the pollution of our planet we help to clean its atmosphere.

We have to empower light, empower the divinity within us. This does not mean denying ugliness and injustice, poverty and disease. It doesn't mean becoming callous or pretending these don't exist. It means providing a healing elixir, not by giving blind hope, which can only create more expectation, more tension and frustration, but only by generating the Light-substance whereby transmutation can begin to happen.

What the world needs at this moment is understanding, re-education. It needs to clean up the rotting thoughtforms, beliefs and ideas that are crippling all action and manifestation.

Individuals need to take notice of how the mind works, what thoughts are, what they do to themselves and what they do to others through their thinking, their feeling, their words and their acts.

If we don't clean up our inner pollution, we will be like the blind leading the blind, one miserable person coming together with another miserable person, thinking that they are going to help each other. In the end we have two miseries, not doubling but infinitely multiplying the intensity of that misery. To be of real service we have to start with ourselves and where we are coming from inside ourselves.

The real ecology begins with our own thoughts and our own feelings. That is what is going to raise this planet's vibratory rate. When we have assumed individual responsibility for our own power, that power joined to others becomes the power of the godhead in action.

Obedience to The Law

When we have understood that we are indeed one at the source point, we know that what we do to another we are ultimately doing to ourselves. But we don't often turn that around to understand that what we do to ourselves we also do to others. Consistently through the ages, self-torture in one way or another has been condoned. Now obedience to the Law would right this misconception immediately.

What is the Law? The Law of Light. The supreme power over everything is of the Light; not the physical light that finds its opposite in darkness, but that Light which is the source of all and goes beyond all duality; the Primary Life Source. To honour it is to obey it.

It's actually very simple. As you honour the Light in you or in another, you honour the Light in another or in yourself. Knowing that you are not the creator but *of* the Creator, that you live and

307

work out of a partnership with that force, allows you to live in humility, and yet with a tremendous responsibility: the responsibility to use the power and strengths wisely, honourably.

I use the word honour when I mean love in a full, active sense. Love is perfect action, the basic feeling of all of Life. It is the creative force. Love adheres to itself and it also gives; it is magnetic and radiatory at the same time. It takes in and it creates. Love is like the sun: the creative power of all that is. It is the basic motor power – the perfect basic feeling.

When we personalise love we contaminate it and proceed to dissect it into a million and one bits and pieces, believing that we own things and people. As we colour it with density it becomes possessiveness. As a perfect force it is the basic impulse or feeling that propels life and sustains it. It becomes energy in movement: a force that can be directed.

Obedience to the Law is the right use of the love force.

As we undergo the planetary initiation at the level of the heart, we are all exploring the different expressions of the love force and experiencing what is one of the most emotionally heightened periods in the history of the planet.

Through our repressions and expressions we are learning to manage, understand, purify and channel love. Instead of condemning ourselves for being emotional, we need to bring the spiritual element into it and see the phenomenon in the light of love.

Emotionality, Sexuality and Spirituality

Because of the nature of the teaching I am involved with, perhaps the greatest number of clients who come to me are those who have had some exposure to spirituality. Most of them already accept the concepts of love, harmlessness, brotherhood and enlightenment. Some of them have had deep experiences in religious practice. For this reason, many of my clients have severe problems with the integration of sexuality into their spiritual belief system.

Most people who come 'into the path' don't know what to do with their sexuality. The choices are to repress it, to hide it (from the self or from others), or to live a duality where the spirit and the body take turns at satisfying themselves. Luckily, some have managed to see and live beyond duality, drawing from the primal energy joyfully and creatively.

For the majority who haven't been able to integrate these two forces, it is important to clarify a few issues. As we open to spiritual unfoldment, we need to deal with the emotional body and its addictions. It is through the desire of the emotional body for supreme fulfilment as Spirit that we have the spiritual drive to begin with. The deepest goal of our lives is to attain to spiritual enlightenment. But because the desire is rooted in the emotional body and this emotional body is sublimating a physical drive which may be embarrassing, frustrating or an otherwise painful involvement with life, we will need to come at some time or another face to face with it; particularly since real spirituality can never escape from life.

Sexual energies intensify emotionality, which is why women feel so much more irrationally during the menstrual cycle and during periods of peak sexual activity or times of intense sexual relating. The excesses produced often cause a person with spiritual leanings to say, 'OK, forget it! It is too distracting; too disturbing!' It is this reasoning that led religions to abolish or condemn sex. And yet you can't go off to the desert or to the mountaintop and hide interminably without sex following you from within yourself.

You will find another person, a situation (real or imaginary). Life will ultimately provide you with a partner to work this out, usually someone who is also on the spiritual path and has the same hang-ups that you do. The sexual energies match and will trigger one another into an awakening and a resolution.

Meanwhile, you can never undo spiritual work. If you can't handle both spirituality and sexuality simultaneously, you will have to handle them separately. Your whole being will seek the equilibrium, until spirituality is embodied in the cells at the level of orgasm.

Orgasm is only the beginning, not the end, of an ecstasy that ripples through universes. It is matter echoing the contractions and expansions of creation. To run from it is to run from godliness. But this does not mean that to indulge in it is to embody godliness. To really understand the nature of this force is to bow in reverence before it; in sum, to honour it.

The lessons within sexuality are another facet within the lessons of love at the planetary level, another mirror through which we can observe how we treat ourselves and others, and how well we are applying the Law of light. It is a lesson that we must all go through – physically, emotionally and mentally.

Our planet is suffering from the misuse of power in the past. Within our hands have been placed the care and administration of the greatest power possible, that we may now place it at the service of Love, that we may refine it into and through the power of Light. If we fail to use the power wisely, the energy itself will reverberate back to us with the same qualities that we lend to it and manifest itself as illness and despair. For more information, the reader is referred to my book, *Karma and Sexuality: The Human Alchemical Experience.*

The only way of making peace with something, as with someone, is to live it through. There is no pretending or lying. Sex is the very epitome of the love force in action at the level of matter. And through it and beyond it are the ecstasies of Spirit . . . infinitely more intense!

Postscript

The New Cycle

Evolution is essentially spiritual and moves in cycles of activity. Each cycle is heralded by a certain leap forward even if it may not seem so. Activity within each cycle is represented by a geographical location that illustrates the achievements of the age or cycle.

The planet we call earth evolves as its individuals evolve. The consciousness of individuals today is moving through the lessons of Love into a point beyond dualities and the paradigms of the past cycle. In essence, the new cycle, or the new age as it has come to be called, embodies not only a quantitative leap but represents concepts and values that are qualitatively new. America, and by this I mean the three Americas, represents this new consciousness.

There is still controversy over the original seat of spiritual power and worldly activity on the planet: whether Africa, North, Central or South America, Asia . . . There is allusion to many great civilisations, in particular to the Amazonian and a great civilisation which flourished in what is today the United States of America, which we are told preceded the Atlantean and Lemurian. Then, we understand, the seat of Atlantis was on what is today the Atlantic Ocean, while Lemuria's spiritual activity encompassed the Pacific.

The next great centre for spiritual advancement was Egypt. Coincidental with this blossomed the civilisations of the East, which seemed to have reached an apex at the times before the Great War of Worlds called the Mahabharata. The Vedic scriptures speak of a culture even more remote. Each of these great civilisations has developed a certain aspect of the godseed expressions and has used a certain methodology, or ideology.

Each civilisation has contributed towards a certain balance or

311

integration between the personality and the spirit. The very remote civilisations lived a life of pure spirit, with little density to obstruct their actions or perceptions. By the time we had reached the Lemurian stage, consciousness was embodying the lowest chakras and wrestling with the spiritualisation of substance. The Atlantean tradition developed powers of will and mind, and the Egyptian endeavoured once again to seed or root consciousness into the very earth. Simultaneously, the East decoded the laws of nature and creation, while in the West the Godman Jesus, came to embody Pure Love.

In order to tap into the source energy or momentum in the Godhead, a certain level of spiritual mastery is called for. The development of consciousness within each tradition, whether past or present, calls for a re-evaluation of the needs of the time. Our times call for an answer to the questions surrounding the use of power – our personal, collective and spiritual power – and our use of individuality and personality.

Spiritual development and material progress go hand in hand. Success is built upon a foundation of underlying spiritualisation or focus of Light power. As we head into the Golden Age, we need to look at ourselves with a fresh perspective. As far as spiritual development is concerned, we are still very much at the effect of the influences set by the previous cycle.

In the previous cycle of evolution, which I call the Buddhic consciousness, the expression advocated by the spiritual teaching of the time was contemplation and the method was surrender. Perfection was attained through purification and surrender to higher will. The process there was to integrate the lower bodies, the physical, emotional and mental, within the vibratory nexus of the solar plexus. The individual emptied himself of the violence of the lower bodies and surrendered to the highest consciousness, reflected outside himself in the teacher or doctrine. The purpose was to attain to a state of bliss and openness: Nirvana.

Nirvana, the state of *samadhi*, consisted of no-ego or a sense of separation from life, which was perceived everywhere with tremendous love and gentleness. *Ahimsa* meant harmlessness and was the highest lesson taught by Lord Buddha. The individual dissolved into a very high state of consciousness, which raised right through the upper chakras or faculties without activating them into an individual identity. One merged into a state of surrender to divine will, into *sunnya* – the void or primordial nothingness.

Buddhic consciousness in our age has been represented in the West by various religious practices, of which the Sufi tradition is perhaps the most dramatic. Here the ego of the lower self is slain at the heart. Instead of aspiring towards the primordial void, the goal is the fullness of everything: God as everything.

At the level of Buddhic consciousness we dissolve all boundaries that separate us from others or that hold us in pseudo-superiority and we connect with the fibre of brotherhood, the oneness of life in preparation for the next step. Very little energy was given to individuality or physicality. This emphasis was reflected in Eastern cultural and political activities up to the very recent past.

We are now experiencing a collective urgency towards activity, individual expression and material and technological advance, which is the hallmark of the New Age. For this, the new cycle, which I have referred to earlier as the Christ-consciousness, requires the formation of a certain individualised will of God. The Western Christ, through the figure of Jesus, unlike the Eastern Christ through the figure of Lord Buddha, possesses an *identity*. He knows who he is and what he is to do. His teaching remains as the highest, most inclusive teaching of all the ages, as the energy which He embodied is the greatest from the Source, or Logos.

Christed Consciousness is action – action from the level of activated higher chakras and faculties, as opposed to the surrendering of them as in the previous cycle. Instead of an ego, the Western Christ possesses a personal identity, a focus of individuation, not separate from the source, yet distinctly individual. He does not dissolve into the whole in the Buddhic sense. He maintains a very conscious union with the whole and within that a mastery, a determined will-activity.

The Three Americas

The seat of the new cycle encompasses the wealth, faculties and attributes inherent to the races within the three Americas. The new cycle marks a return to initial concepts, but at a higher level in the spiral of spiritual evolution.

At the moment, the United States is suffering the effects of its dominance, in the political and economic sense, over the third world powers of the Central and South American governments. The wealth of Central and South America is deep within the soil and soul of its people, its traditions, its individual note or frequency within the ocean of infinite variables.

Central and South America are undergoing a purification by fire, an awakening and a restimulation which will take many years. Out of this will come a strength and clarity beyond our wildest expectations. At this very moment South America is being prepared to host the sceptre of power for the New Age. Its ancient sisters, Africa, Australia and New Zealand, are likewise emerging with a new mastery and an ancient power that will significantly alter our little and limited points of view. We are witnessing, at long last, the end of the dark ages of the soul, the darkness which gives birth to the Christ Child within us all.

Within the traumatic upheavals of this great birthing, Inner Alchemy offers a method, a warning and a supportive understanding to carry us through the second birth.

The keys for the transcendence in this age – the New Age – lie in the joint power and abilities embodied by the land and the peoples of the three Americas, where the sound of the Godhead is the sound of thunder and the Sacred Fire is the essence upon which creation spins.

Fig. 5.1 Co-Creational Symbol for Inner Alchemy

Detailed list of contents

Meditations

For all enquiries concerning the author's trainings, workshops and consultations in Brazil and in other countries throughout the world, please contact the Center for Inner Alchemy in São Paulo, Brazil:

ALQUIMIA INTERIOR
Rua Francisco Dias Velho, 66
Cep 04581.000 Brooklin
São Paulo, Brazil

Fax 0055–11–240–5149